Adventures of a Montana Ranch Family 1880–1964

the KEMPTONS

Trudy Kempton Dana

FARCOUNTRY
PRESS

EARLY PRAISE FOR *THE KEMPTONS*

A fascinating look at one western family whose members reflect the gamut of the American experience—from a signer of the Declaration of Independence to a Wild West performer who wowed audiences in Australia by roping kangaroos. Lavishly illustrated with photographs, artifacts, and manuscripts, the stories of the Kempton family's life in eastern Montana are by turns inspiring and heart wrenching. Trudy Kempton Dana has done a masterful job

—**Donna M. Lucey,** author of *Photographing Montana (1894-1928): The Life and Work of Evelyn Cameron*

I first met Trudy when her grandfather Berney E. Kempton, was inducted into the Montana Cowboy Hall of Fame a few years ago. Her stories reflect our mission to honor the cowboy way of life, American Indian culture, and collective Montana Western Heritage. This book does all that and more—as I personally continue to be humbled by the narrative of those who came before us.

—**Christy Stensland,** executive director, Montana Cowboy Hall of Fame and Western Heritage Center

The past can teach us so much about how to live in the present. Brava to Trudy Kempton Dana for setting down these family stories.

—**Kirby Larson,** Newbery Honor award-winning author of *Hattie Big Sky,* set in eastern Montana

The Kempton family endured the rugged journey westward to Terry, Montana, full of grit and dreams. They left their lasting mark on the town and Trudy's captivating depiction of their lives will surely leave the same!"

—**Megan Pirtz,** editor, the *Terry Tribune*

Trudy Dana makes history come alive. Her skillful writing recounts the adventures and everyday lives of her ancestors who helped to tame our great country. It's not often that a writer who is descended from

individuals who have become household names or who were living in historic places at pivotal times takes the time to do the research and has the ability to pull it off. We are all the richer for it.

—**PJ Dempsey,** career editor (McGraw-Hill, Random House, Simon & Schuster, and M. Evans)

A fascinating story of a descendant of one of the signers of the Declaration of Independence who was raised as a New England Quaker and went west to make his living trading with Indians. He married 7 Indian wives and when the governor pressured him to give up his polygamous way of life and abandon his half Indian family to find a traditional American wife he refused claiming there were no white women within 500 miles and the nearest one was already married. A quintessential piece of American history as gripping as the Lewis and Clark journals.

—**Ken Stuart,** founder and editor-in-chief, Schirmer Books, Macmillan Publishing Co.

I teach high school American literature and it I wish there were more positive, uplifting resources for my students. I found that in Trudy Dana's stories! Her grandmother's journey from Sweden is a great depiction of an emigrant's experience and the hardship they overcame, the true grit and determination they showed. I wish these stories could be included in every American literature textbook.

—**Kim Ferragamo,** high school teacher, Edmonds, Washington

This book is a captivating collection of stories that depict what living was like in the early American West before it was tamed. Funny, heartbreaking, courageous, and uplifting are just a few reactions you'll find upon traveling through her assemblage of real-life Kempton family stories. Ms. Kempton-Dana's ability to bring alive the harsh realities of ranch and range life through the experiences of this strong, tightly knit, loving family is extremely well done and indeed succeeds in immersing the reader into a fascinating time in our extraordinary American history.

— **Matthew Holt,** screenwriter and author

~ *Dedication* ~

For my granddaughters, Annika and Lina.
Time and time again, you asked me to tell
you a story. These are the ones you liked the best.

And to the memory of my father,
Jerry Kempton.

ISBN: 978-1-56037-733-7

For more information about our books, write
Farcountry Press, P.O. Box 5630, Helena, MT 59604;
call (800) 821-3874; or visit www.farcountrypress.com.

 Produced and printed in the United States of America.

23 22 21 20 19   1 2 3 4 5 6

TABLE OF CONTENTS

Four generations of Kemptons.

TO THE READER

*D*o you ever wonder what sparks a book's creation? You see and read the completed product, but there are countless steps and sometimes years between the start and finish. It was that way with *The Kemptons: Adventures of a Montana Ranch Family, 1880–1964.*

When I began, I never envisioned these stories would fill three volumes. I simply wanted to record our family's accounts and memories so they wouldn't be lost. In January 2014, I began collecting stories, artifacts, photographs, historical records, diaries, and personal experiences of the Kempton family. I knew past generations of Kemptons played an important and colorful role in the history of America, especially in the settlement of the West, but I had few details.

Over the years, I had listened to Dad's stories of his boyhood on a large horse and cattle ranch in eastern Montana, near the small town of Terry. Instead of bedtime fairy stories, Dad told true-life stories of cowboys and Indians, horses and cattle, the open range, and early homesteads that extolled the mystique of the Wild West. Despite leaving for college and never again living in Montana, Dad held an everlasting fondness for the Kempton Ranch and the wide Montana prairies.

When I was older, Dad, who was a member of the Anchorage Toastmasters, told more stories of his great-grandparents and grandparents who were some of the first settlers in Colorado and Montana. We learned his grandmother was part Sioux and that our dad was listed on the tribal rolls and held deeds to Indian land due to his Sioux birthright. We discovered that our grandfather, a star rider and roper with Doctor Carver's Wild West Show, had been fluent in the Sioux language and had many friends among the tribes. Dad told us about the Kempton Ranch, the largest horse and cattle spread of its day, and the grueling work involved in ranching. We heard about Dad's brothers, his friends, and Pansy, the young girl whose mother helped Mrs. Kempton in the kitchen, plus the men and women who worked on the ranch and at the Kempton Hotel in nearby Terry.

Over the years, I retold Dad's stories to my daughters and then to my granddaughters, and even to friends. I began gathering family photographs and was amazed at the wealth of American history and bygone days these extensive visual records revealed. Using diaries, papers, letters, personal interviews, accounts, and photographs, I compiled details about family members, including a Mayflower pilgrim, an early American patriot who signed the Declaration of Independence, a powerful Lakota Sioux chief, and some of the first pioneers to settle in Colorado and eastern Montana. I learned that both my great-grandfather, JB, and grandfather, Berney, made Kempton one of the most respected and celebrated names in the valley of the Yellowstone River.

When my father became ill in 1994, my trips from my home in Washington state to see Dad in the family home in Anchorage, Alaska, became more frequent. It was during these visits that I learned more about our family. Dad told me about his favorite devoted teacher, the dangerous childhood adventures and scrapes he thankfully survived, his father's enthusiastic hosting of dudes to the ranch, the death of this great man, and the hard times before the family sold the ranch and eventually the hotel.

As I prepared to return home following a visit, one of the last things Dad said has always been of great comfort. When I told him I would be going home the following morning, he reassured me it was okay, because he, too, was going home soon. He quietly passed away just a day or so later.

My stories are the authentic and compelling lore of Kempton ancestors, but more importantly, they are a genuine, salt-of-the-earth part of our country's history in the nineteenth and twentieth centuries, providing an insightful glimpse into the exploration and early settlement of the American West. I am amazed at the details of Dad's stories

I remembered over the years, but there are some points of which I am uncertain. I have done my best to be accurate and have augmented my memory with research, but a few names, dates, and particulars remain open to interpretation. All the stories are based on true accounts, the people are real, and the ranch and hotel still exist in the small town of Terry, in eastern Montana.

It is my firm belief that family history does not have to fade away. I challenge you to record the details of your own family while the information still exists. When memories become stories told to following generations, this invaluable and priceless family narrative is preserved.

I trust you'll enjoy reading these true accounts as much as I treasured writing them.

Most sincerely,
Trudy Kempton Dana
Edmonds, Washington

ACKNOWLEDGMENTS

Many special people helped make this book possible. First of all, thanks to my husband, Ellis, for the innumerable hours he spent restoring our old family photos. Thanks also to my daughters, Katie and Jenny, for their suggestions. My strongest and sweetest encouragement came from my granddaughters, Annika and Lina, who told me they hoped other people could read these stories, too. Thanks to my brother Tom, who spent a long weekend with me going through boxes of old family photos. I also appreciate all the research my sister Gail conducted on Kempton genealogy before her death.

Thanks to my dear friend Connie Chambers who has encouraged me since nursery school. Most sincere appreciation to Matthew Holt, a fellow author, for his many hours of editing and constant support. Thank you to Christine McCroskey for her unfailing belief in me. When I was stuck, Laurie Isbell often came up with just the right idea. Thanks to Alice Purdy, Lynda Hughes, and my PEO sisters who read the manuscript and provided suggestions. I also appreciate the help of Taylor Teachworth and Elaine Solvang.

Special thanks to Donna Lucey, the author of *Photographing Montana: The Life and Work of Evelyn Cameron,* for advice and encouragement, and to Carol Doig, widow of the best-selling Montana author, Ivan Doig, for her guidance.

Thank you to Christy Stensland, executive director of the Montana Cowboy Hall of Fame, and to Lory Morrow of the Montana Historical Society, my cousin Kay Kempton Nyquist, cousin Jim Kempton and his wife Rose, and Gary Kartevold. Thanks to Steve and Sue Tibbetts for showing me around the former Kempton Ranch.

Sincere appreciation to Pauline O'Meagher and Bill Allen from the Australian family of Gerald Roland Stanley O'Meagher, for their stories, postcards, and photographs. I am also grateful to Linda Schwartz of the Kempton Hotel and Glen Heitz and Carol Larsen of the Prairie County Museum and Cameron Gallery in Terry, Montana. And thank you to Barbara Magnuson, Tracy Ingersoll, and all the relatives I never knew I had, who graciously shared notes and memories of past generations of the Kemptons.

PEOPLE AND SETTINGS

THE KEMPTONS

JERRY KEMPTON

My father, Gerald "Jerry" O'Meagher Kempton (1912–1994), was a confident child, the second oldest of five Kempton children, all boys. Jerry was kind, friendly, and smart. He loved reading and excelled at math.

THE KEMPTON BROTHERS

Berney and Martha Kempton had five sons, from oldest to youngest: James Berney (1910–1983), Gerald O'Meagher (1912–1994), Edmond Foote (1913–2012), John Magnuson (1915–1986), and Berney Edmond, Jr. (1917–1990).

BERNEY EDMOND KEMPTON AND MARTHA MAGNUSON KEMPTON

My grandfather, Berney Edmond Kempton (1870–1942), grew up with a rope in his hand and developed that talent until he was one of the most famous roughriders and bronco busters. As a young man, he spent nearly two years traveling the world with Doctor Carver's Wild West Show as a star rider and roper.

He was a handsome, dashing man, the expansive host of the Kempton Ranch and the Kempton Hotel.

Berney said he wanted to die with his boots on, while he was still active. He got his wish, passing away one evening in the lobby of the Kempton Hotel, still wearing his boots. Berney Kempton was inducted into the Montana Cowboy Hall of Fame in 2015.

My grandmother, Martha Magnuson Kempton (1886–1964), was born on a farm in Sweden and orphaned at a young age. One by one, she and her siblings emigrated to America, against almost insurmountable odds.

She completed all grades of elementary school in one year while also learning English, and she graduated at the top of her high school class.

Martha was a very capable businesswoman, intelligent and forward-thinking, supervising both the ranch and the hotel, while raising five boys. Known for her delicious cooking, she never used a recipe.

JAMES BERNEY "JB" KEMPTON AND MARIA GERRY KEMPTON

JB (1843–1910) was the son of the captain of a whaling ship out of Maine. Maria (pronounced "Mariah") was the daughter of an early mountain man and a Sioux Indian woman. JB was very civic-minded, establishing the first bank in Terry, several businesses, and the new high school, as well as the Kempton Ranch. Maria Gerry (1851–1910), was a strong, quiet woman, well respected in Prairie County. JB and Maria had six sons: Berney Edmond, Asa, Sanford, Joe, Jim, and Henry, and two daughters: Marie and Sarah.

JOSEPH AND ELIZA SABRINA FOOTE KEMPTON

These fifth-generation Kemptons lived mainly in Colorado, but often stayed at the home ranch in Terry. Eliza Sabrina, called Sadie, from the affluent Nathaniel Foote family of Villanova, New York, left a life of ease to marry Joseph Kempton in 1841. Kempton, from Penobscot County, Maine, was the captain of a whaling ship. Together they went West in an ox cart, first settling in Michigan where their children were born, then later moving to Colorado, where they were again early pioneers.

OTHER PEOPLE

PATRICIA "PANSY" MCMILLAN was a young girl about Jerry's age who lived on the ranch. Her mother helped Martha Kempton with the cooking. Pansy was best friends with Jerry and like a sister to all the boys. I met her as a grown woman with a family of her own, when I went to college at the University of Montana in Missoula.

GRAY HAWK was a young Sioux boy from the Fort Peck Reservation in eastern Montana. Gray Hawk was related to Jerry's part-Sioux grandmother, Maria. He sometimes lived at the ranch, attending school with the Kempton children. He was best friends with Jerry.

JEFF DIXON, a transient cowboy from eastern Washington, had a shady past when Berney Kempton took a chance and hired him as a ranch hand. Jeff soon became the trusted, capable ranch foreman whose loyalty to the Kemptons was unshakable.

THE FLORIDA COWBOY was a favorite ranch hand who worked on the Kempton Ranch for many years. He was named for the state he came from, and his horse was called "Miami."

SUSAN PHILLIPS was the competent, enthusiastic young teacher in a one-room schoolhouse that local children attended. She was a good friend of the Kemptons and often stayed at the ranch. Eventually she and ranch foreman Jeff Dixon married and their relationship with the Kempton family continued.

SETTINGS

Most of my stories take place on the KEMPTON RANCH, or in the nearby small town of Terry, in Prairie County (originally called Custer County), Montana. My great-grandfather, James B. Kempton, came from Fremont's Orchard, near Greeley, Colorado, to establish the ranch in 1882. In its heyday, it was one of the largest spreads in eastern Montana. The Kemptons raised horses that were used by soldiers in several wars. They also trained Percheron workhorses, as well as the polo ponies that were prized by royalty in England and France. They shipped beef cattle by the trainload and were respected figures at the great cattle markets.

The Kemptons were advocates of dryland farming, and their early experiments on the ranch were beneficial to many farmers and ranchers. They grew wheat that needed very little rain and corn that came to full growth in just ninety days.

The Kempton land was blessed with some forty natural springs. The ones near the ranch house filled reservoirs and provided water for irrigation. In winter, the springs looked like giant fountains of ice.

THE KEMPTON HOTEL in Terry was built in 1913 to accommodate visitors to the ranch. (Some say the original building was constructed as early as 1904.) The hotel has had several owners since being sold by the Kemptons. The present owners, Russ and Linda Schwartz, say it is one of the oldest continually operating hotels in Montana, still welcoming guests today.

The place is said to be haunted by ghosts of the 1918 Spanish flu victims who died in a makeshift infirmary set up in the hotel attic.

The terrain of PRAIRIE COUNTY is mostly benchlands, valleys, coulees, and rugged badlands. The Indians called them badlands because the area was so hot in summer, cold in winter, and little grew there. The nearby waterways are the Yellowstone and Powder Rivers, plus smaller creeks and streams.

The small town of TERRY, MONTANA, was originally named Joburt's Landing for the man who built a supply post in that location along the Yellowstone River. When the Northern Pacific Railroad arrived in 1881, the town was renamed Terry in honor of General Alfred Terry of the Union Army. Terry had led an early expedition in connection with George Armstrong Custer's campaign against the Indians of Montana. In July 1806, William Clark, of the Lewis and Clark Corps of Discovery Expedition, traveled down the Yellowstone through the area that is now Terry.

Today, Terry is a lovely small community, where neighbors know and care about one another and children play in streets shaded by large old trees. The Prairie County Museum and Cameron Gallery attract many visitors who pull off the interstate and find this friendly little town, steeped in the history of the West.

Terry, which is the county seat, is situated just about midway between Miles City and Glendive in eastern Montana. The area has about two hundred days of sun during the year. Temperatures range from minus 43 in winter to 111 degrees during summer.

The famous Montana photographer, Lady Evelyn Cameron, a former Scottish aristocrat, and her husband, Ewen, a naturalist, settled near Terry in the late 1800s. Evelyn was a friend and neighbor to several generations of Kemptons. Her photos show typical Montana life of that time (see *Photographing Montana 1894–1928: The Life and Work of Evelyn Cameron,* by Donna M. Lucey).

In the 1920s, when many of my stories take place, Terry was a small town of under a thousand people. There was a general store, feed store, livery stable, blacksmith, post office, dry goods store, ladies finery shop, farm supply store, newspaper office, drug store, the State Bank of Terry, a few churches, several saloons, the Kempton Hotel, the sheriff's office, and other assorted shops and buildings, plus private homes, all typical of a small Montana town.

Cattle were shipped from local ranches to the Midwest, and passengers came and went on the Northern Pacific Railway or by stagecoach in the early days.

*T*he **KEMPTON RANCH** was located near the small town of Terry in Prairie County, Montana.

KEMPTON TIME LINE

Manasseh Kempton (1589—1662) arrives at Plymouth Plantation from England	1620
American Revolutionary War	1775–1783
Elbridge T. Gerry (1744–1814) signs the Declaration of Independence	1776
Joseph Kempton (1817–1909) marries Eliza Sabrina Foote (1821–1901)	1841
Elbridge Gerry (1825–1875) opens trading post in Colorado	1842
Joseph, Eliza, and family move to Colorado	1856
American Civil War	1861–1865
Homestead Act passed	1862
James B. (JB) Kempton (1843–1910) marries Maria Emma Gerry (1851–1910) in Colorado	1869
JB Kempton establishes Kempton Ranch near Terry, Montana	1882
Martha Magnuson (1886–1964) is born in Sweden	1886
Berney E. Kempton (1870–1942) tours with Dr. Carver's Wild West Show	1889–1891
Montana Statehood	1889
Martha Magnuson (1886–1964) emigrates from Sweden to United States	1895
Kempton Hotel built in Terry, Montan	1904
Berney E. Kempton and Martha Magnuson marry	1909
Gerald O'Meagher Kempton (1912–1994) is born in Terry	1912
Gerald Kempton (1912–1994) and Phyllis Engdahl marry in Olympia WA	1938
Gerald and Phyllis Kempton move to Anchorage, Alaska	1941
Trudy Kempton Dana is born in Anchorage	1945
Kempton Ranch sold	1946
Kempton Hotel sold	1960
Berney E. Kempton inducted into Montana Cowboy Hall of Fame	2015

WILD WEST SHOW
IN A TRUNK

O ne fall afternoon, Jerry Kempton and Pansy McMillan, both ten years old, helped their mothers prepare for the upcoming Sunday night dinner, an important and popular institution on the Kempton Ranch, a large horse and cattle spread outside the small town of Terry in Prairie County, eastern Montana. Jerry was the second oldest son of ranch owners Berney and Martha Kempton, and Pansy was the daughter of Anna McMillan, a widow who lived on the ranch and helped Mrs. Kempton in the kitchen.

The sign for the Kempton Ranch.

The Kempton Ranch house, from the front.

A crowd was expected that evening, and there was still a lot to do. Jerry and Pansy set tables, put out serving dishes, arranged chairs, and did other chores. But they were anxious to finish and have some free time, so they tended to be underfoot. With sighs of exasperation, both mothers suggested they run along and find something to do until guests arrived. The youngsters, glad to be done with chores, readily agreed. Unfortunately, they soon realized there would no outdoor activities—it was raining.

The dining room at the Kempton Ranch.

"Pansy, I spent a half hour ironing that dress. Don't get wet, and stay clean," Mrs. McMillan warned.

"You too, Jer," reminded Mrs. Kempton. "Those are your Sunday pants and shirt."

"Yeah, Mom," answered Jerry.

"Okay, Ma, don't worry," said Pansy as she tugged at one of the ribbons in her light brown hair.

Usually her hair flew free, but today her mother did it up in ringlets that framed her freckled face and pert button nose. Both the curls and the fancy dress with scratchy crinolines caused her some discomfort since she usually wore overalls or loose skirts that allowed her to ride and play. She was an active girl, friends with all the Kempton boys, but closest to Jerry. She was generally happy and optimistic, even after losing her father and her home just a few years before. Pansy was kind, just about as smart as Jerry, and she always tried to do the right thing.

Jerry and Pansy sat on the covered porch and watched the rain until Jerry spoke up.

"What do you wanna do?"

"I dunno," Pansy replied. "But let's stay outta the kitchen."

Jerry agreed, paused a moment in thought, then said, "I know! Let's explore the attic!"

The attic stretched the full length of the house and was largely unused except for storage. This mysterious and interesting place was full of castoffs, seasonal decorations, and old furniture. Usually the children were discouraged from playing up there, but Jerry and Pansy reasoned that if they were quiet and put everything back as they found it, it would be okay. Besides, probably no one would find them there and ask them to help with any further dinner preparations.

Whispering to one another, they climbed the steep staircase at the end of the upstairs hall of bedrooms and opened the door to the attic. Light filtered in through the high windows, and they could hear the rain patter on the roof close above them. The place smelled dusty. Old sheets covered furniture and boxes were stacked four high. They saw numerous trunks and smaller leather cases, plus all sorts of other treasures that looked interesting to young, curious eyes.

"Hey Pansy, look here!" Jerry said, his face lit up with a playful smirk. He pulled a sheet off a dress form that both mothers used for sewing their clothing, plopped a nearby feathered hat on the neck of the form, and danced around the room with the busty headless lady. The children laughed as Jerry finished the dance and returned the lady to her place.

Jerry caught sight of himself in a large floor mirror. He was tall for his age with lots of thick, black hair that curled back from what his father called a "swarthy" face. His mother occasionally kidded him about being "tall, dark, and handsome," like a movie star. Jerry thought he looked honest but wasn't really sure what honesty looked like in a person. Generally, he liked himself and most people liked him too.

After that quick self-assessment, he turned back to Pansy, who pulled a sheet from an ornate velvet settee. They plunked themselves down on the moth-riddled cushions and watched puffs of dust rise around them, glimmering in the light from the windows.

Jerry turned and noticed an old, battered trunk on the floor next to the settee.

"Hey, look at this trunk. Where'd it come from?" he asked.

"I dunno, but look at all those stickers!"

The sides and top of the trunk were plastered with old stickers advertising hotels and cities. Although the stickers had faded and peeled, Pansy could still read a few.

"St. Petersburg, Melbourne, Vienna, Berlin, Cairo, London, San Francisco," she rattled off. "This trunk's been around the whole world, just about. Who'd it belong to?"

"I dunno. Let's open it and see."

Both children pulled and yanked on the lid until the corroded hasp finally gave way. Jerry carefully lifted the lid on squeaky hinges and they peered in.

Inside on top was a large folded paper poster. They gently opened the folds and smoothed the edges to find that it was an advertisement for "Doctor Carver's Wild America Show." The poster showed Indians in full-feathered headdresses sitting somberly atop ponies and cowboys riding and roping, dressed in vests, chaps, and cowboy hats. At the bottom of the poster was a photo of a cowboy on horseback throwing a rope. Underneath was the name "Berney Kempton."

"Look at this!" Jerry exhaled as he saw the name. "I think that's Dad! He was in a Wild West Show? Why didn't I know about that?"

"That's keen!" said Pansy. "Looks like he was a star, but I wonder why he didn't ever tell you."

They gazed at the poster for a few minutes, amazed at what they had found. Then they carefully folded and put it aside.

Next they found a stack of yellowed newspaper articles from a number of countries that appeared to detail the events of Doctor Carver's Wild America Show. Many were printed in languages they couldn't read, but the pictures showed the same cowboys and Indians that were on the poster.

Pansy pulled out an article from a Melbourne, Australia, newspaper. "This one's about your dad. Look! It says he roped kangaroos!"

"Jeepers! Kangaroos?" Jerry said as he came closer, and they both read the newspaper story. "How'd he do that? He even roped two of 'em in one loop!"

After scanning the stack of newspaper articles, they put them aside. Then Jerry lifted out a professional studio portrait of his father in his younger years holding a lasso and standing stiffly next to a saddle.

"Look at Dad. He was so young then."

"Yeah, and handsome too," Pansy added.

"Kinda like me!" Jerry joked as he posed in what he thought was his most handsome stance.

Pansy laughed. "Ah, come on, Jerry, let's see what else is in here."

Leaning over the trunk, Jerry pulled out a leather vest with colorful, intricate beadwork and a pair of matching chaps.

"This is what Dad wore in that photo."

"I'll bet it was his show outfit!" suggested Pansy excitedly.

The children continued removing things from the trunk. They found a very worn leather jacket, several old white shirts, stained and yellowed, and a pair of well-worn, tooled leather boots covered with mildew.

Under all that was a large envelope stuffed with papers. Jerry riffled through, pulled out several pages and looked them over.

"Gee whiz! Here's the paper Dad signed with Doctor Carver! Let's see—Dad was born in 1870, and he signed this in 1889. That means he was only eighteen or maybe nineteen when he joined the show!"

"Here's the places they went to. Golly, they went all over the world," Pansy remarked as she handed the list to Jerry.

Pansy pulled out a stack of letters tied with string and looked them over. "These are old letters your dad wrote. Here's one to his parents from Egypt. Listen to this: 'Me and two other passengers were strolling about the night of the fifteen of Novemeber, and we seen something that I never since forgot.'"

Berney's letter from Egypt.

"Um, not very good English, is it?" Jerry interjected.

"Yeah, there's more: 'The Egyptians were worshiping Mohamad [sic] and were going through with some of the greatest motions I ever seen, and they would keep it up for two and three hours at a time and all the time repeating the word Ahla in diferant tones of voice. The head priests fixed chairs for us in front of them, and there we drank some of the finest coffee in the land. After the performance was over they gave us some sweet flavored water that had been perserved for a year.'"

"Yuck, I wouldn't drink water that sat around that long," said Jerry with a grimace.

"Me neither," agreed Pansy.

"Look at that last paragraph about a ship steward who killed himself!" Jerry exclaimed. "Yuck, it says he cut his throat with broken glass. Ick, I hope Dad didn't see that."

"And they went into churches built clear back in 1734! Golly, that's so old," Pansy said.

"Let's keep all these letters and stuff out so we can look at it later," Pansy suggested as she set the papers next to her on the floor and turned back to the trunk.

"Now, what's this thing?" she asked, holding up a dark-brown, curved piece of shaped wood.

"I've seen pictures of these before. It's a boomerang," said Jerry, taking it from Pansy. "When you throw it, it comes back to you 'cause of the curve. Australian natives use it for hunting." Jerry stood and made like he was going to throw it but said, "Too bad we don't have more room up here. Maybe we can try it outside sometime."

When the children reached the bottom of the trunk, they found a light-brown, short-haired, tanned skin.

Jerry held up the long pelt and said, "What in blazes is this?"

"Jerry, you know we're not supposed to swear," said Pansy sternly.

"Jesus, Pansy, that's not swearing, but what do you think it is anyway? The fur's too short for a wolf, and the pelt's too long. It's not a cow or horse skin. What is it?" asked Jerry.

"I think it's a kangaroo!" said Pansy as she pointed excitedly to the pouch. "A kangaroo skin! I wonder if your dad roped this one."

Jerry looked up from the trunk and frowned.

"Jer, what's wrong?" asked Pansy. "You look sad."

"Well, it's just—" Jerry sighed. "I wonder why Dad didn't talk about this. He was a star, and we didn't know it. He didn't even tell his own kids!"

"You'd think he'd want to brag about something like that," Pansy said.

"Yeah, I sure wouldn't keep it a secret! I'd tell everyone!"

"I know how we can find out more about this!" exclaimed Pansy. "Let's show this stuff to your dad and everyone else tonight after dinner, right before dessert, and ask him about it!"

Jerry lit up at the suggestion. "Great idea! He'd have to tell us in front of all those people, don'cha think?"

Giving it another thought, Jerry added, "Do you think he might get mad 'cause we got into his stuff?"

"No, how mad could he get with all those people there watching him?" Pansy reasoned.

The children gathered the leather vest and chaps, poster, studio portrait, kangaroo skin, and the envelope full of letters and papers, then returned everything else to the trunk. From the high windows, Pansy and Jerry saw buggies and a few cars arrive and knew Sunday dinner would soon be underway. They brushed the dust off their good clothes, closed the trunk, and headed downstairs, excited about what they found and the possibility of learning more about this unknown phase in the life of Berney Kempton.

Sunday dinner at the Kempton Ranch was a special weekly event. Usually every table in the dining room was filled with townspeople, visitors, ranchers, and anyone else who wanted a great meal and an enjoyable evening. Martha Kempton was known for her delicious beef

The dining area on the porch at the Kempton Ranch.

and chicken dinners with mashed potatoes that boasted some of the best gravy in Prairie County and even possibly in all of Montana. There were vegetables from the ranch garden, and warm Parker House rolls were standard. To finish the evening, dessert always included Martha's famous apple pie.

Jerry and Pansy usually loved Sunday dinners, but this particular one seemed to stretch on forever as the adults ate, laughed, and talked endlessly. The two children anxiously waited for what felt like eons until, finally, there was a pause before coffee and dessert.

The youngsters had rehearsed what Jerry would say, but they were still nervous, unsure how their surprise would be taken. After an exchange of anxious glances, Jerry nodded to Pansy, and they made their way to the head table where Berney was still eating. Jerry tapped his father on the shoulder and leaned to whisper in his ear.

"Me and Pansy have somethin' we wanna show everybody," Jerry said quietly.

Berney looked at him questioningly and said, "What do you wanna show 'em?"

"It's kinda a surprise, Dad, but a good one," Jerry answered.

"Okay, son," Berney said as he stood, raised his hand to silence the conversation, and said, "It appears, my friends, that Jerry and Pansy have something they would like to share with all of us tonight."

When the room quieted, Jerry reached into the box he was carrying and held up the beaded vest and chaps for all to see. He cleared his throat, took a deep breath, and began. "You probably know my dad's an expert rider and roper, but I'll bet you didn't know that when he was only eighteen, he joined the famous Doctor Carver's Wild West Show."

A murmur of interest rippled through the crowd.

Taken by surprise, Berney's eyes widened at the first shock, but then he shook his head and laughed as Pansy held up the poster of a younger version of himself swinging a lasso. Jerry showed the studio portrait of Berney as a young cowboy wearing the beaded vest and chaps.

"Where in the world did you kids get all that?" Berney asked.

"It's really great, Dad," Jerry said, smiling. "We found it in a trunk in the attic."

The dinner guests craned their necks to see what was happening, and some at the back of the room stood to get a better look.

"Hey, Berney, why didn't you tell us about this before?" said Mike Patterson, a neighboring rancher.

A murmur of agreement sounded from the group, and the rest of the diners joined in asking Berney for an explanation. Not usually one to pass up the chance to tell a story, Berney held up the vest and chaps and began telling the crowd about the nearly two years he spent traveling the world with Doctor Carver's Wild West Show.

"I think most of you've heard about Doctor Carver's reputation as a rifle marksman, but do you know he set records that haven't been equaled to this day? He could do things with a rifle that no other man could duplicate, and his work with a shotgun was no less equal. He was one of the first marksmen to advocate shooting with both eyes open.

Some of the members of Doc Carver's Wild West Show, Berney Kempton, far right.

His most amazing feat was hitting fourteen glass balls in the dark just using the sound of the whistling objects to guide his aim."

"He was called Doctor, but he had actually trained to be a dentist, and in his early years, he was a buffalo hunter. I think I have a picture of him in here somewhere," Berney said as he sorted through the envelope, pulled out an old photo, and held it up. "This is how Doc looked all dressed up in showy duds. I actually hooked up with the show in Austria," he continued. "We traveled to France and Belgium then on to Russia. Because I wasn't yet twenty-one, I couldn't enter Russia unless Doctor Carver declared I was his dependent. Dependent? Hogwash! Why, I hadn't depended on anyone since I was eight years old! Kids grow up fast on the prairie. At ten I was sent out on horseback to search for strays with nothing but my gun and a little food. At times I would be alone for days. Before I turned fourteen, I drove both horses and

William Frank "Doc" Carver, 1883.

cattle hundreds of miles, all on my own. Here I was, an adult, yet Russia considered me a dependent child."

"Dad, here's your certificate from Russia," Jerry said as he unfolded a heavy, ivory-colored paper from the envelope.

"Yeah, that's it," said Berney, holding up the official document then passing it around.

"Once we were inside Russia, we first went to Petrograd. Well, now it's called St. Petersburg. While we were there, we gave a special show for Czar Alexander III. My sister, Marie Kempton, and her husband, Ed Phillips, were both with Buffalo Bill's show when it was in Russia years later. Marie told me their troupe appeared before Nicholas Romanov II, his wife, son, and lovely daughters. The royal girls asked them to repeat some of the tricks, and one even wanted Marie to show her how to swing a rope. Marie demonstrated, but the rope kept catching on the girl's skirts. Finally her mother said something to her that made

Berney's permit to enter Russia.

her stop. Marie later heard she told her daughter that she would never be a cowgirl so she had better concentrate on learning to be a duchess! They were just darn nice folks. Unfortunately, as I'm sure you know, the entire family was later tragically assassinated in a civil war in their country. Real shame. To think of anyone killing those sweet girls and that little boy is just horrible.

"After Russia," Berney continued, "we spent some time in Central Europe. As a matter of fact, in Berlin we gave a special performance for Kaiser Wilhelm I. The people were so keen to see a Wild West Show. They were fascinated by cowboys, Indians, riding, and roping—anything from the American West. We did the show for thousands and thousands of 'em, and they always mobbed us afterward, wanting to talk or even get our autographs.

"After we left Europe, our ship traveled through the Mediterranean Sea, and we went ashore at Port Said in Egypt. We nearly killed ourselves eating all the fruit there. It was so delicious, but we just weren't used to that much fruit. I remember eating an orange that was like nothing I ever tasted before. It was so sweet and flavorful. Fruit grew everywhere—there were whole trees full of it.

"The next day in Port Said, I went inside a big building that must have been one of their holy places. It was quiet and restful, and our days were usually almost frantic with all those shows, packing up and getting to the next place. There was little time for just sitting, except for that particular afternoon. I can tell you, there was such a deep sense of peace in that place. Even alone, out on the prairies, I've never felt like that. I tried to explain it to the others, but no one understood so I just enjoyed the memory myself.

"Then we steamed through the Suez Canal towards Melbourne, Australia, where we stayed for five months. It was good to stay put for a while, and those Aussies had such a hankering to know about Indians and cowboys."

Berney thought this was a good time to take a break, since Martha was pouring coffee and handing around slices of apple pie.

"Let's stop and have some dessert, then I'll tell you more. I need some coffee and pie to keep up my strength," he kidded.

As the diners finished dessert, the questions began once more.

"Berney, when did you leave the show?" asked J. W. Stith, the proprietor of the Terry Mercantile.

"After stops in Johannesburg in South Africa, the Samoan Islands, and Hawaii, we finally arrived back in San Francisco. I left the show there in 1892 to come back to Terry. After being gone for so long, it was time to get back to my regular life. You know, I saw the world at a young age, and I came to realize I wanted to spend the rest of my life in Montana," said Berney to rousing applause from the crowd.

When the clapping died and he continued, Berney talked about the other cowboys and the sharpshooters. He told about the stoic Indians who went along on the tour and how difficult it was for them to go from their simple lives on the plains of Montana to perform in European palaces for royal audiences.

"Why, there were many times I wondered what a cowboy from Montana was doing there among European royalty. And if I felt out of place, you can imagine how difficult it was for those Indians," Berney admitted.

Pansy passed around the old envelope stuffed with papers they found in the trunk, and the diners looked through the documents.

Ewen Cameron, a neighboring rancher, waved a folded sheet and asked, "This contract says you joined the Wild West Show in Fort Yates, North Dakota. Why did you join up there?"

Berney explained that Doctor Carver had already been in Miles City, not too long a ride from the ranch, recruiting riders and ropers.

"At that time," he said, "I was passed over, but I didn't give up 'cause I knew I was a better rider and roper than some of the cowboys he hired. So when Doctor Carver recruited Indians from the Standing Rock Reservation at Fort Yates, I rode more than 250 miles over there to try again. I knew I had to do something special to get Doc Carver's attention, so I went and found a wild stallion," Berney mentioned casually.

"What did you do with a wild stallion?" Jerry asked, incredulous. "Did you get a saddle on him?"

"Well, not quite," Berney explained. "Actually, I rode the stallion bareback into the saloon where Doc Carver was having a drink and stopped the horse right in front of him. Then I turned and rode back out. Didn't even say a word," Berney added nonchalantly. Hearing this, Jerry and Pansy's jaws dropped, and those in the crowd who knew Berney's penchant for showmanship chuckled.

"What'd he do?" Jerry asked.

Berney laughed. "Hired me on the spot, of course! Then he arranged for me to meet up with the show in Vienna."

"Berney, whatever are those hanks of long hair the Indian in this old photo has in his hand?" asked Bonnie Patterson, the wife of a neighboring rancher, holding up a photograph from the envelope. "It couldn't be what I think it is, could it?" she continued.

"Well," said Berney, "that's Big Bear, a Hunkpapa Sioux, who wore a number of scalps on his belt when he did the show."

"Ew!" several women exclaimed.

"You gotta remember these were real Indians, and it wasn't too many years before then that warriors commonly took the scalps of enemies they killed and wore 'em on a belt. In fact, many of the Indians with the show fought in Custer's Battle of the Little Bighorn in 1876 when I was only a small fry. During the time we all traveled together in the show, some of the braves and chiefs even showed me their scars from that battle, but they wouldn't say a word about what happened. I think they're afraid of retaliation.

"Some of you know that my mother, Maria Gerry, was the daughter of Molly Red Kettle, whose father was Chief Joseph Red Kettle of the Lakota Sioux. I've always been proud of my Indian blood. I even spent some time on the reservation and learned to speak Sioux. When I was with Doctor Carver, I got to be good friends with many of the Indians. Even though they trusted me, not a one would tell about that day at the Little Bighorn. They took those secrets to their graves."

"Berney, can I speak up here?" asked Asa Kempton.

"Sure, but it depends on what you're gonna say," laughed Berney. "You're my brother and we have a lot of secrets together."

Asa stood and said, "I hafta to tell you this about Berney. When he was in the Wild West Show, he befriended many of the Indians hired

Big Bear with scalps.

directly from the reservation. Like he told you, he spoke Sioux, and the tribes trusted him. When I asked him about this, he said those Indians were overwhelmed, going from the plains of Montana to the palaces of Europe, performing for royalty. It was even a more difficult adjustment for them than it was for him. He said this was simply his way of making things a little easier for them. He said nothing about their skin color. To Berney, they were just people who needed a hand. That's just the kind of man he is," Asa said, sitting.

Left to right, Red Horse, Big Bear, and Painted Horse.

The crowd applauded as Berney stood there, embarrassed but secretly gratified. To get the focus off himself, he turned and asked Jerry, "What else you got in that box, son?"

Jerry pulled out a paper and said, "I can't read the language of this newspaper, but it shows you riding a big black horse bareback, with a bunch of military men watching. What's that all about?"

"Yeah, we gave a private performance in St. Petersburg for the Dowager Empress of Russia. She was a real sweetheart, kind of like a friendly grandma. That big Cossack horse was brought to the show one night. He had thrown off an entire regiment of riders, one after the other. No one could stay on that devil. He was bucking and kicking when they forced him into the ring, but within minutes I was able to ride him. The Empress was real impressed. She even said in English, 'He outrides my Cossacks.' I guess I just have a knack with wild horses. I speak their language," Berney joked.

"Mr. Kempton," said Pansy, "here's an old *Ripley's Believe It or Not* cartoon about how you roped two kangaroos in one loop."

Berney took the yellowed newspaper clipping from Pansy. "That's right. One night in Melbourne, a number of kangaroos were herded into the ring,

Ripley's Believe It or Not featured Berney's two-kangaroo roping stunt. This particular panel appeared after Berney's death.

and I was told to rope 'em. Actually, it was just the same as roping horses, cattle, and an occasional wolf here on the range. On my third try, by chance, I caught two kangaroos in the same loop. The crowd went wild thinking it was part of the show. From then on, people expected that trick at every performance. Word got out, and a fellow from *Ripley's Believe It or Not* showed up one night. His cartoon appeared in a number of newspapers. In fact, a family friend in Astoria, Oregon, saw the drawing in the *Rogue River Courier* and sent it to the family in Terry. My brothers told me that when JB looked at the cartoon, he dryly remarked that it was high time I got back to roping horses," Berney added.

For the next hour, folks continued to ask Berney about his famous past. Finally, when it grew late, they finished seconds of pie and coffee, bid one another goodnight, and headed home. After Berney said goodbye to the last guest and came back in the house, he gathered the keepsakes from the Wild West Show and put them carefully on a side table in the dining room. He stopped and looked back at the collection once more. What an unforgettable evening it had been, stepping back in

Doctor Carver's Wild West Show in Copenhagen
Berney Kempton top row, fifth from left

Doc Carver's Wild West Show members in Denmark.

time to when he was a young man seeing the world and earning more money than a cowboy ever dreamed of.

When he left the Wild West Show, he was a twenty-year-old star—a cocky, handsome young man. But when he returned home, he stepped back once again into the hard life of ranching. Instead of being a celebrated rider and roper, he was just one of the six Kempton sons.

Berney knew it was difficult for some of the Wild West stars to return to their previous lives. He heard a number turned to drink, and some still tried to catch the glamour they once experienced. Berney made a successful transition because he put fame behind him and moved on. By hard work, he eventually became the owner of the Kempton Ranch, one of the largest spreads in Montana, as well as a respected family man.

Berney was still handsome, with thick, black wavy hair and perfect posture. He dressed well, usually in a white shirt and tie, English riding pants and jacket, high leather boots, and a trim-brimmed hat. He always pulled a lock of thick hair forward so it showed under his hat.

The mantle clock striking ten brought Berney out of his daydreams. He turned out the gas lights then headed upstairs. *Ah, the difference between my life then and my life now,* Berney thought.

The life I have now is what I really wanted," he said aloud as he went to find his wife, Martha.

A short time later when Jerry was in his room almost asleep, Berney came in and sat on the bed beside him.

"Dad, I hope you weren't mad that we got into your stuff, but why didn't you ever tell us you were famous?"

"No, son, I'm not mad. In fact, it was fun reliving all those memories tonight. I never bragged about being in that show because a man needs to be known for the good he is doing in the present, not for what he did way back in the past. I did all that when I was a young man, long before I met your mother. My time with the Wild West Show was a grand adventure, but the importance of my life is how this ranch supports all of us and helps Prairie County."

Doc Carver's Wild West Show members in Melbourne, Australia.

"I guess I understand that, but maybe you could've quietly told us," suggested Jerry.

Berney chuckled and said, "Your mother took the vest and chaps and plans to frame 'em to hang in the dining room. That'll be interesting for our guests." Berney paused and then said, "But remember, son, we can't live in the past. We have to make the present something we can be proud of and plan for the future. That's the real measure of a man," he added as he hugged his son.

"I love you, Dad," Jerry said as his father stood.

"I love you too, son," his father replied, leaving the room and softly closing the door.

Jerry soon fell asleep dreaming of wild Russian Cossack horses, hopping kangaroos, and the dashing young man with a lasso who became his father.

Author's note: The dark-colored ironwood boomerang is still in our family and hangs on the wall of my brother's home. We never saw it in use.

Ewen Cameron was the husband of the famous prairie photographer Evelyn Cameron. He was a naturalist who studied the birds of the area. The Camerons' ranch was nearby, and they were friends and neighbors to two generations of the Kempton family.

ORPHANS FOLLOWING
THEIR FATHER'S DREAM

*M*artha Kempton quietly opened the door to her son's bedroom to make sure he had finally stopped reading. If she or Berney didn't enforce Jerry's bedtime, he read until the wee hours of the morning and was tired the next day. That boy loved to read.

Jerry had put away his book but was still sitting up in bed with a thoughtful look.

"Hi, Mom. I was just thinking about you."

"Oh, you were, were you?" Martha replied with a chuckle.

"Yeah, I was wondering what it was like when you were a kid."

"Well, my life wasn't as easy as yours, and you'll probably tell your children that your life wasn't as easy as theirs. Most parents hope their children have a better time growing up than they did."

Martha Kempton.

"Was life really bad for you as a kid?"

"Yes, it was extremely hard for me and my sisters and brothers and doesn't make for a pleasant story. I sometimes wonder how I survived, let alone came to Montana and thrived."

"You were an orphan, weren't you? Is that why it was so bad? Tell me about it?" Jerry asked, interested, but also hoping to delay his bedtime.

It was a rare, quiet night on the Kempton Ranch, and Martha had some free time. Although she didn't like reliving those painful memories, she realized Jerry should know about her childhood, and perhaps this was a good time to tell him.

With a deep sigh, she said, "Okay, I'll tell you because you should know our family history—but only if you promise to go to sleep afterwards." She pushed a lock of dark curly hair off her son's forehead.

"I promise. Sit here," Jerry said, patting the bed. "I'll move Tucker. Come here, boy," he said to the family dog.

"You should also ask your father to tell you about his childhood. Did you know that his family came from Colorado?"

"Yeah, I know some of that," answered Jerry.

"Ask him about Elbridge Gerry. He was called the 'Paul Revere' of Weld County, Colorado. Once, he rode all night to alert settlers to a planned Indian attack. Lives were saved because of his warnings."

"Wow! I'll ask him," said Jerry.

"You should know about your heritage so you can someday pass it on to your children. It's not all good, but then life isn't all good, is it? Let me get a few things in my dresser that are important to the story," Martha said as she left the room.

"You gotta move over, Tucker," Jerry said as he gently pushed the family dog awake. "Momma's gonna sit there and tell us a story."

Tucker obediently got up from where he usually slept and resettled himself at the bed's end.

"Good boy," Jerry said, plumping up his pillow.

Jerry simply thought of his mother as just that, a mother. He knew she came from Sweden, and he grew up hearing her pleasant accent, but he never really thought of it as foreign.

Soon Martha came back, handed Jerry two small photographs of a woman and a man, an aerial photo of a farm, an old worn and faded head-scarf, and a beautiful ornate hair comb with blue stones on the swirled top. Jerry had never seen the photos or the scarf, but he recognized the hair comb his mother wore when she dressed up for special occasions.

Old memories came alive for Martha as she looked at the keepsakes and wondered where all the years had gone. *How does time pass so quickly?* she thought. *And how can we slow its passage?*

Martha settled herself on Jerry's bed as Tucker licked her hand, snuffled, and went back to sleep. She stroked the dog's soft ears and began.

"This old scarf is one of the few things I have from my childhood. It's linen that was made from flax we raised on our farm. My grandmother wove the flax into cloth and colored it with natural dyes from her garden. I remember watching her sit at a big loom, weaving and singing to me."

"Jeepers, that scarf is really old!"

"Old? Son, are you trying to tell me I'm old?" Martha asked with mock alarm.

"I didn't mean that—you'll never be old," Jerry said, but he remembered the other day he noticed his mother's brown hair was streaked with gray and the skin around her eyes wrinkled when she smiled. Jerry always thought his mother was pretty in a friendly, motherly way. She was kind and smart, a constant, dependable ally in his life, and he hoped she would never grow old.

Martha held the first photo near Jerry's bedside kerosene lamp so they could both see and said, "Here's what the family farm in Sweden looked like when I was a young child. It was called High Hill, *Höga Berg* in Swedish, and the land had been in father's family for generations. My grandfather, Elof, built the large two-story house, the smaller hired man's place that included a carpentry shop, the barn, and other buildings when he was a young man in about 1820. He constructed it on the site of an older house. Most buildings were made of wood and painted red. All the roofs were slate, and the long barn was made of stone. That barn was such a fun place for us children with the animals, all snug and warm. We used to play with the sheep, and they were clean, not greasy like Montana sheep. Part of the barn was called the granary, and the floor there was made of hardwood. I remember my father beating or 'flailing' the grain and also a horse going 'round and 'round to thresh grain."

Höga Berg, the family farm in Sweden.

"Why was some threshed and some flailed?"

"I don't remember why that was, but I do remember that there was another not-so-nice use for the granary in the winter. When the ground was frozen, people from the village laid out their dead in our granary. We children didn't like that at all."

"I can see why!" Jerry said.

Martha laughed, looked at the photo again, and said, "That building to the right of the house in front of the barn was the most wonderful storehouse. It was there we kept our rye, oat, and wheat flour, casings for sausage, salt pork, salt herring, and the dry codfish we made into lutefisk. The lye with which lutefisk was made came from the wood ashes in our fireplace. In the storehouse, we also had large longhorn and caraway cheeses and rye crisps—round with holes in the middle—strung up on long poles hung across the room. Lingonberries were put in large kegs and covered with water. In winter, we cut chunks of this frozen water and berries and made a sauce sweetened with brown syrup. I think the sugar for the syrup came from Cuba in fifty-pound, triangularly shaped hunks. We used an ax to cut what we needed. This storehouse was a fairyland for us children, and we always watched for our mother or one of the hired girls when they went out there, so we could go along. It was built like an Alaskan cache, up on stilts."

"Why stilts?" asked Jerry.

"That prevented animals from getting into the foodstuffs. There was also a flax house out back and a few other smaller outbuildings that don't show in the photograph."

"What's a flax house?" Jerry asked, peering closely at the photo.

"It was a small house where the harvested flax plants were woven on large looms to become the linen cloth used for many of our clothes. You can see some of the fields planted in flax on the left and the orchard on the right. We frequently chased magpies out of the apples, currants, cherries, and orchard fruit so they wouldn't eat it all. The farmland in front extended all the way down to the lake, and in back was forest timber."

"It all looks neat and tidy."

"It was. I remember it was a very pretty place. My grandfather worked the land with his sons, but my father, Magnus, who was probably not yet twenty, decided to go to America to learn about new farming methods. Sweden had just endured several years of devastating crop failure, and the land was already overused. Magnus heard about farming experiments in Kansas that helped increase soil productivity. He hoped to study agriculture and then bring the knowledge back to help Swedish farmers. And he did just that.

"He studied at an agricultural school somewhere in Kansas for seven or more years, learned English, and became familiar with American customs. He returned home to Sweden after his father had a stroke, but when he tried to make suggestions about farming, his brothers and other Swedish farmers wouldn't listen. They said farming was better understood in Sweden, and the things Father told them about agriculture in America couldn't possibly be true. They accused him of thinking he was better than they were because he had lived in America. That must have been very discouraging for Father. Also during the years he was gone, his brothers somehow took over his share of the farm and left little for him."

"So they took his land while he was in America learning things that would have helped them all?" Jerry asked, frowning.

"Yes, I guess so. But all that happened before I was even born. Soon after his return to Sweden, Father married my mother, Kajsa. Look at these pictures of them. I still have the photographs because I kept them between the pages of my Bible."

Magnus Elofson.   *Kajsa Anderson.*

"Those are your parents?" Jerry asked, looking closely at the two oval photos. "You look kinda like your mother, I think."

"Well, maybe," said Martha thoughtfully.

"Did your father feel cheated when his brothers took the land? Did he get it back?"

"He tried to force them to make it right, but it never happened, and he was bitter about that for many years. His bitterness did no good and probably hurt him more than it did his brothers. You know what they say, 'The acid of bitterness burns the vessel that contains it.'"

"Yeah, I can see that," Jerry said.

"Yes. I'm getting way ahead of myself. I should start at the beginning."

"I was born on December 18, 1886, in the Village of Byn, county of Gunnarskog, Province of Vermland, Sweden, and I was the fourth of six children. Our early years were good. We had plenty to eat and lots of brothers, sisters, and cousins to play with. However, that all ended abruptly when our mother died."

"That must have been terrible."

"Yes, life changed completely."

"How old were you then?" Jerry asked.

"I was eight years old."

"How'd she die?"

"Well, she died just a few days after Betty was born," Martha began. "She was only thirty-eight years old, but she never recovered from that difficult birth. I remember I was allowed in her room for just a minute and saw her lying in bed, so pale and weak, holding tiny Betty. She died just a day or so later."

"That's sad."

Martha quickly composed herself, then said, "I don't remember Mother's funeral, but I clearly remember when we all got home from the church. I went into her closet, where I still smelled her scent. I put my hand up the sleeve of one of her dresses and pressed it to my face. I can see it yet—the dress was a pretty blue, trimmed with black braid. I stayed there in the closet hugging the dress and sobbing until my sister Mary found me. I also remember how Father stood alone in the bedroom, holding little Betty, just staring out the window and looking lost. Finally, Mary took the baby from him and told him that we would all help him care for Betty. Betty was a darling child, so easy, happy, and loving. She was a joy to all of us."

"Your mother sure died early, but I remember hearing you tell someone that your mother's father lived until he was 102 years old, was never sick a day in his life, and only died when he fell off a hay rake."

"That's right. My grandfather lived a long and healthy life and so did my grandmother, who died when she was eighty-six. But Mother didn't have their constitution. I think Father's father also lived until he was ninety-four, although his wife died quite early."

"Mom, I sure hope you and Dad live a long time. I love you both and don't know what I'd do without you."

Martha leaned over, gave Jerry a hug, and said, "I hope so too. We just never know when the Lord will take us, but I plan to live a long time."

"Then what happened?"

"After Mother died," Martha continued, "Father cared for us as best he could, but he was not well. He often told us about America and the unbelievable opportunities for farming on the Great Plains. He told us that crops grew quickly with very little rain in the rich soil. He often talked of his desire to take all of us back to America. When he became ill, he strongly urged us to emigrate, even though he probably knew he wouldn't live to go with us. He wanted us to settle on the West Coast or Great Plains. He taught us English and told us about life in the United States.

"Then just a few years after Mother's death, Father died of tuberculosis —a horrible disease of the lungs. I remember he coughed day and night and gradually became weaker. One of the last things he told us was that our family would prosper when we all lived in America. Eventually we children prospered, but it was a long road with much heartache."

Jerry was silent for a time before he asked, "What was your father like?"

"He was kind and loved us children very much but had a heavy mood, unlike his own father who was always full of fun. Our father loved our mother and was heartbroken when she died. I remember that he detested vanity in any form, and I often wonder how Mother, with her slow sweet smile, managed to have all those pretty dresses."

Tucker whined and put his cold nose in Martha's palm, and she reached down to pet him.

"Good boy," said Jerry. "You go to sleep now."

"Our oldest sister Mary was sixteen when Father died, and she tried to take care of us children. Little Betty was less than three years old. Mary wanted to keep us all together and stay on the farm, but Father's relatives didn't permit that. Father and his brothers didn't have a good relationship, and I think it grew far worse after Mother died, but they hid most of that contention from us children. After Father's death, his older brother took dreadful advantage of us, cheating us out of Father's small share of the land, our land. We were powerless children without our parents. No one spoke up for us, and sadly, none of our uncles or aunts or even grandparents took us in. All six of us quickly went to different places."

"Why in the world didn't your aunts or grandparents keep you?" Jerry said angrily. "Isn't that what family is for?"

"Yes, of course, they should have taken us in, but they didn't," Martha said with a sigh. "That's still a mystery to me because they were nice people, and aunts, uncles, and grandparents commonly adopted orphaned children of their relatives. Father's father, our grandfather, was a respected sort of scribe for all the neighbors, a wonderful writer, full of fun, who helped settle disputes and acted as an informal mayor, but he died before Father, so he couldn't help us either. I know that Father's older brother—and I don't even remember his name—was very jealous of Father and reviled him as the know-it-all brother who had lived in America. That man was a mean bully, and perhaps he strongly influenced the family not to take us in."

"Reviled means hated?" asked Jerry

"Yes, but we know there are always eventual consequences for one's actions, even if they're not judged here on earth. But I've never understood why we weren't taken in by family, and it's sad, even to this day."

"What happened to your aunts and uncles in Sweden?"

"I don't know. We didn't stay in contact, and there wasn't much love lost."

Tucker interrupted the conversation, sound asleep on his back, with his legs in the air, pedaling as if he were running.

"I'll bet he's chasing something in his dream," Jerry said. "He looks so funny."

They laughed, and Tucker roused with a whine and a big stretch.

"What do you think he was dreaming about?" Jerry asked.

"I don't know. Maybe chasing a rabbit or running after one of you boys."

Tucker wagged his tail, licked Jerry's face, and jumped down off the bed.

"Keep on with your story, Mom."

"I could finish up another night. It's getting late."

"Ah, please. Usually you're so busy. This is more important than sleep."

"Okay, but this is the saddest part. After Father died, I remember how we cried and pleaded to stay together, but it did little good. No family in the village would take all of us, and they wouldn't even take two of us together. I remember our oldest sister, Mary, tried to comfort us and promised she would keep in touch. She said someday we would all go to America and be together again. I think we wondered how in the world that would happen with all of us just thrown to the winds."

"That's really sad."

"Yes, it was, and that's why I almost hate to bring up these memories. But we know that the outcome was eventually positive and most of my brothers and sisters are here in Montana, living close to one another, even after all that."

"Where'd you go when they split you up?" Jerry asked.

"I first went to live in an orphanage in Oslo, Norway, and that's where I learned to speak Norwegian, along with my native Swedish. Mary, true to her word, kept in touch. She began working right away and sometimes sent me candy or a new dress, but she saved most of her money to pay for passage to America."

"She was a really good sister. How old was she?"

"She would have been about sixteen. It was due to her that we're all here. She was always close to Father and told him she would do her best to honor his wishes of settling the family in America."

"She was a hero! I'm gonna thank her next time I see her."

"She'd like that," Martha laughed.

"How long were you in the orphanage?"

"I think I was there a year or two, and I kept busy helping care for the younger children. I wasn't paid, but I had enough to eat and lots of company. Then, unfortunately, the orphanage sent me to live with an older man and woman who were very cruel. They only wanted a child to work for them, without pay. I was essentially their slave. I was constantly tired, hungry, and oh so lonely. Most nights I clutched that old linen headscarf grandmother made for me back in Sweden and cried myself to sleep. If I complained or didn't work fast enough, they beat me with a willow switch."

"Really? Didn't the orphanage know they were bad?"

"I don't think they did much checking on potential parents' characters or living situations back then. They were mostly interested in just finding homes for their orphans."

"I don't know how it happened, but after a year, I went to another family as a nursemaid for their children, even though I was young myself. Swedish girls were prized by rich families as governesses and ladies' maids. I was a smart girl, able to read and write in Swedish, Norwegian, and some English too. That kind family fostered my learning and treated me well. I'll always be grateful to them. Eventually, I became their cook, and that's where I first learned to make the cinnamon rolls you love so much.

"True to her word, Mary kept in touch and reminded us of Father's dream of living in America. Soon both August and Mary emigrated and made their way to Miles City, where other Swedish families settled. August worked in a tin shop, and Mary had a job with a wealthy family. They both sent money to Anna in Sweden, and soon she joined them."

"That's keen how all of you helped each other come over," Jerry said, wondering if he and his brothers possessed such intense dedication.

"Yes, we worked hard to save money for each other's passage. I hoped to be next with my brother Wilhelm, and knew I needed to get a paying job."

Martha looked at the clock on Jerry's nightstand.

"Is your clock right?"

"I think so. Why?"

"I'll be back in a minute. I've got to get the cinnamon rolls in the oven," Martha said as she left the room.

Mmm, cinnamon rolls, Jerry thought. *Maybe if we talk long enough, they'll be baked and I can sneak down and get one. Mom is such a good cook. Of all the mothers I know, she's the very best.*

Soon Martha returned, bringing the waft of cinnamon with her as she sat on his bed and continued the story.

"Eventually I left that wonderful family to look for paying work. I had become an experienced cook, so I applied to be the cook on a packet ship."

"What's a packet ship?"

"It's a small ship that mainly carries mail from one place to another. Ours went between Norway and Sweden, and sometimes our boat carried passengers too. I first talked to them about the job when I was fifteen, but they told me I was too young. So I went home, put my hair up, put on makeup, borrowed a sophisticated-looking dress, then went back a few days later. They hired me! I saved almost all the money I made because I had my own small room on the boat and didn't have to pay for meals.

"My brother Wilhelm also saved money, and we planned to travel together to America. Unfortunately, at the last minute, he couldn't go, and I had to travel alone, but he did come a few months later. The thought of making such a trip by myself was daunting. I was scared, but if my sisters had done it, then I could do it too. And I did! When I look back, I'm amazed at how brave I was."

"I don't think I could do it."

"I'll bet if it ever came to that, you would find the strength within yourself too. I know you would, Jer."

"I hope I don't have to find out. What happened next?"

"I bought my ticket, and then everything took place quickly. First, I had to get from Sweden to Liverpool, England. I took a boat from Gothenburg, Sweden, to the English city of Hull and from there a train to Liverpool. The boat to Hull, called an 'America Boat,' only sailed two times a week. Finding my own way to the docks and then later to the train station was so difficult, and I almost missed the boat. The America Boat and the train took two days, and I hardly slept at all. When I did take a quick nap, it was sitting up. There were many others going from Sweden to America, and most were helpful and kind to me.

"I heard a rumor that young, unmarried girls might not be allowed to enter America alone, and I seemed to be one of the few girls my age traveling by myself. I was terrified that I had come so far but might be turned back. Luckily, an older Swedish couple I sat beside on the train and saw again in Liverpool told me I could travel with them. They even offered to say I was their daughter, but I didn't need to do that after all."

"On April 7, 1905, the day before we sailed, I stood on a high dock and looked down at the SS *Lucania*. That ship took us across the Atlantic

SS Lucania, *Cunard Line.*
PHOTOGRAPH BY JOHN S. JOHNSTON, LIBRARY OF CONGRESS, LC-D4-22369.

Ocean to New York. From New York, I took a train to Montana, where I finally joined Mary, Anna, and August."

"You remember the exact day the ship left?"

"Oh yes, and the day it arrived in New York, April 15, 1905. Some things you don't forget."

"Was it fun to go on a ship?" Jerry asked.

"No, it wasn't. The *Lucania* was a nice, fairly new British ocean liner, but my ticket was for steerage."

"What's steerage?"

"It's the lowest class of accommodations on a ship and the cheapest. It certainly was not nice down on those decks, but I didn't know that at first as I was so excited about the trip. When I boarded, there was so much to see with sailors loading crate after crate of goods and more people coming on board. Some of the passengers looked very rich, dressed in fine clothing. For them, the trip was luxurious. Others, like me, wore plain country clothes.

"Soon I was directed to my quarters and found it was a small section for unmarried girls on the side of a large open room for women. We each had a tiny bunk of our own, and bunks were stacked four high with very little space between. The large room was dirty and smelly, but I planned to make the best of it. Several women wept when they found themselves separated from their loved ones. Most families had their own small space, but not all. The large areas were divided into group quarters for men and for women."

"Separated? How would that work if a mother was traveling with a son about my age? Would they separate them?"

"I don't know, but the trip was certainly not fun for any of us. Even before the ship left the dock, we gathered to be questioned by the ship's officers."

"What'd they ask you?"

"Oh, they wanted to know our names and ages, if we could read and write, our nationality, and how much money we had. They asked the men if they were polygamists."

"What's a polygamist?"

"It's a man who's married to more than one wife at a time," Martha answered.

"Oh, that sounds complicated."

"We were also asked if we had ever been in prison or an institute for the insane, or if we were deformed or crippled"

"Those are pretty personal questions."

"Very personal, but they wanted to make sure people entering the United States were fit. Let's see, now where was I? Oh yes, the crossing. I remember the first day at sea, I visited with other young people from steerage on the deck where we were allowed or in a common room. The next day there were fewer people, and on the third day only one girl showed up. After that, no one came. They were all ill from something called 'ocean sickness.' That sickness didn't seem to bother me."

"You mean seasick?" asked Jerry.

"Yes, seasick. Most people were."

"What'd you eat on the ship?" Jerry asked, thinking of the sweet rolls that were almost ready.

"The food in steerage was pretty good, but was served like slop— just thrown onto plates, and there wasn't much of it. Oatmeal, bread, and coffee for breakfast, midday dinner was soup and a bit of meat, and supper was usually just bread and butter. Once there was a type of custard, but the ones first in line got it all, so there was none for the rest of us. There was never seconds on anything."

"They had bathrooms, didn't they?"

"Yes, a communal bathroom for women and one for men, but there was no hope of really keeping clean. Then there were stormy days when we were tossed about, and one night, water sloshed over the ship. I remember saying a Swedish prayer over and over asking God to keep me safe. I thought leaving Sweden was a bad choice that night."

"Do you remember the words?"

"*I Faderns ah Sonens ochden helige Andes namm. Amen.* It means, 'May God in heaven protect us. Amen.'"

"That must have been scary."

"It was, but later that same year in October, a huge wave battered the side of the *Lucania* and some steerage passengers who were out on the small deck were washed overboard and others inside were injured."

"Jeez, it's lucky you made it!"

"Don't swear, young man," Martha said with mock severity, trying to hide her smile.

Martha reached over the nightstand, picked up the old scarf, and carefully folded it.

"Keep on talking. I wanna know more."

"Well, as we finally neared the coast of America, we were permitted more time out on deck. It was a pleasant day, and we could see land in the distance. A purser told us it was the city of New York. Soon we passed the Statue of Liberty, welcoming us to America. Do you remember the poem you had to memorize for school that's on the base of that statue?"

"Let's see, does it start, 'Give us your tired, your poor'?"

"Yes," said Martha. 'Give us your tired, your poor, your huddled masses yearning to breathe free.' I believe it's by a woman named Emma Lazarus."

Jerry added, "'The wretched refuse of your teeming shore. Send these, the homeless, tempest tossed to me. I lift my lamp beside the golden door.' But Mom, you weren't 'wretched refuse.'"

"No, Jer, but I was really homeless, and to me, my brothers, and sisters, America was a golden door of opportunity that we didn't have in Sweden."

"Yeah, I guess it would've been. But then how'd you get to Montana?"

"Well, our ship docked at a high pier. The rich people who had stayed in cabins above deck were the first to leave. Finally, we were allowed to go up the gangplank to the dock. After all our days at sea, we had trouble walking on land that was not rolling under us."

"Kinda like we feel after being on a horse all day?" asked Jerry.

"Yes, probably much the same feeling," said Martha, with a chuckle. "That first day in America, I went from official to official on Ellis Island, checked in, answered questions, and received papers. It was a long process that went on for hours. It was good I could speak some English, but I had a slight fever that day, and I worried someone would notice I was ill. I stood up straight and tried to look alert, even though I felt awful. I was afraid I would be banned from entering America and sent back to Sweden."

"They would do that? Send you back?"

"They worried about foreigners bringing diseases into America. No one noticed I was unwell, and I went through the endless processing at Ellis Island. That's when an official changed my name from the Swedish 'Marta' to the American 'Martha' because he didn't think *Marta* sounded right. And that's how my name has remained."

"Is that why Aunt Mary called you *Marta* when she was here? I was about to ask you, but her baby started crying and you both were busy. Which name do you like best? Do you want people to call you 'Marta,' instead of 'Martha'? Some official shouldn't have been able to just change your name like that."

"Many foreign names were 'Americanized' when immigrants came to the United States, and often it was by their own choice. Perhaps they thought it would help them fit in. And I like the name Martha just fine," she added.

"That first night, I slept in a large drafty building with many others who had been processed that day. I remember being so hot and then so cold with fever and wrapping that linen scarf around my head and taking comfort that it was from my home. The next morning, I, along with other Swedes who were going West, made our way through strange and busy streets to an enormous station where we boarded a train bound for Montana. The journey took days, but time passed quickly talking together. Most families planned to farm, and they discussed the good land that would be available, the crops they would plant, and the new lives they would lead."

"In school, Miss Phillips told us the immigrants who came from Sweden, Denmark, Norway, and that part of Europe worked really hard and valued education," said Jerry.

"She's right. Our family was hard working and wanted to get as much education as we could. We planned to fit in and finally live our father's dream for us."

"You deserved it, Mom."

"It was worth it, wasn't it? I don't know what future I would have had in Sweden."

"Then how'd you meet Dad?"

"Well, I stayed with my sisters in Miles City, and by that time our brother August had been promoted and managed the tin shop. We all saved money

Martha Magnuson, valedictorian.

to bring over Wilhelm and Betty as soon as we could. I enrolled in school, and even though I was older than the other students, I was put in elementary school, where I went through all grades in just one year. All of us spoke English, though we still used Swedish when we were alone together."

"Can you still speak Swedish?"

"Absolutely. It's the language I use and write when I want to keep secrets from you boys," Martha said with a laugh.

"Can you teach me some Swedish words?"

"Ja. Well, maybe, but then it wouldn't be my secret language."

"Ah, Mom, maybe just a few things like 'good night' and 'hello'— easy words like that," suggested Jerry.

"How about if I teach you to say 'goodnight' in Swedish and you practice it right now?"

"No, Mom, keep going. I wanna know how you met Dad."

"Okay, but I'll make it quick because you need to get to sleep."

"All of us loved to dance and knew most of the steps, plus the special dances from Sweden we did together, like the *Schottische*. One weekend my sisters and I went to a dance. There were five boys there from the Kempton Ranch who took turns dancing with all the girls. They were all good dancers, nice-looking, and everyone knew their family was doing well."

"Those were Dad and his brothers, weren't they?"

"THIRTY-SIX FEET OF KEMPTON"
Top row: Joe, Jim, Sanford and Henry Seated: Asa and Berney

The Kempton men, Berney seated right.

"Yes, one of them didn't come, but I can't remember who was missing," said Martha. "The oldest one, who introduced himself as Berney Kempton, danced with me several times that first evening. With his good looks and wavy black hair, he was easily the most handsome man in the room. He told me he had spent nearly two years with Doctor Carver's Wild West Show, but said he was now back home and would eventually take over the Kempton Ranch."

"Yeah, Pansy and me just found all that Wild West stuff in the attic. Dad was famous!"

"You mean *'Pansy and I,'* son. Yes, he was famous, but at first I thought he was just making it up to impress me."

"Woo, woo! Was it love at first sight?" Jerry joked.

Martha laughed and continued, "I was the smartest girl I knew, but your father was even more intelligent and seemed to know about almost everything."

"Yeah, he still does." They snickered.

"He began calling on me, and we were engaged about six months after we met. My sisters and brothers all liked him and thought he had a good future. We married the same year I graduated high school as valedictorian of my class."

"Wasn't that kinda young to get married?"

"No, back then women sometimes married in their mid-teen years."

"Not me! Or is it *'not I'?* I'm never gonna get married," Jerry said with determination.

"We'll see, son. You may change your mind."

"Anyway, soon your father and his brothers took over the ranch from your grandfather and grandmother, JB and Maria. Berney was the oldest, and eventually his other brothers began ranching in other areas, and when they did, your dad ran the Kempton Ranch alone."

"Why'd they all move away?" Jerry asked.

"Well, your father bought out their shares of Kempton land. Some stayed in Prairie County, and that's why there are so many Kemptons around here."

"Yeah, we have a lot of relatives, don't we?"

Maria and JB Kempton.

"Soon JB became ill with pneumonia that took him in about a week. That was such a shock since he was a healthy, active man. Then Maria also passed away just months later. She was ill with cancer and lost heart when JB died. They're both buried in the Terry graveyard."

"Yeah, I've seen their graves," Jerry said, turning his head so his mother couldn't see him yawn. He wasn't bored, but the late hour was making him sleepy.

"The ranch house was large and bustling with family, visitors, and townspeople coming and going. Here I was just out of high school and newly married, but I soon took over running the household."

"What was Grandma Maria like?"

"She was the daughter of Molly Red Kettle, who was the sister of Chief Red Kettle, a powerful Sioux Indian leader. Some say Molly Red Kettle was the daughter of Chief Red Kettle instead of his sister, so I'm not exactly sure. Her father was Elbridge Gerry, the man I mentioned who alerted the settlers before the Indian attacks. He was related to the Elbridge Gerry back east, the American patriot who signed the Declaration of Independence."

"What? My relative signed the real Declaration of Independence?" asked Jerry, wide-eyed at this revelation.

"Yes, he did, but he was also responsible for some other things not quite as admirable. A system of dividing an area into voting districts in order to give unfair advantage to one party in an election, called 'gerry-mandering,' was also named after him."

"That doesn't sound too good," Jerry grimaced.

"No, it doesn't, but let's get back to your grandmother, Maria. She was well known in eastern Montana as a capable and solid rancher. She was an imposing woman, as tall as most men, and very robust through the middle."

"You mean she was fat?"

"Well, yes, she was a very big woman," Martha responded, stifling a giggle. "She was also very intelligent, although she could neither read nor write."

"Really, she didn't know how to read or write?" said Jerry, shaking his head.

"That's a mystery to me because Elbridge Gerry, even as a mountain man living in the wilderness married to Sioux wives, always kept his desire for the culture he knew as a young man, growing up in a rich Boston family. He wanted his family to have a good education and know the white man's ways.

"Maria may have been illiterate, but that certainly didn't mean she wasn't smart. It just means she missed learning to read and write. When she and JB married and lived in Colorado, where most of their children were born, they had tutors because they were far from any schools."

Maria Gerry Kempton.

"Huh, why didn't she learn to read and write when her kids did?" said Jerry.

"Well, probably by the time children came along, she was just too busy with all the household work."

"Yeah, you're plenty busy, but you and Dad read a lot."

"You're right. I guess we'll never know why Maria didn't, but she was still a prominent woman in early Prairie County history. When I married your father and came to the ranch, Maria was glad to hand over the cooking to me, and I was glad to take it. I soon made all the meals, and although it was hard work with little help at first, I loved being known for my apple pies, cinnamon rolls, and Parker House buns. We almost always served beef, and my gravy was said to be the best around."

"It still is!"

"Thanks, son. You're easy to please, as long as it's meat and potatoes! Just like your father."

"Now for the last memento," Martha said as she picked up the hair comb and held it in the lamplight.

"Your father gave this to me the first Christmas we were married. It's made of hand-carved tortoise shell, and those blue stones are semi-precious gems."

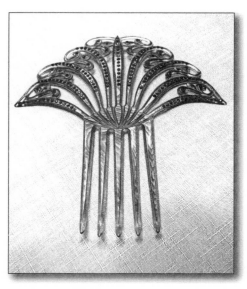

Martha's hair comb.

"It's pretty," Jerry said as he took the comb from his mother and looked at it, turning it over, watching the stones twinkle in the light from his kerosene lamp.

"Just after we married, one night as your dad and I were getting ready for bed, I sat at my dressing table brushing out my long hair.

I usually wore it in a braided bun on top of my head during the day. Your father took the brush from me, swept my hair up, and said I needed some pretty hair ornaments. I told him hairpins did just fine, and we needed to save our money, but that Christmas he gave me this beautiful comb I wear for special occasions. It was far too expensive, and the money should have gone for farm equipment, but it's always meant a lot to me. If you ever marry, son, maybe I can pass it down to your wife."

"Nope, don't count on me. You'll have to give it to someone else."

"Oh, we'll see. We'll see. Now it's way past time for you to be asleep, young man," Martha said as she got up and tucked the blankets around Jerry. *"God natt."*

"Now that's my first Swedish words!" Jerry said, hugging his mother.

"Here's another for you. *'Gubben.'* It's a Swedish term of endearment used for sons who are much loved."

"Ah, Mom, I love you too. Thanks for telling me that story. And I won't forget to ask Dad about his relatives some time too."

"Knowing your family roots is fascinating," Martha said as she thought about the past, present, and future of the Kempton family. Then she added, "I wonder what your history will be, Jer. I wonder what stories your future family will tell or write about you a hundred years from now! Maybe they'll be about your childhood on the ranch!"

"Huh, if they're interested, I hope they tell all the good things and leave out the bad parts," Jerry laughed.

"Well, life isn't all good, is it? It's a little bit of both, and we have to deal with the good and the bad," Martha said.

"I guess so," Jerry said with a sniff. "Mmm, I can smell those cinnamon rolls. Can I have some for breakfast?"

"Of course you can, but that reminds me that I should go and check them right now," Martha replied. "Close your eyes and sleep tight," she whispered as she kissed Jerry's forehead and then closed his door.

We just never know where life will take us, do we? Martha thought as she walked down the stairs to the kitchen. *My journey from a Swedish orphanage to this large horse and cattle ranch in Montana seems too amazing to be true. We really lived our father's dream of coming to America, one by one!*

Author's note: In 2015, as I wrote this story, the scarf had long-since been lost, but today I still have the photos of the farm in Sweden and of Martha's parents and the ornate hair comb that Martha wore and eventually passed down to my mother. A note in my mother's handwriting tells the history of the hair ornament.

These mementos remind me of the incredibly courageous journey of six orphaned children as they made their way to America and the ranch woman who was my favorite grandmother. I am now a grandmother of two little girls, and I will someday pass these keepsakes down to them.

THE KEMPTONS
AND THE LAND

"What is this you call property?
It cannot be the earth, for the land is our mother,
nourishing all her children, beasts, birds, fish, and all men.
The woods, the streams, everything on it
belongs to everybody and is for the use of all.
How can one man say it belongs only to him?"
Chief Massasoit, of the Wampanoag Indians in 1620

"We come and go, but the land is always here.
And the people who love it and understand it
are the people who own it—for a little while."
Willa Cather, from *O Pioneers!*

The Indians who lived in North America and the Pilgrims who arrived in 1620 had two very different and often clashing views of the land and man's rightful use of it. Kempton ancestors belonged to both groups. Early relatives were said to be among the American Indians, who had lived here for eons. My grandfather, Berney, often bragged that past members of our family were the welcoming party for the arriving Pilgrims, but the name of the tribe of our forbearers is not known. A Kempton ancestor was also one of the Pilgrims who established Plymouth Plantation.

The arriving Pilgrims, looking at the seemingly uninhabited landscape before them, did not comprehend this land was already home to thousands of flourishing Indian tribes that had lived meaningfully and successfully here for countless generations, long before the Mayflower set anchor in Plymouth Bay.

Massasoit on his way to meet the pilgrims and
sign the 1621 peace treaty, by Alexander Gilmore.
LIBRARY OF CONGRESS, BIOG FILE - MASSASOIT, INDIAN CHIEF, 1580-1661.

The Pilgrims came to the New World with their own set of preconceived European notions of land ownership, believing land was personal property to be used to produce material wants and needs.

They reasoned that terrain not actively in use was available to obtain for their own personal benefit, although they did acknowledge the New World was previously claimed for England when the first English settlers came to Jamestown in 1607. They were also aware the Jamestown colony failed when most of the group succumbed to disease or mysteriously disappeared.

The concepts of real property and personal property also differed between the Pilgrims and the occupying tribes. (Real property is the land and any permanent structures on it. Personal property is essentially anything that can be picked up and moved.) The American Indians believed they owned only what they made—physical things like bows, arrows, tools, and their movable tepees. Indian tribes collectively had rights to territory for hunting, fishing, or food gathering. For example, a village might have exclusive rights to hunt in a particular area, but many tribes might share the use of a single river for fishing.

The Pilgrim's voyage to the New World was reluctantly sponsored by a group of English investors who agreed they would receive a large share of the land to be held in common by both Pilgrims and investors. After Plymouth Plantation was established, this shared system quickly proved unworkable, as some Pilgrims refused to work, some were slow, and others were busily industrious. This was settled when the land was divided, with every family receiving a parcel according to the size of the household.

The land the Pilgrims worked was converted into private property at the end of seven years and then split between the investors back in England and the Pilgrims. Eventually, under the wise leadership of Plymouth Governor William Bradford, property was further transferred from public to private ownership. Bradford's journal provides the only surviving account of these transactions and the rationale for the decisions.

It was the strong desire to worship God in his own way that caused the first member of the Kempton family to come to the New World.

Manasseh (sometimes written "Manasses") Kempton was born in Northumberland, England, in 1589 at Berwick-upon-Tweed. He died in Plymouth, Massachusetts, in 1662. Manasseh's younger brother Ephraim also came to Plymouth.

In Plymouth, Manasseh Kempton lived with Governor Bradford, the most important figure in the early years of the colony. Kempton served as a deputy to the Plymouth General Court and also sat on a number of juries and committees. Kempton soon married Juliana (Carpenter) Morton, the widow of George Morton, who died the first winter in Plymouth. Juliana's sister married Governor Bradford. Together both Kempton and Bradford raised the five children born to Juliana and George Morton.

The popular children's book *Sarah Morton's Day: A Day in the Life of a Pilgrim Girl,* by Kate Waters, tells about the young daughter of Juliana Morton soon after her mother married Manasseh Kempton. Sarah was concerned about pleasing her new father and gaining his acceptance. It proved to be a happy adjustment for all.

Manasseh eventually owned a twenty-acre share of Plymouth Plantation, plus extensive property in several other towns, including Eastham, Dartmouth, and Scituate, Massachusetts. The family prospered, and its land holdings increased as years passed.

Manasseh died in 1662 after having lived and good a full life. At his funeral, it was said, "He did much good in his place and in the time God gave him." He gave the land he owned to his stepchildren.

Decades came and went as arriving European settlers claimed more land for themselves. Eventually the thirteen American colonies formed, and the people began to push for an end to English domination. The next well-known Kempton ancestor, Elbridge Thomas Gerry, became one of the American patriots who were instrumental in ending the rule by England.

Gerry (1744–1814) was born in Marblehead, Massachusetts, the son of a wealthy merchant. He graduated from Harvard in 1762, and as a member of the Continental Congress he argued for independence from England. He was one of the signers of the Declaration of Independence. Unfortunately, he also had the dubious distinction of devising "gerrymandering," a system bearing his name that unfairly divides voting districts to benefit one party over another. Gerry became the governor of Massachusetts and was eventually elected vice president of the United States under President James Madison in 1813.

At this point, there are contradictions regarding the Kempton genealogy. Some say the next Kempton of note, Elbridge Gerry (1818–1875), an early Colorado mountain man and Indian trader, was not related to the Elbridge Gerry who signed the Declaration of Independence. Other sources claim the Colorado Elbridge Gerry was indeed the grandson of the great patriot. Still others explain that the reason the aristocratic family in the East was reluctant to claim the Colorado man was due to his unusual lifestyle of marrying multiple Indian women. East-

Elbridge Thomas Gerry (1744-1814), a signer of the Declaration of Independence.

ern highbrow society looked askance at Gerry's polygamy and wanted nothing to do with this man, whose own contributions to society were heroic but mostly overlooked.

After studying numerous sources, I hold the point of view that Elbridge Gerry of Colorado was the grandson of the famous patriot with the same name. Many reliable sources, such as the Daughters of the American Revolution (DAR), agree with this opinion. The DAR, after a great deal of research, even formed an Elbridge Gerry Chapter, citing sufficient information favoring his descendency.

It is known that Elbridge Gerry of Colorado was born in 1818 into an elite Boston family. He was well-educated, a man of breeding and refinement. Following the death of his mother and his father's remarriage to a stepmother, however, he left his privileged situation to go west.

After leaving home, he was

Elbridge Gerry of Colorado.
COURTESY OF HISTORY COLORADO.

always very secretive about his past, telling the truth only to one friend, who died at a young age before he revealed the information to anyone else. Gerry did not even tell his children about his former life, although the tattoo of a ship on his arm seemed to indicate he had been to sea at some time.

In the mid-1830s, Gerry came to the wilds of Colorado, the first white man to settle in what was to become Weld County, where he trapped and traded. At that time, beaver were highly prized for fashionable hats and clothing. A skilled trapper could earn at least $6 a pelt. But by 1840 beaver were hunted almost to extinction. In addition, clothing trends changed, and this fur went out of fashion.

Gerry then set up a trading post at Fort Laramie, in what would become Wyoming, where he did a brisk business supplying Indians, early settlers, and eventually gold seekers with goods, often in exchange for buffalo skins. His commerce was very successful, and entries in his account books showed he sold sugar by the cup and buffalo skins by the thousands. In the 1940s, my grandmother, Martha Kempton, came upon these account books stored in the attic of the Kempton Ranch. She later donated them to the Colorado Historical Society, along with the likeness of Gerry shown here, which she found in one of the family albums.

At Fort Laramie, Gerry married Molly Red Kettle, daughter of the powerful Sioux Indian chief Red Kettle. My great-grandmother, Maria Emma Gerry (1851–1910), who eventually married JB Kempton, was their second child.

By custom, when a white man married a Native American woman, he was considered to be a part of the tribe and expected to follow its lifestyle of having more than one wife. Being married to a Sioux woman was also of benefit to Gerry's Indian trade. He later married Polly Red Kettle, the twin sister of his first wife, and still later married Millicent and Minerva Swift Bird, another set of twins. His last wife was named Big Woman, for whom he paid five ponies.

It was said that Gerry's wives respected him and all his children loved him. What greater historical record can any man leave than this? When it was suggested that Gerry would be more readily accepted in early Colorado society if he divested himself of his multiple Indian wives, he was outraged and indignant, and he refused.

In 1860, Gerry established a large horse ranch east of Greeley near Fremont's Orchard. At that time, relations between Indians and settlers were often tense. One night in 1864, Sioux relatives of Gerry's Indian wives came to warn him of a planned massacre of white settlers from Denver to Julesburg that would take place within days. That night, Elbridge Gerry made his famous Paul-Revere-style ride to warn settlers, thus averting the attack and saving many lives. In angry retaliation, the Indians stole Gerry's horses and cattle while he was away.

It is not known how Gerry first acquired his early land, but as one of the original white settlers in the area that became Colorado, he certainly had his pick. Gerry was said to be worth $40,000 in 1860 but only $1,500 ten years later. At one time, he owned an entire block of land in downtown Evans (now a suburb of Greeley), where he built stores and the famous Gerry House, an elegant hotel. Ironically, most of his wealth disappeared before his death in 1875. Elbridge Gerry died without a will, and his heirs received very little.

Elbridge Gerry settled in Weld County, Colorado, and began a successful trading post, though the property deeds remain lost to history. We know, however, that he built Fort Gerry near the Overland Trail on land licensed by the Indian agent Twiss on November 24, 1857. In addition, the U.S. government, in gratitude for Gerry's heroic night ride that saved many settlers from an Indian raid, later gave him land and compensated him for the theft of his stock.

My great-great-grandfather, Joseph Kempton (1817–1909) was born in Hampden, Penobscot County, in the state of Maine, the son of Seth Kempton and Lucy Brown Kempton. As a young man, he sailed on whaling ships, and some reports said he was a ship's captain.

Joseph Kempton met Eliza Sabrina Foote (1821–1901), who was born to a wealthy family in Villanova, Chautauqua County, New York. She was related to Nathaniel Foote (1592–1644), an early English immigrant to Connecticut, who founded Wethersfield, the oldest town in that state. He owned extensive land in and around Wethersfield.

Joseph and Eliza Sabrina (often called Sadie) married in 1841 and soon set out by ox cart for Michigan, where they were some of the first pioneer settlers at Cutler's Corners, near Jackson. Later they moved to North Adams, Hillsdale County, Michigan, where they were once again the first whites. It was here their nine children were born, one of whom was my great-grandfather, James Berney (1843–1910), known as JB. He had very little education as a boy because there were no schools nearby, yet he became a well-educated man. His mother, as the daughter of affluent parents, probably taught the children at home, and JB became an avid reader.

Little is known about Joseph Kempton's land ownership in Michigan, but his father, Seth Kempton, owned a large tract of land in North

Adams Township. Perhaps Joseph and Sabrina settled on that property during their years there. At some point, they also lived in Amity, Iowa, in Page County.

How did Sabrina, from a background of wealth and ease, cope with life as an early settler? Did she ever curse the new land? Did she rue the day she fell in love with a man with "itchy feet" who wanted to conquer new frontiers and see new vistas? Born to a wealthy Eastern family, she could have had any number of rich beaus, content to live a civilized, cultured life. Did she ever long to be back with her family in New York in her luxurious childhood home where there was always plenty to eat, nice dresses to wear, and social events to attend? Or perhaps Sabrina was as adventurous as her husband and craved the challenge of the wild American frontier. Unfortunately, none of her diaries or writings survived, so we don't know.

In 1856, Joseph, Sabrina, and their children moved farther west once again, this time to Fremont's Orchard, not far from Greeley, Colorado. As before, they were some of the first white settlers in the area. Over time, they prospered and established one of the largest hay farms on the South Platte River. Their outpost, typical of the times, was composed of two long wooden buildings built parallel with a large area between. At each end was a high stockade of sturdy, sharpened wood posts. At night, they drove their animals into the safety of this fortress, protected from Indian raids.

How did pioneer settlers like Elbridge Gerry and Joseph Kempton acquire land in the early to mid-1800s that became the foundation of their wealth? To whom did the seemingly endless landscape of virgin territory belong, and how was it purchased before passage of the Homestead Act of 1862?

Common private acquisition of land in western territories began in 1781 when the eastern states surrendered their claim to the unsettled territory west of the Mississippi River. Then, during a period of national expansion from 1781 to 1867, vast tracts of land were purchased from other countries, such as the Louisiana Purchase, Mexican lands, and the Alaskan Purchase from Russia. At that time, the public domain totaled 1.8 billion acres.

To encourage settlement of the West, Congress passed laws in the 1800s authorizing disposal of some public lands to citizens, states, and private companies. The General Land Office, the predecessor of the U.S. Bureau of Land Management, was established in 1812 to oversee this dispersal and keep land records. District land offices opened in settlements, and when most of the land in an area was disbursed, the office closed.

From the 1820s through the 1840s, westerners pushed for more liberal land laws, for free homesteads or donations for those who would settle on the land. Congress occasionally offered land at no cost in regions it wanted settled, but before 1862, public lands were distributed primarily through auctions. Some states and individuals received land through grants. Over time, squatters were allowed redemptive rights to the land they claimed as their own.

One of the most important decrees for the welfare of the people ever passed in the United States was the famous Homestead Act of 1862, which turned over vast amounts of public land to private citizens. This declaration, signed into law by President Abraham Lincoln, completely changed land ownership and was in large part responsible for the settlement of much of the American West.

President Lincoln described the benefits of the Homestead Act, saying, "So that the wild lands of the country should be distributed so that every man should have the means and opportunity of benefiting his condition." People from all walks of life—men, women, newly arrived immigrants, and former slaves—all took advantage of this program to better their circumstances by owning land.

Ironically, most of the land given away by the Homestead Act was originally taken forcibly from American Indian tribes. If living and working on a piece of land gives someone the legal right to be there, it is difficult to understand how Congress justified the removal of Native Americans from their age-old home territory.

THE UNITED STATES OF AMERICA,

To all to Whom these Presents shall come, GREETING:

Homestead Certificate No. _1141_

APPLICATION _1162_ } Whereas, There has been deposited in the General Land Office of the United States a Certificate of the Register of the Land Office at _Denver Colorado_ whereby it appears that, pursuant to the Act of Congress approved 20th May, 1862, "TO SECURE HOMESTEADS TO ACTUAL SETTLERS ON THE PUBLIC DOMAIN," and the acts supplemental thereto, the claim of _____ _Joseph Kempton_ has been established and duly consummated, in conformity to law for the

North half of the South East quarter, and the south east quarter of the north east quarter of Section seventeen, in township four north of range sixty west of the Sixth Principal Meridian, in Colorado, containing one hundred and twenty acres

according to the Official Plat of the Survey of the said Land, returned to the General Land Office by the Surveyor General:

Now Know Ye, That there is, therefore, granted by the UNITED STATES unto the said _Joseph Kempton_ the tract of land above described: To Have and to Hold the said tract of Land, with the appurtenances thereof, unto the said _Joseph Kempton_ and to _his_ heirs and assigns forever; subject to any vested and accrued water rights for mining, agricultural, manufacturing or other purposes, and rights to ditches and reservoirs used in connection with such water rights, as may be recognized and acknowledged by the local customs, laws and decisions of Courts, and also subject to the right of the proprietor of a vein or lode to extract and remove his ore therefrom, should the same be found to penetrate or intersect the premises hereby granted, as provided by law.

In Testimony Whereof, I, _James A Garfield_ President of the United States of America, have caused these letters to be made patent, and the Seal of the General Land Office to be hereunto affixed.

Given under my hand, at the City of Washington, the _nineteenth_ day of _August_, in the year of our Lord one thousand eight hundred and _eighty one_, and of the Independence of the United States the one hundred and _sixth_.

BY THE PRESIDENT: _James A Garfield_

By _Wm H Crook_ Secretary.

S H Clark Recorder of the General Land Office.

Recorded, Vol. _4_ Page _100_

13694
Filed for Record the _25_ day of _June_ A. D. 1884, at 11 15 o'clock A. M.

H. A. Nice County Clerk.

Joseph Kempton's 1884 deed for land in Colorado.

The Homestead Act stated that any man or woman at least twenty-one years old or the head of a household was eligible for 160 acres of undeveloped land simply by fulfilling a number of requirements and paying minimal fees. The filing fee to claim the land was $10 and homesteaders had six months to begin living on the property. They were required to build a dwelling and cultivate or improve the land over five years, during which they could not be absent for more than six months a year.

Settlers interested in homesteading first filed their intention with the nearest land office, where a check was conducted on any prior ownership of the plot in question, which was usually described by its survey coordinates. Besides the fee to claim the land, there was also a $2 commission to the land agent, who kept the records and handled paperwork.

With improvements made and requirements met, the homesteader asked two neighbors or friends to attest to this. After paying a $6 fee, the settler received a patent or deed for the land, signed by the current president of the United States.

An early photo of the Kempton Hotel shows a land office in the front corner of the building called Redwater Empire Land Company.

The Redwater Land Office was housed in the Kempton Hotel.

Later, in 1877, Congress passed the Desert Land Act, which gave 640 acres—four times the amount granted by the Homestead Act—to any settler who irrigated the land within three years. This act appealed to cattle ranchers in eastern Montana.

The Civil War broke out during the years Joseph and Sabrina lived in Colorado. Although the territory was far removed from the conflict, their eldest son, JB, felt he should do his part to keep the country united. Consequently, he joined the Union Army in Page County, Iowa, in 1864. In November of the same year, he was among the 62,000 men who set off with General Sherman in Atlanta headed south toward the Atlantic Ocean—Sherman's historic "March to the Sea."

Those months were the worst in JB's life, and for the rest of his days, he pushed the memories far back in his mind. When his children asked him about the war, he adamantly refused to talk about it. He told them only that he lost many good friends in the fighting.

As the Union Army moved, it attracted a growing group of ex-slaves who greeted the soldiers as conquerors. Sherman treated the blacks with courtesy and expected his troops to do the same. Perhaps this example was a source of the Kempton racial acceptance that continued through the generations.

Luckily JB went through the war without being wounded or captured and was mustered out at St. Louis, Missouri, in September 1865. All he wanted to do was get as far away from the military as he could, although in later years he took an active part in the Grand Army of the Republic, a fraternal organization of veterans of the Union Army of the Civil War.

Out of the military and heading west, JB took a job driving a bull train transporting goods from St. Louis to Colorado. Back at his family home in Colorado, he met Maria Emma Gerry, the daughter of a neighboring horse rancher, the well-known mountain man who had alerted settlers to an Indian raid—Elbridge Gerry. JB and Maria Gerry fell in love and married in Evans, Colorado, on April 12, 1870.

Maria and JB settled in Weld County, thirty-five miles west of Greeley, and it was there they raised their children. Their firstborn son, Berney Edmond Kempton, was my grandfather. Eventually JB had the largest hay ranch on the Platte River, and in 1869 he established himself in the cattle business. His ranch was not far from Elbridge Gerry's first outpost.

During the next ten years, JB continued to expand his ranch, but over time he gradually felt crowded with all the new settlers moving into the area. Since he liked the wide-open spaces and was most comfortable when not a house or person was in sight, he started looking for land farther afield.

In 1880, JB first saw the land in eastern Montana that would become home to generations of the Kempton family. At that time, eastern Montana was practically uninhabited. One could travel for miles without seeing another human. Thousands of buffalo dotted the plains, and in the whole territory during those years there were only 250,000 head of cattle. The Montana grassland was lush, and natural springs were abundant in the area now called Prairie County. JB Kempton recognized the blue grama grass, buffalo grass, western wheatgrass, and other species that all stood instead of flattening, so the cattle could feed on it even in winter. The bluebunch wheatgrass also greened early and grew well in almost all soils. Montana snows were not as deep and not as long lasting as in Colorado, and the winds frequently blew the snow off the grass, further allowing cattle to feed all winter. JB observed the abundant streambeds that provided water and shelter for cattle and saw the deep soils and good groundwater. He believed this eastern Montana rangeland would be a good place for his family to settle.

JB first selected a site for his cattle on the Tongue River, a temporary location, known as the J Mule Shoe Ranch. He was an original settler on his second ranch on Cedar Creek. He remained there until the early 1880s when he moved to his third location, known as the Kempton Home Ranch, part of which he had acquired earlier. He eventually turned the Cedar Creek property over to the XIT Company, the largest cattle concern in Montana.

The Kempton Home Ranch soon contained more than 3,500 acres adjacent to thousands of acres of public lands on which JB raised both horses and cattle. Maria and JB had six sons and two daughters. Their eldest son—my grandfather Berney—eventually took over the ranch. Both JB and Berney were advocates of dryland farming, and their experiments helped both farmers and ranchers who grew feed for their livestock. The Kemptons raised record crops—dryland wheat, ninety-day corn that proved especially valuable in the semi-arid country, and noteworthy Irish potatoes. With irrigation systems drawn from the springs, there was always a huge, flourishing kitchen vegetable garden.

Both father and son loved the wind-swept prairies, valued the land, and treated it with respect. They anticipated the first green of springtime and the clean white after a snowfall. To them the land was life. They were some of the first to express concern about overgrazing and fire control.

Perhaps Prairie County was getting too crowded for JB's liking in 1910. Whatever the reason, he began making plans to move his horse herds to the Wind River Reservation in Wyoming. His unexpected death from pneumonia cut those plans and many others short. Friends said one day they saw him in town looking hale and hearty and the next week they received word of his death. It was a shock to his family and came at a time when Maria was also ill, fighting the cancer that would take her only four months after JB's death. Family, friends, and the community mourned the death of this great man of Montana, and soon after they also grieved for the passing of his respected and popular wife, Maria Gerry Kempton.

In JB's eulogy, he was remembered as a visionary and driving force in the growth of the town of Terry and the county. Remembered as a friend to all, a good husband, and a kind father, it was also noted he helped establish Terry's first bank and was its vice president when he died. He was also a main stockholder in the Ranchman's Supply Company in Terry, an institution that did an immense business for many years. He was a promoter of schools, and in the early days he provided a private teacher for his own children and those of nearby ranchers in a one-room schoolhouse.

The Union Church in Terry.

The Union Church today.

Later he encouraged the building of larger schools, and although not a resident of town, he took the lead in the planning and construction of a splendid high school. Unfortunately, he died before it was completed. He was also a supporter of the Union Church in Terry, which still stands today.

As a successor to his father in ranch activities, Berney took over after JB's death. At first, the ranch continued to prosper under Berney's care, but soon times became difficult.

A number of factors led to the difficulty. Cattle prices dropped to a low. The ranch had prospered by selling cavalry horses to the military for use in several wars, but now there was little need for military mounts as armies became more dependent on motorized vehicles. The Kempton Percheron workhorses that helped make the ranch famous were soon replaced by farming tractors. These trends threatened the continued success of the Kempton Ranch.

Berney and Martha Kempton decided to turn their focus to attracting city folks interested in the Montana Western mystique and willing to pay grandly to spend time on a working ranch. The Kempton Ranch, with its proximity to the nearby Kempton Hotel in Terry, began taking in visitors. This proved successful, with Martha doing the cooking and Berney leading trail rides and regaling "dudes" with his stories. But Berney's death in 1942 changed all that. Several of the Kempton sons tried to revitalize the ranch without much success since times were difficult in Montana and across the United States.

Finally, a few years after Berney's death, Martha Kempton sold the ranch to a man named Barnam who later sold it to a well-known

Steve Tibbetts and his sons now own and operate the former Kempton Ranch.
COURTESY OF *AGWEEK.*

Prairie County rancher, Steve Tibbetts. Steve and his three sons still own the former Kempton Ranch, and the land is once again highly profitable through their dedicated efforts and modern ranching techniques.

The land of the famous Kempton Ranch is still incredibly beautiful. The reservoirs that JB scraped out more than 100 years ago still attract waterfowl. Black Angus cattle dot the hillsides, and crops line the lowlands. The trees, in early photos appearing as just seedlings, now tower over the remaining buildings. Although the original ranch house, no longer occupied, has fallen into disrepair, you can still see the grandeur of the large, welcoming living room and dining areas. Only the memories, the ghosts of the Kempton family, remain. As Willa Cather said, "We come and go, but the land is always here."

From the earliest generations of my family, even before the Pilgrims, my ancestors had a deep regard for the land. From England to Plymouth to the Eastern Seaboard to the Midwest and finally to the prairies of

Ranchland near Terry.

Colorado and Montana, the Kemptons loved the land, and it gave them life. The land was indeed their good mother.

Martha and Berney at the ranch.

IS THE KEMPTON
HOTEL HAUNTED?

The Kempton Hotel.

he Kempton Hotel in Terry, Montana, built by Berney and Martha Kempton in 1914 to accommodate visitors to the nearby Kempton Ranch, still welcomes guests today. Photographs taken around 1900 show a smaller similar building, so the hotel actually dates back to the turn of the century. The Kempton Hotel provided first-class lodging and dining for travelers passing through eastern Montana, and its present owners, Russ and Linda Schwartz, claim it is the oldest continually operating hotel in Montana. My husband and I recently enjoyed a few days there, and it brought back many memories of my childhood.

In the 1920s, Berney and Martha Kempton divided their time between the hotel and the ranch, which was a few miles from town. Although they hired personnel to operate the hotel, they still oversaw this establishment and often spent time there, Berney at the front desk and Martha in the kitchen. Jerry, his brothers, and Pansy explored the hotel from basement to attic, racing up and down the halls, peeking into open rooms, and sliding down the laundry chute. Pansy and Jerry sometimes played chef, mixing up concoctions on tiny plates, custard cups, and assorted dishes stored in the basement. One of their favorite games was hide-and-seek between the storage shelves while their mothers washed their long hair in the soft water of the natural artesian springs spigot in the hotel basement.

The Kempton Hotel and dining room provided an elegant welcome for many a traveler, from the famous to the ordinary. The place also saw some very grim times. The Spanish Flu pandemic of 1918 hit hard in Terry. (Worldwide, more people died from this illness than all those killed in the First World War.)

When eastern Montana medical offices and hospitals overflowed with patients, doctors begged Berney to allow them to use the hotel attic as a sick ward to isolate patients and care for them more easily. Berney and Martha felt it was their civic duty and agreed.

Rows of metal beds were set up, nurses attended to the ill, and doctors divided their time between patients in the hospital and those in hotel attic. Meals were prepared in the hotel kitchen for patients who were well enough to eat. The attic functioned as a makeshift infirmary for several months until the epidemic began to wane.

Unfortunately, a high percentage of patients succumbed to their illnesses. Death from this influenza came quite quickly; often a patient felt okay in the morning, feverish at noon, and was dead by nightfall. It was a horrible way to die. The victim's lungs filled with fluid, and simple breathing became a struggle. Within hours, the patient agonizingly suffocated. Unlike other illnesses, this flu often struck the young and able-bodied more than any other segment of the population.

None of the Kempton family or ranch hands became ill. Berney said they were just "too ornery to get sick," but it was probably because they stayed mostly on the ranch and limited their contact with other people. Martha thought her healthy meals also made a difference.

Fortunately, the Spanish Flu outbreak in Terry was short-lived, and hotel operations soon became normal once more. Hearty appetites returned, and the kitchens at both the ranch and hotel were busy cooking and serving the food for which they were famous.

KEMPTON HOTEL
By Jim Kempton
(Submitted by Mary Haughian)

In 1914, when the Kempton Hotel was built, many people speculated that it would go broke because it had not been built by the railroad. But time has proven those speculators wrong.

An integral part of the hotel was the restaurant located on the first floor. It was in operation from 1914 to 1946. The linens matched the napkins and the tablecloths. Finger bowls were used for each person to wash his hands. Mrs. Kempton always had fresh flowers around the restaurant.

Mrs. Kempton was famous for baking pies, but at times hired cooks to help. Berney Kempton served as a cook many times. A familiar saying of his was, "Heck, coffee isn't good if it won't float a horseshoe."

The meals were priced very low. One could buy a meal ticket, 21 meals for $7. This would be about 33 1/3¢ per meal. A regular meal would cost 50¢ even though steak was served.

The hotel had the honor of lodging at least two very important persons. Theodore Dreiser, author of "An American Tragedy", came to Terry by way of the Yellowstone Trail and stayed at the hotel. The other person was Madam Schumann-Heink, a famous contralto, who visited the hotel on her tour of America.

But not all visitors at the hotel have been famous or wealthy. In 1918 it was used as a hospital during the flu epidemic in Terry.

This famous landmark has seen many changes during the years. When the hotel was built a horseshoe was placed right side up over the front door. This was so good luck would not run out.

Jim Kempton penned a piece on the hotel's history for the local newspaper.

While both the hotel and the ranch served excellent fare, dining experiences at the two locations were distinctly different. The hotel dining room was elegant, with courses presented on bone china dinnerware imported from Limoges, France. Ranch meals were more casual, with plain white, heavy-duty dishes. This large stock of many-sized sturdy dishware was stored in a small room dubbed "the china room," adjacent to the large ranch kitchen.

One quiet afternoon, several shelves in the ranch china room suddenly collapsed under too much weight. Hundreds of tiny sauce dishes and small bowls crashed to the floor. Most of the dishes broke into tiny pieces and could not be salvaged. The mess was swept up and thrown away. (There was no garbage service on the ranch in those days, so debris was taken out to a dump area and thrown onto a pile that was regularly turned. Even today, small pieces of this white china can still be found in the soil.)

A menu for dining at the Kempton Ranch.

"Thank goodness it was just the everyday china," Martha said to Mrs. McMillan, "but any dishes are just too costly to lose. Fortunately, there are boxes of extra bowls and sauce dishes in the hotel basement. Gray Hawk's here with Jerry, so if we send them into Terry, we'll have the dishes in time for dinner."

Gray Hawk, a distant Lakota Sioux relative of the Kempton family who often visited the ranch and sometimes went to school with the Kempton children, was staying at the ranch for a few weeks. He and Jerry were looking for something to do when Martha asked for their help. The boys willingly agreed and hitched up the wagon, remembering that often she paid them each a nickel for errands like this.

"You'll find the boxes in the hotel basement, right by the large wash tub. Here's a sample of what I need to help you get the right ones. And thanks, boys, for doing this errand," Martha said as she pressed a nickel into each of their palms. "The workmen will be gone for the day, and the hotel'll be empty. Better go right away before it's too dark to see, since the gas lights have been disconnected."

The Kempton Hotel was temporarily closed to guests as workmen installed electric lights to replace the gas ones. They also modified several rooms on the first floor. With construction underway, all regular personnel were given time off. The only people in the building were workmen trying to finish the job as quickly as possible.

If the boys hadn't dawdled, there would have been plenty of afternoon sunlight coming through the hotel windows. But they had stopped to talk with friends who were fishing in Cherry Creek near the ranch. Consequently, when they got to the hotel, it was close to dusk.

The lobby, usually bustling and busy, was empty and lifeless when the boys arrived, the workmen having left an hour or so before.

"You wanna see the dining room?" Jerry asked. "It's really keen."

The dining room at the Kempton Hotel.

Jerry pushed open the double doors that led into the large dining room. The tables were bare except for a coating of construction dust, but the room still looked elegant.

"Mom makes sure the tablecloths and napkins match. See all those vases over there? She puts flowers on each table. There are all kinds of glasses too and dishes that came all the way from France. She even puts fingerbowls on the tables."

"What's a fingerbowl?" asked Gray Hawk.

"Oh, it's a fancy bowl to dip your dirty fingers in before dinner, or something like that," Jerry explained, not exactly sure himself how fingerbowls were used.

"But if people got dirty hands, why don't they wash up?" Gray Hawk asked. "A little bowl wouldn't do much for dirty hands. Then what'd you do with the dirty water? You don't hafta drink it, do you?" Both boys laughed at the thought.

"Why, Mr. Gray Hawk," joked Jerry, faking an accent and strutting around the room. He picked up a goblet and held it with his little finger extended.

"Indeed, sir, this is a *most* fancy place, where people dine in high style. It is certainly not a place for boys with dirty hands, who don't know what a fingerbowl is for. You simply gotta have proper manners to come to this joint!"

"Yeah, Jerry. Or should I call you Count Gerald? Oh, Sir Count, I hate to bother you, but we really must descend to the basement, while there's still some daylight, sire," said Gray Hawk, bowing before Jerry and offering his arm.

"Certainly, my good man!" Jerry responded as he closed the doors to the dining room, and the boys strode arm-in-arm through the lobby and down the dark hall that led to the basement stairs, still laughing.

Luckily, some outside light still came through the small basement windows as they started down the stairs. Halfway down, Gray Hawk stopped abruptly, grabbed Jerry's arm, and pointed to something white lying on a step.

"What's that?" Gray Hawk asked.

Jerry leaned down and picked it up. "Just a rag someone left," he said, holding it up.

"What're those long strings?"

"I dunno. It's kinda like a doctor's mask to keep out germs. Let's just get the boxes before we run outta light," Jerry answered.

The hotel basement had never been one of Jerry's favorite places. He remembered when his older brother Jim used to lure him down the steps to a corner of the basement with the promise of a toy or something interesting. Then when Jerry wasn't looking, Jim ran back up the stairs, slammed the door, and left Jerry alone in the dark. Jerry remembered sitting in the blackness, afraid to move, screaming for his mother. This happened a number of times when he was about four or five. Looking back, Jerry wondered why it took him so long to catch on to Jim's mean trick. Finally Martha figured out what was happening and told Jim that if he ever did that to any of his brothers again, she would take a belt to him herself. Now these years later, Jerry wasn't exactly afraid of the dark basement, but he admitted he liked it better in the daytime.

Jerry and Gray Hawk took down a few boxes labeled "dinnerware" from a row of open shelves. They brushed off the accumulation of dust and cobwebs and opened each one. A mouse scurried from its hiding place near the shelves, and the boys could hear the scratching of some other small creature in a far corner.

"It's spooky down here," said Gray Hawk. In the quiet, his voice sounded unnaturally loud.

"Yeah, let's find the stuff and get out."

"Here they are," said Gray Hawk as he opened a carton and held up one of the small sauce dishes inside.

"Good, now let's find the bowls," said Jerry as he continued to search.

"Ugh! Spiders!" Gray Hawk groaned, brushing off a spiderweb on one of the shelves.

Jerry finally found the bowls next to the washtub. He noticed the light from outside was dim, and the dark basement was eerily quiet.

"I don't like it down here," Gray Hawk whispered as he restacked the boxes.

"Yeah, let's just get upstairs," Jerry agreed.

Suddenly, without warning, water poured from the spigot into the washtub near the boys. They jumped back in fright, nearly knocking over a stack of dinner plates.

"Who—who did that?" Gray Hawk stammered.

"You musta hit it," said Jerry as he looked at the stream of water and twisted the knob firmly to stop it.

"Not me! I didn't touch it," said Gray Hawk, his voice high-pitched and shaky.

"Well, me neither, but it couldn't turn on all by itself. Uh, let's just get these upstairs and get outta here," Jerry suggested, trying to make light of this strange situation.

Each boy picked up a carton of dishes and headed for the steps. They were almost at the landing when the basement door slammed shut with a bang. Both boys gasped and nearly dropped the dishes. The stairs were now pitch black, and they had to feel their way up to the door.

"It's locked!" said Gray Hawk, in a whisper as he tried the doorknob. "Somebody locked us down here!"

"Maybe the wind just blew it shut," Jerry said, trying the door. "You're right. It is locked!"

Gray Hawk set his box down on a step and put his shoulder against the door, pushing as hard as he could. The door flew open, and he fell into the hall by the lobby.

"It musta just been stuck," Jerry said in a trembling voice.

The boys picked up the boxes of china and headed for the main door, warily glancing behind them. As they reached the door, they noticed the white gauzy thing they had found on the basement stairs, or at least one just like it, hanging on the doorknob.

"How'd that get here? It wasn't here before," Gray Hawk said as he grabbed it.

The boys went out onto the front porch, glad to be out of the hotel.

"What is this thing?" Gray Hawk asked as he looked at the piece of gauze in his hand.

"Like I said before, I really think it's a face mask that doctors or nurses wear over their mouth and nose. I saw something like it in the old photos Dad has of the Spanish Flu, when a hospital was set up in the attic, because so many people were sick."

"Yeah, you told me about that," answered Gray Hawk.

"Did I tell you a newspaper man from Butte wrote a story about it and took pictures? He thought it was great Dad let sick people stay here. Some of the pictures even showed dead bodies covered with dark blankets. Dad told us there were lots of 'em."

"Let's just get outta here," said Gray Hawk as they loaded the boxes of china into the wagon and set out for home.

"I don't like that place," said Gray Hawk. "How'd that water turn on by itself?"

"I dunno," Jerry said. "Maybe it was under pressure, or we probably just hit the faucet and didn't know it. I don't believe in ghosts, so there's some explanation."

"We weren't close to the faucet. And how'd the door slam, huh?" Gray Hawk asked.

"Well, it musta been the wind," Jerry said with a conviction he didn't feel. "And one of the workmen probably used that old mask to keep out the dust and just left it behind."

"There was a black feeling in that place," said Gray Hawk quietly.

"Oh, Gray Hawk, you and your black feelings. Everything's got a reason."

"Oh yeah?" scoffed Gray Hawk.

"I guess it did feel sorta spooky," Jerry said. "Even though I don't believe in that ghost stuff," he added.

The boys arrived back at the ranch and took the boxes to the kitchen. Martha thanked them and told them to wash up for dinner. Dinner sounded like a good idea since their trip to the hotel had left them hungry.

At the dinner table, Berney, knowing Jerry and Gray Hawk had been to the hotel, asked, "How's the construction going?"

"Well, Dad, we didn't exactly hang around and look."

"Oh?" Berney said.

"That's a spooky place in the dark with no one around," said Gray Hawk.

"Yeah, maybe a little scary," added Jerry.

"Scary? What do you mean, Jer?" Berney asked.

"Well, it was kind of spooky, Dad." Gray Hawk shook his head in agreement.

"Spooky? What was spooky?" asked Martha as she passed the gravy.

"Well, Ma . . ." Jerry began, interrupted by his father who stood up, put a white napkin over his head, and held out his arms.

"Uhhhhhh, ohhhhh," Berney moaned dramatically. "I am the spirit of Les Moore. Shot in the back with a forty-four. No less, no more. Ohhhh, ohh."

"Dad, that's dumb," said Jerry as the younger boys howled with laughter.

Berney moaned again, then sat down and put the napkin back on his lap.

"Well, you know," he said ominously, dropping his voice to a whisper, "some people think the hotel is haunted by ghosts of the flu victims who died there."

Jerry and Gray Hawk looked at each other but didn't say a thing.

Then Berney leaned back in his chair and laughed. "But I think that's all a load of hogwash."

Dinner conversation turned to the Spanish Flu. The oldest Kempton boy, Jim (who was eight at the time of the pandemic), said he found some neat things in the attic when he helped clean it out months after all the doctors and patients left. Jim was the only child who had any memories of that time.

"What kind of stuff did you find?" asked Jerry.

"Well," said Jim, "a bunch of old letters and a sack with ten silver dollars. I guess the people who wrote the letters died 'cause they never got sent. I gave the money to Dad, and I think he still has the letters, don't ya, Dad?"

"Yeah, a lot of them. We mailed the ones we could, but most weren't properly addressed," Berney replied. "I kept those, just in case we could ever figure out who to send 'em to."

"Jeepers! Dad, can Gray Hawk and I read some of 'em tonight?" asked Jerry.

"You bet. I'll show you where they are. They're interesting and sad at the same time," Berney replied.

After dinner, the boys followed Berney into his study, where he took some papers and envelopes down from a high shelf and handed them to the boys.

"You're welcome to look 'em over. I'm gonna go check something in the barn," Berney said as he left the room.

The boys unfolded the papers and looked at the handwriting.

"It's strange to think the people who wrote these died, and the letters never got sent," said Jerry

"Yeah, it is spooky," said Gray Hawk.

"Listen to this. It's from a girl to her sweetheart in Butte," said Jerry as he began to read.

Dearest John,

Things are fine here, but I miss you so very much and wish we were together again. I know you feel you must earn a sum of money before we marry, but I worry about you going down in the mines.

I took a long walk out on the prairie earlier this week. I blushed when I passed our special picnic spot. I thought about how wonderful it will be when we are married.

I am planning to make the trip to see you in Butte two weeks from now and arranged to stay at the Anderson rooming house.

I will make this letter short because I have not been feeling well and plan to take a nap this afternoon. I am looking forward to a lifetime with you.

Yours forever,

Ann

P.S. I have enclosed a photo I had taken at the studio in Miles City.

"Look in there. Is there a picture of her?" Jerry asked.

Gray Hawk felt around in the large envelope and pulled out a photo of a young woman with dark hair wearing a white dress.

"She was real pretty, but I'll bet she was getting the flu. She musta been one of the sick people in the attic who died, and that's why her letter wasn't sent," said Jerry. He shivered and put down the letter. Both boys were silent as the weight of this knowledge settled on them.

"Who was John, do ya think?" asked Gray Hawk quietly.

"I dunno," said Jerry. "There musta been lots of men named John in the mines in Butte. I wonder if he knew what happened to Ann."

"They were gonna get married," said Gray Hawk, with a sigh. "I wonder where she's buried. Maybe John found her grave."

"I dunno. Dad said they ran outta coffins 'cause so many people died, so they had to put some of 'em in one big grave. Most of their names were on the headstone, but Dad said they didn't know all the names, so John maybe never knew what happened to her. This envelope wasn't even addressed, so it couldn't be mailed."

"Too bad," murmured Gray Hawk. "She was just about to get married."

"I wonder what she was like," said Jerry quietly. "I'll bet she was nice."

The boys read other letters, equally as poignant. Then they found an envelope in the stack, still sealed. The address read, "To Sally Evans, San Francisco." The line for the street name or box number was blank, as if the writer planned to complete that information later but never had the chance. The boys carefully slid Jerry's pocketknife under the envelope flap and took out the letter. It was from a man named Jim Evans to his sister. The letter said Jim was leaving all his worldly possessions to her, along with the money in his bank account in Missoula. He also wrote about a poke of gold he planned to send when he was better but would keep with him until then.

"If that man died in the hotel attic, what happened to that poke of gold? And what's a 'poke' anyway?" Jerry asked.

Jerry looked up the word in the big dictionary on his dad's desk and said, "Well, one meaning of the word poke is a small bag, often used for storing gold dust or nuggets."

"You mean there might be gold in the attic?" exclaimed Gray Hawk.

"Gee whiz, if the workmen are tearing out boards to put in electricity, this'd be the time to look!" Jerry responded excitedly.

"Yeah!" Gray Hawk said. Then they heard the boom of thunder and the sudden sound of heavy rain. "But not tonight."

In his dreams that night, Jerry saw the girl named Ann dressed in the gauzy white dress, her face covered with a veil, holding a bouquet of flowers. She looked like a bride as she walked down the aisle, but she kept on walking and walking off into space.

The next day, Jerry and Gray Hawk made another trip to the hotel since they knew workmen wouldn't be there. They left the ranch at noon to have plenty of daylight to explore the attic. They didn't want to get caught in the dark again. Jerry brought a hammer and crowbar to pry off the wallboards. They looked for Tucker to take along as a guard dog but couldn't find him. Berney said he was probably off chasing rabbits.

They told Martha they wanted to see how construction was coming and promised to bring her more small bowls. Knowing the boys' penchant for exploration, she figured they must have ulterior motives, but she wasn't too concerned and didn't want to spoil their adventure.

When they got to Terry, before they went inside the hotel, Jerry proudly pointed out the horseshoe above the front door.

"Dad nailed that up when the hotel first opened. He said a right-side-up horseshoe is supposed to hold in all the good luck. He says it's worked all these years 'cause the hotel's done really well. When he first decided to build it, people told him that any place that wasn't built by the railroad wouldn't be a success, but they were wrong. Dad says the railroad can't be the boss of everything! And he was right," Jerry said, proud of his father's initiative and perseverance.

A horseshoe for luck.

Inside the front door, Jerry clomped heavily across the lobby. Gray Hawk, more accustomed to a quiet approach used when hunting game, asked him why the heavy foot.

"I want anyone here, ghost or human, to know we're comin' so they can get out," Jerry explained. "I read somewhere that if you let spirits know you're coming in, they scram."

Gray Hawk noticed there were more footprints in the dust of the floor than he had seen yesterday.

He pointed out a set of small prints probably made by a child or girl, and said, "Who else's been here since us?"

"Well, ghosts don't leave footprints, so it was probably just the workmen," Jerry joked.

"I don't know about that, Jer. I don't think they work much over the weekend."

Jerry just shrugged and looked around the lobby at the furniture covered by old sheets and dust covers.

"Anyone could hide under those sheets," said Jerry. He jokingly ordered, "Come out, come out, whoever you are! Friend or foe, whoever you are!"

Gray Hawk suppressed a giggle as the boys crossed the lobby and climbed the stairs to the second floor then up to the attic. He whispered, "It's creepy being where so many people died."

Jerry cocked an eyebrow and answered, "Nah, you never say that on Indian battlefields when we're looking for lead balls. More people died out there than here, ya know."

"Yeah, those places should have more darkness than here, but this just seems scary," said Gray Hawk.

"Too bad we couldn't find Tucker and bring him along 'cause that dog's not afraid of anything, not even spooks," said Jerry.

Jerry pushed open the attic door and just stood there looking around the long room, lit only by three windows.

Gray Hawk, right behind him, said, "You going in, Jer?"

"Oh yeah," Jerry said as he stepped into the room and pointed to an empty wall. "The old photos show a row of beds over there with curtains between 'em."

"So anyone in bed could've slipped something behind the wall and no one would've seen 'em," said Gray Hawk.

The boys checked the wall and found some boards were loose.

"These boards are so flimsy. It'd be easy to hide something behind 'em," suggested Jerry. "Let's see if we can get 'em off."

Handing Jerry the crowbar, Gray Hawk said, "Probably no one's ever checked behind here."

"Yeah, but before we pull 'em out, I gotta use a bathroom. I gotta go really bad," said Jerry. "I'll use the one at the end of the hall. It has windows. Be back in two shakes." Rushing out, he called back in a loud whisper, "Don't start without me!"

Gray Hawk found an old wooden box, turned it over and sat down. While he waited for Jerry to return, he looked around the room. There were a few boxes, some old furniture, and a bunch of metal beds stacked at the end of the room. He wondered if the beds were used by patients or hotel guests.

A few minutes later, Jerry, white-faced and out of breath, burst into the attic. He looked behind him down the dark hall and whispered, "There's a—a—a someone down there!"

A hallway in the Kempton Hotel.

Gray Hawk's eyes widened in fear as Jerry continued, "When I came outta the toilet, I saw a girl in a white dress down the hall. She—she, uh, had dark hair and was singing to herself. I—I don't think she saw me."

"Sounds like the girl in the photo," said Gray Hawk. "Maybe you saw a ghost!"

"I dunno, but when I ducked back into the washroom, the place smelled sweet like things girls use, and there was still some water in the sink."

"Maybe you saw the ghost of that girl—what's her name? Ann, who died up here."

"It couldn't a been a ghost—ghosts don't need to wash up," said Jerry, trying to be logical.

"Then who was it? Your dad said no one's staying here. Maybe workmen?" asked Gray Hawk.

"Nah, they're gone today. Besides, workmen don't wear dresses!" Jerry pointed out, again trying to be logical. "You wanna sneak down there and check?" he asked.

"Nah! You crazy?" Gray Hawk whispered. "Not me!"

"Let's lock the attic door," said Jerry.

"Let's just get outta here and ask your dad or one of the ranch hands to come back with us. The Florida Cowboy would come—he likes adventure," said Gray Hawk, looking at the closed door.

"Nah," said Jerry, "They wouldn't want us pulling off wallboards, and we'd never get to see what's behind there. Let's just take a quick look and then get outta here. Come on, lock the door and we'll stick together. That's the only way we'll ever find out what's up here. With the door locked, we'll be okay, don't ya think?"

Gray Hawk agreed. The boys locked the door and looked for a place to start their search behind the wallboards.

Jerry kept glancing at the door and thought, *I really saw someone down there. I know I did. First, I have a dumb dream about that girl and then I think I see her. That's crazy. There's no such thing as ghosts. I'm being dumb.*

Trying to be brave, Jerry said, "If we wanna find that gold poke, let's just forget about what I thought I saw. Maybe it was just my imagination."

"Yeah, you got a good one."

Ignoring his friend's comment, Jerry said, "If they found silver dollars on the other side of the room, maybe no one's ever checked here. Let's try it," he suggested.

Jerry put the end of the crowbar under the wood and began prying the first board. Both boys were alarmed at the loud screeching noise, but they continued. Within minutes they had pulled out all the boards along one wall but found nothing but dust, old spiderwebs, and the desiccated bodies of two long-dead mice. They were looking for another likely wall to pry when they heard the loud bang of a door slamming on a lower floor.

"What was that?" Jerry whispered as both boys grabbed each other's arms.

"Sounded like a door. I don't like this. . . ."

"Shh, be quiet and listen," gulped Jerry. "Maybe the wind slammed it."

"Jer, there's no wind today," Gray Hawk whispered as the two slid down the wall and sat quietly on the floor listening for more noises.

After a few minutes, Gray Hawk poked Jerry and whispered urgently, "I hear footsteps on the floor below us. Listen." He put his ear to the floor. "They're light footsteps like a kid. Or maybe it's the girl in the white dress you saw," he added.

Jerry swallowed loudly and whispered, "I don't believe in ghosts."

"How can we get outta here without going down that hall? I don't wanna go past whatever is down there," Gray Hawk said.

"Maybe we can climb out the window onto the roof, hold on tight, and go down that ladder in back," suggested Jerry, who also didn't want to go down that hall again.

Both boys pushed hard on the attic windows, but they wouldn't budge. It had been too many years and too many coats of paint since they had last been opened.

"There's no other way out. We're gonna have to open the door and go down the hall," Jerry whispered in a shaky voice. "We gotta get outta here."

They quietly unlocked the attic door and tiptoed down the stairs to the dark hall.

"Did you bring the crowbar or hammer?" Gray Hawk whispered.

"No. Too bad 'cause they'd be good weapons. But we got this far, so let's just keep going and get out," said Jerry as they walked as quickly and quietly as they could.

Suddenly, one of the guestroom doors in front of them in the hall flew open, and a large figure burst out in front of the boys, blocking their way. The boys hollered. The light from the room windows showed the outline of a man holding a gun.

"Hold it! Don't move!" the man shouted. "Step into the room and keep your hands up!"

Jerry and Gray Hawk complied, too frightened to feel relief that this was a person, not a specter.

"Dad! No! It's just the young boy I saw!" said a girl, who was sitting on the bed in the room. "Put the gun down. It's just him and his friend!"

The man lowered the gun and put it on the dresser. He slumped from his intimidating posture and said sheepishly, "Oh, heavens! I apologize to you both." He looked back at his daughter and added, "I am so very sorry."

When Jerry got his voice back, he said, "You—you—you're the girl I saw in the hall. Who—who are you, and what're you doing here? This is my dad's hotel, and it's closed now," he added in a voice that sounded braver than he felt.

The girl stepped forward. She was pretty with dark hair that curled around her face and a white dress. Jerry and Gray Hawk were startled at her resemblance to the photo they found of the tragic Ann who had written to her sweetheart before she died.

"I am, once again, so terribly sorry to have frightened you boys," the man said, "but I didn't know who you were and if we were in danger. Please forgive me." He held out his hand and continued, "My name is Dr. Jonathan Bonner, and this is my daughter Elizabeth. We are just passing through Terry on our way to Spokane where, at last, I have a job waiting," he added.

Jerry kept glancing at Elizabeth and finally said, "Uh, you look like a girl in a photo we saw named Ann. She, uh, stayed in this hotel."

"I do?" Elizabeth asked. "Was Ann a guest here?"

"Well, uh, not exactly," stumbled Jerry, "More like, uh, kind of like a patient or something." Then he gained more courage and said, "But why are you here in the hotel when it's closed?"

"I can explain," said Dr. Bonner. "I knew the Kemptons to be kind, generous folk from the time I came through and stopped at your ranch, hoping for a handout. A woman and a little girl invited me in, gave me dinner, and sent me on my way with food for several days. The woman even gave me two silver dollars."

"That was Mrs. McMillan and Pansy," Jerry said. "But Mom would have done the same."

"You see," continued Dr. Bonner, gesturing to his daughter. "I was recently on my way to get Elizabeth, who was staying with my brother and sister-in-law in Fargo. There was a bit of a disagreement, and they didn't want me to take her. They said I was an overeducated, no-account individual who would never be able to take care of a daughter."

Elizabeth spoke up. "We tried to tell them that Dad had a good job waiting at a college in Spokane, but they didn't believe it and said it was just another of Dad's many pipe dreams. No one in that family gives much credence to higher education, I'm afraid."

"She's my daughter, but they would not let her go with me—her own father. Finally, with no other options, we said we were just going out for an evening walk," explained Dr. Bonner, "and we kept going with just what we could carry in our coat pockets. It was the only way to get Elizabeth away from there. That's why she has only her good white dress and a coat."

"Dad and I got a ride as far as Terry," said Elizabeth, "but we had no place to stay when the storm began last night."

"In desperation, we tried the hotel door and found it open," said Dr. Bonner.

"Yeah, the door's never locked," Jerry said. "In fact, it doesn't even have a key, so it's always been open, since it was built."

"We could tell there's construction going on," Dr. Bonner continued, "but we hoped your family would not mind if we took shelter here, in light of the circumstances."

"Look here," said Elizabeth, walking to the nightstand, opening the drawer and holding up an envelope that was stamped and ready to post. "It's to your mom and dad."

Dr. Bonner said, "It's an explanation and a thank-you with a note saying that I promise to send money for the room from my first paycheck."

"I'm so sorry Dad scared you with the gun. Why, it isn't even loaded."

"Gee," said Jerry, "if you need a place to stay, why don't you just come out to the ranch with us and spend another night. Dad can find someone who's driving west and can take you to Spokane."

Elizabeth and her father smiled at the boys and told them that would be wonderful and much appreciated.

"I'll bet Mom has some clothes you can wear instead of that dress, but it's real pretty," said Jerry, who was now back to his talkative self.

Gray Hawk just shook his head. He hadn't said much and was still shaking from the scare.

The four rode back to the ranch in the wagon the boys had driven to the hotel. When Jerry and Gray Hawk took Dr. Bonner and Elizabeth inside and explained their situation, Mrs. Kempton said she was glad to have them stay with the family. Mrs. McMillan and Pansy recognized the man from the previous encounter and greeted him warmly.

At dinner that night, the family heard the story of Dr. Bonner and his daughter. Bonner made it clear he was not a medical doctor but rather a doctor of English literature. He added he had the great fortune to have found work as a professor of English studies at Gonzaga University in Spokane. Elizabeth said she hoped to obtain a scholarship in voice.

After dinner, she sang a number of songs for the Kemptons, and her beautiful singing met with generous applause.

During the evening, Jerry frequently looked at Elizabeth and thought of her resemblance to Ann, the ill-fated bride-to-be. He even found the letter, took out the photo, and showed his dad, who said, "Hm, there is quite a resemblance, isn't there? I'm sure Elizabeth will have a better future than poor Ann."

A day later, Dr. Bonner and Elizabeth caught a ride with Mike Patterson, a neighboring rancher, who was driving to Spokane to pick up his daughter. He was glad for the company, and they were happy to get to their new and promising life.

A week later, Jerry and Gray Hawk asked Berney if he thought there were any treasures still behind the walls of the hotel attic.

"Oh, I doubt it. All the boards were pulled off and every inch was checked years ago after the hospital moved out."

Jerry mentioned the letter telling about a gold poke.

"There's no gold poke in that attic. If there ever was, it was taken years before," said Berney. "Your brother Jim did find some silver dollars that we donated to the church."

With that, the boys ended their treasure hunt, although Jerry had dreams about Ann for several more weeks. She was always in her white dress, so pale and sad, still walking and looking for someone. Finally, in his last dream, there was a young man coming toward her with a smile and open arms. Jerry hoped John had found his Ann at last.

The Kemptons kept in touch with Dr. Bonner and Elizabeth for years. Although they talked about it, the father and daughter never made a trip back to Montana. Almost every year, however, the Kemptons received a Christmas card from them with a handwritten note telling of their activities. Elizabeth became an opera singer, eventually married, and had a family. Dr. Bonner lived with them in Spokane, where he was a much-loved professor of English at Gonzaga for many years until his death.

Author's note: Modern travelers who spend a night or two in Terry sometimes report the Kempton Hotel is haunted. It is said the spirits are those of the unfortunate souls who died in the hotel attic from the Spanish Flu.

Some say they've even heard the clink of Berney Kempton's spurs on the hardwood floors, but I'm sure any apparition of Berney would not have stayed in the hotel. His vital spirit would be out riding the Montana range he loved so well!

It was, however, in the lobby of the Kempton Hotel that Berney Edmond Kempton passed away from a heart attack in March of 1942 at the age of seventy-one. A Greyhound Bus driver, who routinely stopped in Terry at about two in the morning for a break and a cup of coffee with Berney, found him slumped in his favorite chair. The newspaper he was reading had fallen to the floor. And yes, Berney Kempton died with his boots on, just as he hoped to.

GUMBO MUD
AND FAMOUS GUESTS

If you can talk with crowds and keep your virtue,
Or walk with Kings—nor lose the common touch. . . .

here are many more lines to that poem called, "If," by Rudyard Kipling, but the above stanzas describe Berney Kempton, the owner of the Kempton Ranch and the Kempton Hotel in Terry, Montana. This poem was one of his favorites.

In his lifetime of some seventy-one years, Berney entertained countless people—first as a star rider and roper with Doctor Carver's Wild West Show as it traveled the world, and then as the owner of an immense ranch and a popular hotel. He loved being the charismatic showman, the expansive host.

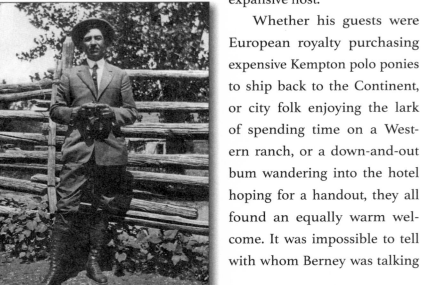

Whether his guests were European royalty purchasing expensive Kempton polo ponies to ship back to the Continent, or city folk enjoying the lark of spending time on a Western ranch, or a down-and-out bum wandering into the hotel hoping for a handout, they all found an equally warm welcome. It was impossible to tell with whom Berney was talking

Berney Kempton

simply by listening to what he said, because he treated all his visitors with the same goodwill and acceptance. This was partly a hallmark of general Montana hospitality in those days, but it was mostly Berney's own particular attribute.

Another personal trait was Berney's love of poetry and good literature. His personal collection included works of many famous authors and poets, and most of the books were well-worn from multiple readings. Whether it was an evening around the campfire during a cattle drive or a winter afternoon gathered close to the stone fireplace in the ranch house, Berney could be counted on to recite a poem, many of which he knew by heart. Who would have thought this Montana rancher, this cowboy's cowboy, was such an ardent lover of poetry and literature? Perhaps Berney Kempton was an early Montana Renaissance man.

Berney also seemed knowledgeable about almost every topic relevant at that time. In fact, this knowledge was one of the qualities Martha noticed during the months Berney courted her. Martha, a Swedish immigrant, learned English quickly and completed all grades of elementary school in one year, then went on to graduate high school at the head of her class. She quietly realized she was the smartest young woman she knew. When introduced to Berney Kempton at a dance in Miles City, she met her intellectual match.

Martha and Berney married and had five sons, one of whom was my father. Any time the boys had a question, Martha advised, "Go ask your dad—he'll know." And he did. This intellect continued into the following generation. My father, Jerry, also knew about almost anything. Our mother often said the same thing when we came to her with questions: "Go ask your dad—he'll know." And he did.

One rainy Montana spring evening, while tending the front desk at the Kempton Hotel, Berney heard a car pull up out front. It was a terrible night to be outdoors—it had rained hard all day and was now a time when travelers should be inside, comforted by a fire.

Even before he laid eyes on his new guests, Berney heard snatches of their angry conversation.

"I told you, we should have stayed in Miles City!" the woman whined. "You never listen to me, do you?"

"But it should have been a short drive. Who knew it would take so long to go just forty damn miles," was the man's response.

The Kempton Hotel.

The couple straggled into the lobby, dripping wet, in bad spirits, and in desperate need of some comfort. The man's expensive suit pants were caked with muck up to his knees. It was obvious they had been driving on wet Montana gumbo roads.

"Damn roads. Damn mud!" the man growled as he looked around the lobby.

"I told you we should have just stayed in Miles City," the woman complained again, trailing behind and shaking out her wet umbrella.

"Yeah, I know, I know, but it was only forty miles to here. Just forty miles!" the man retorted as Berney stepped from behind the counter and handed them small towels. They thanked him and gratefully mopped their faces.

"Bad night to be out, I'm afraid. I'm glad you made it," Berney began.

"Yeah, it took over eight hours to drive the forty miles from Miles City. Forty stinking miles, and I can't remember how many times we got stuck in that blasted mud," the man growled.

"Your roads are terrible, just terrible!" the woman chimed in.

"Yeah, looks like you both had a bad deal, and I'm sorry. But around here, we say that any road in Montana that gets you where you're goin' is a good road! It's too bad you ran into gumbo at its worst," Berney said, hoping to disarm the angry couple with a sympathetic smile.

"Gumbo? What in the hell is gumbo? The only gumbo I've ever heard of is seafood soup in New Orleans," the man said.

"Around here, that's the name for clay soil that turns to gluey mud when it rains," Berney said. "It's slicker than you know what, sticks to tires, shoes, and the undercarriage of cars. I'll see that your shoes are cleaned, and I'll have our man hose off your car as soon as he can. If you don't get it before it dries, the stream from the hose will only amuse that mud. We'll do our best on your pants too," Berney added.

"Good luck with these shoes," the man said. "I feel like I'm five inches taller," he added as he lifted his foot to show thick mud caked on the soles of his expensive loafers. "I'll leave 'em here," he added, stepping out of his shoes and leaving them near the door.

"How long will you be staying with us?" Berney asked.

"Just one night, thanks. We're on our way to New York," the man replied as he scribbled his name in the guestbook and took out his wallet to pay for the room.

"Now are you folks hungry?" Berney asked. "We don't have many people staying in the hotel tonight, and our dining room closes in about a half hour. I can tell you everything's great, but the pot roast is the best around, and my wife Martha's apple pie is well known all the way to Seattle! You'll have time to change clothes, if you want," he added.

A few minutes later, the couple came down for dinner, stopping to talk to Berney.

"We're doing much better now," the man said with a smile.

"Yes, dry clothes make a world of difference," the woman added. "We're sorry if we were rude when we came in."

The man stepped forward and extended his hand to Berney, who shook it heartily. "My name is Ted, and this is my wife Helen. Would you do us the pleasure of joining us at dinner? We'd like to hear more about this area of Montana, if you're free," the man said to Berney.

Berney never passed up an opportunity to talk about his beloved prairies, so the three went in for dinner. Ted had questions about the town, cattle ranching, and the nearby badlands. Helen asked about the people in Terry and remarked that the food was as exceptional as Berney said it would be. Both men had seconds of apple pie and coffee. Finally, Helen yawned and excused herself, saying she was going up to bed. She told Ted he could stay and talk as long as he wanted, and Ted seemed glad for someone to visit with.

The two men chatted for a while as the restaurant staff cleared the tables and set them again for the morning meal. Knowing they wanted to close up the place and go home, Berney suggested that he and Ted take their coffees into his den, where they could continue their conversation.

The desk, a table, and several chairs in Berney's den were piled high with heaps of books, some closed and others lying open.

"You've been doing some serious reading, I see," Ted chuckled as he glanced at the mountain of books, noting some of the authors. "You've got some great books."

"Yeah," said Berney as he lifted books from a chair, put them in a corner, and motioned for Ted to sit. "I had these out since yesterday when a man stopped in for a meal on his way to Chicago. He wasn't quite in your circumstances," Berney said as he looked at his guest's cashmere jacket and flannel slacks. "In fact, he was mighty down on his luck, but that fella sure knew his poets. I think he said he was an English professor at some famous university back East before he lost his job. Now he's riding the rails like so many men nowadays, just looking for any work."

"Ah, yes. There but for the grace of God go we," said Ted soberly, shaking his head.

From his comment, Berney wondered if Ted's past was a "rags to riches" climb. He certainly appeared to be successful now. Before the couple came downstairs for dinner, Berney stepped out on the hotel porch to get a quick look at their car parked in front. It was a brand-new Duesenberg, costing far more than a "pretty penny."

"How 'bout a shot of Jim Beam?" Berney asked. "Prohibition never really happened out here," he added with a wink, taking a bottle of bourbon and two glasses from a cupboard on the wall in back of his desk.

"I surely would! That's my favorite brand," Ted replied as Berney poured two fingers into each glass.

"Mine too," said Berney, handing Ted a glass. "Cheers, and to good times!" Ted said heartily as both men hoisted their glasses and took long swallows.

Ted looked around at the shelves of books and said, "You've got quite an extensive collection of good authors and poets."

"Yeah, I do a lot of reading, and I especially enjoy poetry," Berney said as he picked up a well-worn volume of *The Rubaiyat of Omar Khayyam*. "I like the words of these ancient Persian poets. In fact, I've got my own version of one of their poems right here." He took a small, worn, blue spiral-bound notebook from his breast pocket, opened it, and handed it to Ted."

Ted took the notebook and looked at the page. "Ah, it's the poem 'Look To This Day.'

A page from Berney's notebook.

It's said to have been written by an ancient Persian poet named *Kalidasa*. It's one of my favorites too, along with so many of the poems of the *Rubaiyat,"* he said, then read aloud Berney's version of those famous lines. "Yeah, there's something enduring about the Persian poets, he continued. "Why, I used to read poems from the *Rubaiyat* to Helen quite often. 'A Book of Verses underneath the Bough, A Jug of Wine, a Loaf of Bread—and Thou Beside me singing in the Wilderness.' She would finish it with the line, 'Oh, Wilderness were Paradise enow!'"

Ted added thoughtfully, "You know, I guess we don't do that much anymore. It's funny how life changes and things cool down, isn't it?"

Berney didn't have a good answer for that enigma asked by generations of lovers, so both men sat quietly for a while, savoring their whiskey.

Then Berney said, "I like Robert Service a lot, and his ballads are great to recite," he added, picking up a small book with a faded green cover. "I took this one on our last roundup, and it's a little worse for wear from the weather that week, but the boys loved hearing 'The Cremation of Sam McGee' and 'The Shooting of Dan McGrew.' My favorite is 'The Spell of the Yukon.'"

Berney stood with a faraway look in his eyes and began to recite:

> "I wanted the gold, and I got it—
> Came out with a fortune last fall,
> Yet somehow life's not what I thought it,
> And somehow the gold isn't all."

Ted recited the second verse:

> "No! There's the land. (Have you seen it?)
> It's the cussedest land that I know.
> From the big, dizzy mountains that screen it
> To the deep, deathlike valleys below."

Then they both took turns reciting from memory until they reached the end of the poem. They laughed as Berney took a photo from the

Robert Service's cabin in Dawson, Yukon Territory.
COURTESY OF THE CITY OF VANCOUVER ARCHIVES

front of the book, showed it to Ted, and said, "A friend of mine was up in Dawson City and sent me this photo of Service's cabin."

"Not exactly a palace, is it?" was Ted's response. "Don't think I'd want to live there for long, but I can remember worse places I've laid my head," he added.

Berney refilled both glasses, then Ted asked, "What have you been reading lately?"

"Well, I just finished *The Jungle*, by Upton Sinclair," Berney answered. "And boy, oh boy, even as a cattleman, it sure changes the way you think of the meat-packing industry."

"Yeah, I agree. It was enough to make me consider giving up meat, but your steaks tonight were sure delicious."

"I've also just read Jack London's *White Fang* and *The Sea-Wolf*," said Berney.

"Is that so? I'm reading his novel *Martin Eden* right now. The main character is an ignorant seaman who dreams of education and literary fame," said Ted.

"Literary fame? Why I reckon that none of those famous authors are any happier than we are, even though they've achieved literary fame!"

Berney ventured. "Like the nobility who come out to the ranch to buy our polo ponies, they're full of money, but not full of human happiness and haven't a shred of contentment."

"Yes, you're probably right," Ted agreed pensively, and the two men sat quietly in companionable silence.

"But that's enough philosophy," Berney said. "How 'bout I get us some more pie?" Ted agreed that this was a good idea, so Berney left and came back with two slices of apple pie.

As he looked at an apple slice skewered on the end of his fork, Ted said, "Your wife's an excellent cook, Berney. You're lucky. Helen can hardly cook an egg."

"Yes, Martha's a gem, she is, and smart too. My second-oldest boy, Jerry takes after both of us and almost always has a book in his hand."

"How many children do you have?" asked Ted.

"Five, and they're all boys!"

"You're fortunate to have children," said Ted. "I'm from a large family, but sadly I've never had children of my own."

"That's too bad," Berney responded. "It's a part of a man that stays behind, even when he's gone. Maybe you'll have some yet, you know."

"Maybe . . ." Ted answered quietly.

To get the conversation going again, Berney said, "I just finished Zane Gray's *Riders of the Purple Sage,* but it's not a very good depiction of Montana. What do you think of his writing, Ted?"

"Well, for a dentist who lives in New York City with the first name of Pearl, it's not too bad!" Both men laughed.

"Hm! You seem to know a lot about that fellow, don't you?" Berney asked.

"Yeah, well, maybe I met him a time or two." Ted responded mysteriously but said nothing further.

"Most of the Westerns I read are dime-store novels from the Terry Drug Store. I've got a deal with the owner that if two desperados aren't killed on every other page, I can return the book," Berney said with a laugh.

At one point in the conversation, Ted asked Berney what he thought of the new novel *Sister Carrie*, written by Theodore Dreiser.

"Can't really say," Berney responded. "I haven't read that one yet. I'll try to get a copy sometime. In fact, I haven't read much of Dreiser's writings, except for an article he wrote for *The New York Times*. I read it while waiting in my attorney's office in Miles City a few weeks back. It was

Theodore Dreiser in 1933.
PHOTOGRAPH BY CARL VAN VECHTEN,
COURTESY OF THE LIBRARY OF CONGRESS,
LOT 12735, NO. 34.

a good article—Dreiser wrote about his style of portraying characters whose values lie in their dogged persistence against all obstacles. Yeah—persistence. I liked what I read. How 'bout you? What do you think of Dreiser?"

"Uh, well, he's okay," Ted stammered, and he quickly changed the subject. "I really like Frost's new collection of poems called *A Boy's Will.*"

The two men discussed writers, novels, and poetry far into the night. Their conversation became more and more animated as the level of bourbon crept lower in the bottle. Finally, Ted looked at his watch and exclaimed it was nearly two in the morning and he better get some sleep.

As they left Berney's den and walked down the hall, Berney asked Ted if he and Helen would like to see the ranch in the morning.

Ted thanked him but said that they needed to make up for lost time getting back to New York. Both men reluctantly bid one another good night and went to their rooms.

Nice guy, Berney thought as he fell asleep. *He sure knows a lot about books and writing.*

Nice guy, Ted thought as he fell asleep. *For a Montana rancher, he sure knows a lot about books.*

The following morning dawned clear and mild—a perfect day for motoring. At breakfast, Berney stopped by Ted and Helen's table in the dining room to tell them the hotel handyman had washed the car and scraped the dried mud off the tires. "A lot of good it's going to do you, though. You'll soon be on dusty roads, but it's a great start, at least," he added.

Ted thanked him then said, "Won't you join us?" pointing to an empty chair at their breakfast table. "I'd like to hear more about your ranch, and Helen is interested as well."

Berney sat and began telling them about the large Kempton Ranch and the nearby badlands. Both Ted and Helen could see Berney's pride and were sorry they couldn't add a day to their trip and go out to the ranch.

When the conversation ended, Ted and Helen went upstairs and came back carrying suitcases, ready to be on their way. Berney took the luggage and led the way outside to their car.

As they got in the car, Helen hugged Berney, and Ted warmly shook his hand and said, "When we get back to New York, I'll write you a letter. We both wish we could stay longer, Berney. You're a great host, and didn't we have an excellent conversation last night? It's rare to talk to someone as well-versed in literature as you are. Maybe someday we'll come back, see the ranch, and stay up late again just talking."

"Yeah, we had a great discussion, and I hope we can do it again," Berney replied. "Have a good trip and stay safe. Next time you come, I'll show you the ranch and take you on a horseback ride out in the badlands! Why, I'll have the both of you roping cows and riding broncs before you know it!" They all laughed.

Berney waved and watched until the car was out of sight, then went back into the hotel, thinking of the long list of things he had to do that day.

Days passed, people came and went, and Berney put the memories of Ted and their rousing talk about literature in the back of his mind.

Several weeks later, on a day when Berney was again at the hotel, Martha came in with an opened letter for him.

"It's from your millionaire friend, Theodore Dreiser, in New York City. It's a thank you."

Puzzled, Berney responded, "Who the hell is Theodore Dreiser? I don't recall anyone by that name except for the famous novelist."

"Here, see for yourself," Martha said as she handed the envelope to Berney.

As he read the letter, Berney suddenly realized that Ted, the man with whom he had discussed poets and novelists far into the night, was Theodore Dreiser, the famous novelist and author of *Sister Carrie* and *An American Tragedy!*

"Well I'll be damned," Berney muttered.

"There's a package for you too, from the same man," Martha said as she handed Berney a parcel tied with string.

Berney cut the string and ripped

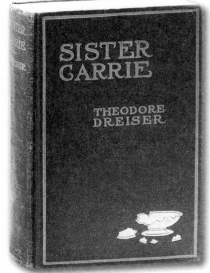

The cover of Sister Carrie.

open the package to find a brand-new copy of *Sister Carrie.* On the flyleaf, Dreiser had written, "To my cowboy friend, Berney Kempton. Thanks for a memorable evening in Terry. Cordially, Theodore Dreiser."

There were many other famous guests who stayed at the Kempton Hotel over the years, but Theodore Dreiser was the only one Berney entertained unaware—at least, the only one he knew about.

Author's note: Since I too am a lover of poetry, many of Berney's books were handed down to me and still sit on my shelves: four volumes of poetry by Robert Service, an early edition of Robert Frost, a well-worn, leather-bound copy of the *Rubaiyat,* and more. Many of the inscriptions in these books are intriguing: *Love from Dolly; Fond recollections of the past and brighter hopes for the future; To Bernie [sic] from your biggest fan; I'll always remember our time on the prairie—* plus other equally enigmatic phrases.

THE NAME O'MEAGHER
(PRONOUNCED *OH-MAR-HER*)

*B*erney Kempton looked over a stack of bills in his office at the ranch. He was troubled when he added up the amount the family had already spent to retain attorneys since 1895, when the Northern Pacific Railway sued the Kemptons over rights to the water on their own land. Berney's father, JB Kempton, was first named in the suit, but it now fell to Berney, since JB died in 1910. Here it was 1920, and the suit was still pending.

The natural spring in question was clearly on Kempton land, some three miles from the railroad track, but the powerful and rapacious Northern Pacific of those days often sued landowners not even in proximity to their rights of way to obtain water for their massive steam engines. Many ranchers and homesteaders simply caved in and turned over their land rather than fight the mighty railroad, but Berney and his father before him both believed in the power of law and justice. They had faith that the courts would be as fair to the rancher as they would be to the railroad, with its unlimited resources and hundreds of attorneys.

For hours, Berney had been studying bills and legal papers. His eyes were tired and his brain befuddled. He was sorting the documents into order when Jerry burst into the room.

"Dad, it's happening again," Jerry said, stamping his foot. "Mom told me to just ignore it, but that doesn't work at all."

"What's happening again, son? What doesn't work?" Berney asked, turning his chair toward the boy and holding out his arms.

Jerry remained stock still with his arms stiffly at his sides, trying to gain control before he spoke.

"The kids at school are teasing me again about my middle name. I hate it! Why'd you gimme the dumb name O'Meagher? It's stupid, and no one can say it right. It's not normal like my brothers' names. You should'a called me David, Pete, or Joe—real names like that!"

Jerry was a confident boy, who usually handled his own problems with a surprising amount of diplomacy. Since he rarely complained, Berney realized this was bothering him a great deal.

Berney shuffled his papers into a pile, looked at his young son, and said, "Let me tell you where your name came from. It's a really fine story of friendship."

Jerry loved the stories his father often told about his life in the "olden days," as he called them.

"Yeah, Dad, tell me."

Berney motioned for Jerry to sit on the chair next to his and began.

"You know about the years I was with Doctor Carver's Wild West Show. Well, that's where your name came from."

"Really? How's that?" Jerry asked.

Jerry Kempton, in about the 5th grade.

"Well, the show spent time in many countries, but some of the most memorable performances were the private ones for royalty."

"You met kings and queens, didn't you?" asked Jerry, as he listened intently.

"Yes, son, kings, queens. And you know, your aunt Marie and her husband Ed were also in a Wild West Show and they even met czars," Berney said.

"And some of 'em got killed, didn't they?"

"You're right. Sadly they did. Your aunt and uncle gave a private show for the children of Czar Nicholas Romanov II of Russia. His daughters loved it, and one of the girls even asked Marie to show her some roping tricks."

"Didn't the whole family get killed later, even the kids? I read about it in a book," said Jerry.

"Yes, unfortunately the Romanovs were assassinated—all of them—during a civil war in their country."

"Well, we had a civil war in our country. Did we do things like that here?" Jerry asked.

"Yes, we had a civil war in America. In fact, your granddad JB fought in the Northern Army, but both sides tried to keep innocent women and children out of the fighting."

"Good," Jerry breathed.

"We can give thanks for the protection Americans have against the cruel use of power, and we're fortunate our justice system looks out for the rights of all people," Berney added, thinking about the lawsuit with the railroad.

"That's good. Yeah, we're lucky to live here, but, Dad, how 'bout my name? Tell me 'bout my name. Was I named for a king or something like that?"

"No, son, you were named for someone far more special to me than any king or queen I ever met."

"Well then, who?" asked Jerry. Normally he enjoyed his father's long stories, but today he wanted to get to the point.

"Whoa! Hold your horses, boy, and you'll find out. The longest stint we had was in Melbourne, Australia, where we stayed for five months. The Aussies just couldn't get enough of the Wild West, and every performance was packed.

"I was the main bronc rider and roper, and my special trick was 'the California Catch,' where the horse's front foot and neck were both caught in the same loop. Actually I had been doing the California Catch

Berney Kempton during his time with Doc Carver's Wild West Show.

since I was a kid, because it was easiest on the horse, but the crowds always thought it was amazing."

"Can you teach me to do it, Dad?" asked Jerry.

"Sure, I'll teach all you boys and Pansy, too, if she's interested. Just remind me.

"All of our show was exciting, but one highlight was a stunning, daredevil act where a horse and rider climbed a long ramp up forty feet and then jumped into a large water tank far below."

"Jumped? Gosh, really? That far? How big was the tank?" Jerry asked.

"It was a pretty large tank, big and deep enough for the horse and rider to land in, but they had to be right on the mark. Doctor Carver said this trick came from an incident years before, when Indians were chasing him. He and his horse came to the edge of a cliff, with the river far below. There was nowhere else to go, so his horse jumped.

A diving horse with Doc Carver's Wild West Show.

They both landed in the deep water of the river and escaped unhurt. He thought a reenactment of that incident would be exciting. And it certainly was.

"This act had been done successfully hundreds of times, but one night it went wrong. As horse and rider neared the top of the ramp, something gave way. The horse jumped anyway, but the animal was off center. Both of them grazed the edge of the tank below, instead of landing in the middle."

"That's awful!"

"Yes, it was," said Berney soberly. "The crowd saw it all. There was a hush for several seconds, then screaming and shouting. It looked pretty bad. The rider broke several ribs, and an arm, and was carried out of the ring. The horse turned out to be okay when they got him on his feet. It could have been far worse."

"I'm glad it wasn't you, Dad."

"Me, too. I'm not good with heights. You couldn't get me up that ramp for all the tea in China. Anyway, the audience was very disturbed, and Doctor Carver worried they might panic."

"Yeah, I'll bet," Jerry responded, now totally engrossed in his father's story.

"In order to take the focus off the accident, Doctor Carver had a number of kangaroos released into the ring, and I was told to rope those critters."

"Rope kangaroos? Was it hard? How'd you do it?" asked Jerry.

"Just the same way you rope cattle and horses, but those kangaroos could sure hop!" Berney said, as he got up from his desk and began to twirl an imaginary lasso around and around, then pretended to let it fly.

"Go, Dad!" Jerry said, laughing at his father's antics.

"After a few tries, by chance, I caught two animals in the same loop. The crowd went wild, cheering, hollering, and thinking this was part of the show. I tried a second time, and on the third try, I caught two kangaroos together again."

"That's the trick written up in *Ripley's Believe It or Not,* right?" Jerry asked.

"Yep. That's the one, and it was such a hit that I had to repeat it at every show."

"That's nifty, Dad, but how does my name fit into all that?" Jerry asked once again.

"Okay, okay, I'm coming to that," said Berney. "One of the local men, who was hired to set up show tents and help with horses, came by and congratulated me after the performance. He was the one who herded the kangaroos into the ring. I remember his Australian accent and that he called me 'mate.'"

"Mate?"

"It's an Australian term for friend. Then he said, 'Blimey, that was ripper!'"

Jerry looked quizzically at his father, trying to figure out the foreign slang.

"That meant that he thought the trick of catching two kangaroos was pretty darn good," explained Berney. "We sat there and talked for a while, and then he asked me if I wanted to 'go a meal.'"

"I'll bet that means to get somethin' to eat, huh?" said Jerry. "That's sure strange English."

"Maybe. Anyway, we went to get a bite to eat and sat there talking for a long time. He was about my age and a real nice fellow. We hit it off and got to know each other during the five months the show was in town. When we both had time off, he showed me the Australian Outback from horseback and introduced me to his family."

"That was awful nice," said Jerry.

"He was the one who gave me that boomerang you and Pansy found in the trunk in the attic. It was hand-carved of ironwood by Australian Aborigines, and he taught me how to throw it."

"You know how to throw that thing?"

"Well, let's say that I used to know," Berney answered, cocking his head and frowning.

"Golly! Will you teach me, Dad? Then I could show the kids at school."

"Sure. Sometime," Berney answered.

Berney continued, "The weeks in Melbourne passed quickly, with performances almost every night and sometimes Saturday afternoons. But, all too soon, we got word we would be moving on. I think the months we spent in Australia were my favorite of all the time I was with Doctor Carver. We didn't have to pack up and travel as often, and we had time to get to know the people. I met many nice folks and became very good friends with O'Meagher. That was his name—Gerald Roland Stanley O'Meagher."

"So that's where my name comes from!" exclaimed Jerry. "And not just my middle name, but my first name, too!"

"You got it! You were named after him."

Gerald Roland Stanley O'Meagher.

"Hmm," Jerry said, thoughtfully, trying to digest this new information.

"Before the last show in Melbourne," Berney continued, "O'Meagher and I took a walk. I can't remember who suggested it, but we agreed when we became established, got married, and had sons, we would name them after each other."

"That's really ripper, Dad!" Jerry laughed. "Whatever happened to him?"

"I invited him to come to the ranch in Montana for as long as he wanted, and he extended an invitation if I wanted to stay in Melbourne."

"Did you do that?" asked Jerry.

"Yeah, he came out here not too long after I got back. He actually worked on the ranch for years, and we had some great times together before he went back to Australia. That was before any of you boys were born. I never went back to Australia, and I should have, but there were always so many things that needed doing here."

"Gee, did you write to O'Meagher?" asked Jerry.

"After he went home, we wrote letters and postcards back and forth, quite often. But, after all you boys came along and he married and had children, we didn't write as often. I'm not very good at letter writing; I leave most of that to your mother, but I often sent him postcards. We kept it up for years, but I haven't heard from him in a while. Life just got so busy."

"Will he ever come to Montana again?" asked Jerry. "I'd like to meet him."

"I don't rightly know." Then thoughtfully, he added, "He's a fine man, honest, hard-working, dependable, and kind. And he made the best scones on the face of the earth."

"What's a scone?" asked Jerry.

"It's kind of like a biscuit, but his were even better than the ones your mother makes, and usually no one can top her cooking. Now you best not tell her I said that, son."

"I won't say a word, Dad."

"You know," Berney said, almost to himself, "I do believe O'Meagher is one of the best friends I ever had."

"Will you keep in touch with him?" Jerry asked.

"While I'm thinking about it, I'll write him a letter this afternoon," Berney said thoughtfully. "And Jer, I guess I should have told you about your name years ago."

"That's okay, Dad, at least now I know it's not a stupid name," Jerry said. "In fact, I think it's pretty great," he added, with a change of heart.

Berney, too, had a change of heart that day. After Jerry left, Berney looked at the paperwork and realized that no matter what the outcome of this official wrangling by the railroad, the Kempton family would remain strong. That's what mattered most—the family.

Berney smiled, got up from his desk, stretched, and went outdoors where his sons were playing baseball and his wife was weeding the garden.

You know, Berney thought, as he looked from his wife to his sons, *I never imagined life would be so good to me. I need to quit worrying over things that haven't even happened and concentrate on what's most important.*

Berney walked through the garden to the row Martha was weeding. He bent down, kissed her, and told her how much he loved her. Surprised, she stood up and hugged him. Then he joined his sons at baseball, and he even hit a home run!

Jerry's new knowledge of the source of his special names made all the difference. From then on, whenever anyone teased him or asked about his name, Jerry proudly told them a condensed version of the story of his dad's time with the Wild West Show, and how he became good friends with a man named Gerald O'Meagher in Australia.

Author's note: Both the names "Gerald" and "O'Meagher" continued down through the generations. The Montana Jerry of these stories grew up, married, and had a son who was named Thomas Gerald O'Meagher Kempton. When that boy grew up, married, and had a son, he named his boy Gerald William O'Meagher Kempton, and the special names continued. Although the present Gerald (Jerry) is an unmarried young man studying to become a doctor, I wonder, if he has a son someday, will he name the boy after the Australian man who became good friends with the young Montana cowboy in the Wild West Show?

The name "Kempton" also continued, as the young Australian man kept his word and named one of his sons, Bernie Kempton O'Meagher. Those names speak of strong friendship, faith in the future, and a deep regard for a rich past. They're names to be proud of.

While writing this story in 2015, my son-in-law, Jens, asked if my father knew what happened to the Australian man he was named after or his son who bore the Kempton name. Dad did not know what became of either one. Of course, that was before the advent of the internet, which now gives us worldwide information at the touch of a few keys.

That evening, I searched the internet, and to my surprise I found a man by the name of Bernie Kempton O'Meagher who lived in western Australia and had dates of birth and death similar to my father's. In an official census, he was listed as a "motor driver." He married in 1941 in East Coolgardie, and lived in Scarborough, Australia. The only additional information I could find was that he had once received a minor citation for allowing gambling in his home. (I wondered if it was a friendly game of poker with buddies.) When I tried to find any relatives of this man, I reached only dead ends, and finally gave up.

Then, astonishingly, the very day the first version of this book was ready for an initial printing, I received an email saying that Gerald Roland Stanley O'Meagher's granddaughter, Pauline O'Meagher, in Australia, was doing some internet sleuthing herself to find more information about her grandfather's Montana friend, Berney Kempton!

With an exchange of emails, I learned that Pauline and her cousin Bill Allen both had information about the friendship between the Montana Berney and the Australian Gerald. They sent a few photos, postcards, and letters that helped fill in the missing pieces about this friendship. A subsequent packet of correspondence the two men exchanged over the years may provide additional facts for stories yet to come.

The Gerald O'Meagher family in Australia.

THEODORE ROOSEVELT AND THE KEMPTONS

heodore Roosevelt first came to the badlands of North Dakota in 1883 when he was twenty-four years old. Falling in love with the area, it quickly became his favorite lifelong retreat.

JB Kempton first came to the badlands of eastern Montana in 1880 when he was thirty-seven years old. He also loved the area and remained there all his life.

Roosevelt eventually became the twenty-ninth president of the United States. JB Kempton became a successful rancher, the family patriarch, and the town father of Terry, Montana. These two great men met and became friends during their time in the West, and that friendship continued down to JB's son, Berney Kempton.

Roosevelt had long romanticized Western culture and was enamored with the image of the

JB Kempton.

cowboy. Intrigued with the massive buffalo, he wanted to hunt these great beasts before they disappeared completely from the prairie landscape. Kempton, a successful Colorado rancher, came seeking a home for his family and good grass for his growing cattle business. He was enamored with the lush Montana grassland and the abundant natural springs in the area that is now Prairie County.

Theodore Roosevelt, 1885.
PHOTOGRAPH BY GEORGE G. BAIN, LIBRARY OF CONGRESS, DIG-PPMSCA-35995.

A cabin at Roosevelt's Maltese Cross Ranch near Medora.
PHOTOGRAPH BY JOHN A. BRYAN, LIBRARY OF CONGRESS, HABS ND, 8-BISMA, I—I.

Roosevelt wanted to adopt the Western lifestyle and became interested in the new business of cattle ranching. He invested $14,000 in property he called the Maltese Cross Ranch and later purchased additional land. Kempton first selected a site for his cattle on the Tongue River, and this temporary location became known as the J Mule Shoe Ranch. He later moved to Cedar Creek, then to his third location known as the Kempton Home Ranch. He eventually sold the Cedar Creek property to the XIT Cattle Company, the largest livestock concern in Montana.

Roosevelt's property, south of Medora, North Dakota, was less than twenty-five miles from the Montana border. Kempton's property, near Terry, Montana, was about sixty miles from the border of North Dakota. The ranches of these two men were less than eighty-five miles apart.

Since the great buffalo herds had been mostly decimated in previous years, Roosevelt's first hunting trip to the badlands was nearly fruitless,

Roosevelt's trophy room at Sagamore Hill.
LIBRARY OF CONGRESS, LC-USZ62-136255.

although, he did bag a large bull bison. That trophy head still hangs in his former home of Sagamore Hill in Oyster Bay, New York.

Kempton also found the Great Plains almost devoid of buffalo. He took advantage of this by driving large herds of cattle north from Texas and east from Washington, Oregon, and Idaho to feed on the nutritious grass of the Dakotas and Montana. He also trailed his extensive horse herds from Colorado to Montana. Some of these were Morgans and Kentucky-bred animals that eventually made the Kempton Ranch famous. The arrival of the Northern Pacific Railway in 1881 offered an easy way for Montana ranchers to get their cattle to East Coast markets, and cattle ranching boomed.

Roosevelt returned to New York and took up his legislative duties in Albany in 1884, but soon his life was upended by the deaths of both his wife and his mother within hours of one another.

"The light has gone out of my life," he wrote.

To deal with his loss, he immersed himself in his work, but when the session ended in the spring of 1884, Roosevelt again turned his sights west, traveling to his ranch in North Dakota, hoping to assuage his grief. He thought he might spend the rest of his days as a Western cattleman.

Kempton brought his family from Colorado, built a large two-story ranch house, and expanded his cattle operations. He invested in the nearby town of Terry, helping build the Union Church and the State Bank of Terry and establishing the Ranchman's Supply Company.

The State Bank of Terry.

The Ranchman's Supply Company in Terry.

In later years, he was a main supporter of the new high school. Folks in Terry called JB Kempton their town father.

Both Roosevelt and Kempton helped establish early cattle associations in North Dakota and eastern Montana. Roosevelt began his region's first Stockman's Association, and Kempton was involved in establishing the Eastern Montana Livestock Association. The aims of these groups were to enforce stock laws, curb thefts, and promote the growth of the cattle industry in both regions. Meetings of these associations included representatives from all of North Dakota and the Glendive, Miles City, and

Terry areas of Montana. Both Roosevelt and Kempton attended meetings and joint conferences of these associations.

Theodore Roosevelt, JB Kempton, and thousands of other ranchers suffered greatly during the infamous winter of 1886–1887. Numerous factors led to this historic disaster. The previous summers were cool and the winters mild, which meant grass was plentiful for the great cattle herds of Montana and the Dakotas. With abundant range grass, few ranchers felt the need to raise hay for their livestock. The range gradually become overgrazed, and newly introduced sheep herds also competed for grass in some areas.

Barbed wire, introduced to the West in the late 1860s, changed the history of ranching. It was also a factor in the heavy stock losses during the disastrous winter of 1886–1887. Ranchers increasingly used barbed wire to fence in their herds, limiting the area where cattle could roam. Unfortunately, barbed-wire fences also prevented cattle from moving to find shelter and food.

First came the blazing hot summer of 1886 that scorched the prairies, leaving little grass. In the fall, there were signs of a coming bad winter—birds flew south earlier than usual, beaver collected more wood than normal, and cattle had uncommonly thick coats. But after the lean summer with little grass, the herds were ill equipped to survive a hard winter.

Snow began on November 13 and fell almost continuously for a month. Then an unexpected December thaw turned the snow to slush. The hard freeze that followed turned the slush to ice, making it impossible for cattle to dig down to the sparse grass below. Their hocks were injured, and their feet bled from the sharp ice.

Worse yet, a storm in January raged for seventy-two hours, preventing ranchers who had raised feed from getting it out to their cattle. During the blizzard, temperatures dropped to thirty below zero; some said it was more like fifty below, as high winds howled across the prairies, blasting the unsheltered herds. Some cattle, too weak to stand, were blown over and died frozen to the ground. Hundreds piled up against barbed-wire fences and froze where they stood. In desperation, ranchers cut the barbed wire, hoping the cattle would move to shelter, but they were so badly frozen the skin on their legs and feet cracked open, and they were unable to walk. Some ranchers reported the hooves dropped off their animals. These gruesome deaths were pure hell for ranchers to watch. Many, like JB Kempton, truly cared about the welfare of their herds, and their desperate suffering was almost more than ranchers could bear.

Cattle in Montana and the Dakotas perished by the thousands. There were carcasses as far as the eye could see. In some areas, about 90 percent of the open range cattle died that winter, and the damage was most horribly evident when spring came. The stench of rotting meat filled the air, and dead cattle clogged the waterways. Countless bloated carcasses floated in the rivers with the spring ice, rolling, sometimes with all four legs up. This macabre scene continued for days. Ranchers called that winter "Death's Cattle Roundup" or "Hell without Heat" or "The Great Die-Up," a grim parody on the term "roundup."

Thousands of ranchers went bankrupt, and many others simply packed up and moved away, giving up everything they had worked so hard to gain. Both those who stayed and those who left bore the indelible marks of severe hardship etched on their personalities.

Roosevelt, in a letter to his friend Henry Cabot Lodge, wrote, "We have had a perfect smashup all through the cattle country of the northwest. The losses are crippling. For the first time I have been utterly unable to enjoy a visit to my ranch. I will be glad to get home."

JB Kempton reported, "I lost 110 percent of my cattle. One hundred percent of my herds perished, and I spent another 10 percent just trying to find where they all went." He was nearly forced into bankruptcy, but with his business foresight, he succeeded in tiding over his difficulties. He restocked with Texas cattle that were tolerant of summer drought and able to survive harsh winters. In addition, these longhorns had the ability to defend themselves and their young against predators.

That disastrous winter permanently altered ranching in the West— ranchers reduced the size of their herds and began growing food for their animals, and many former open ranges were fenced into smaller grazing areas. This was the beginning of the end of the untamed western wilderness that both Roosevelt and Kempton had known.

Roosevelt often rode alone for days through the badlands and the prairies of the Dakota and Montana Territories. It could have been then that he and JB Kempton met and became friends, a relationship that continued into Berney Kempton's generation. Or perhaps they met at one of the joint Montana-Dakota stock association meetings. There are stories that Roosevelt stayed at the Kempton Hotel in Terry and at the Kempton Ranch, but he never signed the guestbook, and no one living remembers the exact date of his stays. No matter how the relationship between Theodore Roosevelt and JB and later Berney Kempton began, it was strong enough that Roosevelt personally helped Berney when he encountered difficulty with a government livestock agent when shipping cattle from Terry to the Midwest. Ed Kempton (1913–2012), Berney's third son, told the following story during an interview conducted in 1991.

In the mid-1900s, a new shipping agent named William Adams was assigned to the post at the railroad station in Terry. He came from the East Coast and was openly disdainful of the small towns of Terry, Miles City, and Glendive. Although folks tried to make him feel welcome, he didn't want to mingle and said he hoped his stay in Montana would be brief, so he could return to the civilized life he had known. After several declined invitations to dinner at both the hotel and the ranch, Martha and Berney gave up. Ranchers complained that Adams made shipping cattle more difficult, and some joked that his last name should be changed to "Adamant" because of his hide-bound adherence to the vagaries of regulations that had never before been enforced. Berney tried to be open-minded about this newcomer in hopes he would mellow.

That all changed when Berney made plans to ship a load of cattle from Terry to market in the Midwest. Berney wanted to ensure his stock would be loaded on their own train, as was the custom, if he shipped at least ten carloads of cattle. This had always been the procedure except for one disastrous time when JB shipped a trainload of cattle in 1899 and lost most of them due to avoidable delays of the Northern Pacific Railway (see page 143 for that story). Since then, when the Kemptons shipped cattle, they had their own train, and there were very few problems.

When Berney entered the train station, the door to the agent's office was partially open. He knocked, opened the door, and went in. Adams, clearly irritated, looked up from his desk and said, "Mr. Kempton, in the future, please do not enter my office until you have been invited." Berney, taken aback by this inhospitable greeting, answered good-naturedly that he would knock in the future. Adams responded, "Yes, that's the way we do things back East, with a little more formality."

Berney shook his head, wondering why Adams had such a big chip on his shoulder. He tried to overlook this cold reception and talk about the upcoming shipment he expected to send to the Midwest within a week.

"Hold on now, and give me a minute to get my book out so I can record all this," Adams said as he slowly reached into several drawers and finally found the book he needed. Berney patiently stood, thinking the man was purposely taking his own sweet time.

When Adams found the book, he proceeded to ask Berney for details about the shipment, and for every detail Berney cited, Adams presented a difficulty.

Finally, in frustration, Berney said, "But that's the way it's always been done here."

Adams retorted, "That is not the way we do things back East."

Berney answered, "That could well be true, but we are not back East now, are we?"

"No, but that is the procedure we will follow while I am in charge," countered Adams.

"Sir," Berney said with growing annoyance, "you are not back East. You are in Montana now, and you should do things the way they do in Montana."

Adams pointed to a thick book on the shelf and said, "We will do things according to these rules." He opened the book and found the pages that dealt with Berney's question and said, "It says right here . . . um, right here. Maybe it is on the next page," he faltered.

Berney stepped closer, looked at the open book, pointed to a paragraph, and said, "Look, here's the answer. It's just as I said. Read this right here."

Adams sputtered, stammered, and read that section of the page to himself. "Well, there are many other considerations that you do not know about, but I will permit it, just this once," he said with practiced officiousness. "Now, I have a meeting, so I will have to ask you to leave my office," he said, waving Berney off.

At home that night, Berney related the story to Martha, who frowned and responded, "Sounds like you didn't make a friend there, dear. Remember, he has power over ranchers around here."

"That may be true, but even he has to adhere to the rules. That is, unless he tries to change them," Berney answered.

Jeff, the ranch foreman, overheard the conversation and added, "Yeah, he's giving all the ranchers trouble telling them how things are done back East."

"How do we get him to realize that he's in Montana and should do things the way we've always done them in these parts?" Berney said. "He just started out bad with that colossal chip on his shoulder."

A week later, Berney and Jeff prepared to ship some 600 head of cattle to market in Sioux City, Iowa. Arrangements were finalized with livestock agent Adams, the cattle were in great shape, and both Berney and Jeff speculated at the good price they would bring.

The Kempton ranch hands herded the animals from the ranch to the livestock pens at the Terry station, and by midday the animals were ready for loading on the next train, expected in a few hours. Adams, who had been watching this work, came out of his office to look over the herd.

With a smirk, he walked over to Berney and said, "We can't take these cattle. I believe they have scabies, and we won't transport them."

"Scabies? What the hell?" Berney almost shouted. "These are prime animals in great shape! There's no scabies, and there never has been. What the hell are you talking about?"

"Mr. Kempton, may I remind you that I am the agent in charge here, and I detect that your cattle have scabies. My word stands on all shipments from this station!"

"Show me any sign of scabies," Berney demanded. "Just show me!"

"These cows are clean," added Jeff. "There's not a thing wrong with them, Adams, and you know it!"

"I am the agent, and I cannot allow them on our train, and that's the end of this conversation," Adams declared. He turned on his heel, walked back into his office in the station, and closed and locked his door.

"What're we gonna do now?" asked Jeff.

Berney was furious. His face was red, and he could hardly speak. He didn't often get angry, but this situation was untenable.

First Berney sought out the sheriff, who unfortunately said he had no authority regarding civil railroad disputes. He looked over the herd and thought they were fine in his estimation, but he could do nothing more.

Berney steamed, swore, and paced up and down the street. Finally, he said, "Well, I've still got one ace up my sleeve, and I guess this is the time to use it. We're not done yet, Jeff. This is not over!"

When the train came and went without the Kempton cattle, Berney and Jeff were in the telegraph office in Terry.

"I've got a friend in a high place," Berney said. "A very high place, and this is the time to call on his goodwill. He said if I ever needed a favor to let him know, and I need one now." He wrote a message and handed it to the telegrapher.

"Mr. Kempton, this is to the president of the United States!" the stunned telegrapher whispered as he looked at the form. "You know President Roosevelt?" he asked.

"Well, yes, I do," Berney answered, further astonishing the young man as well as Jeff, who stood open-mouthed. "Go ahead and send it," Berney said to the telegrapher. "We'll be at the hotel waiting for an answer."

"Well, I'll be damned," both Jeff and the telegrapher said in unison. Berney walked out of the telegraph office and called back, "Please send a runner when you get an answer."

The telegraph was sent to Theodore Roosevelt, the president of the United States, in care of the White House, while Berney and Jeff enjoyed a leisurely steak dinner at the hotel. They were just finishing dessert and coffee when a young boy entered with a return telegram. Berney opened the envelope, unfolded the page, and read aloud:

> "Sorry for trouble STOP You are best judge of healthy cattle STOP Have ordered agent to accept your shipment for next available train STOP Hope to make trip there later this year STOP Best to you STOP Theodore Roosevelt."

When Berney and Jeff returned to the station, William Adams was not around, but a railroad man told Berney his cattle would be loaded on the eastbound train due in several hours.

The 600 head of prime Montana cattle made the trip to Sioux City with no further delay. Within several days, there was a new livestock agent in Terry, and no one knew what happened to William Adams. Berney almost felt sorry for the man but knew Adams had forced him into the situation. He had no regrets for calling on a powerful friend, the president.

Roosevelt made trips to the Dakotas and Montana a number of times after that. He spoke at public gatherings several times in Medora, North Dakota. Berney and his sons were in Medora for Roosevelt's last speech. After he finished, the great man greeted Berney and reminisced about the old days of ranching and the bad winter of 1886–1887. He told Berney how fortunate he was to have a fine family of five boys, and then he shook hands with each youngster. Young Jerry was awed to meet Roosevelt and shake his hand. Little did Jerry know that in his future he would interact with other U.S. presidents when he traveled to Washington, D.C., in his work as chief of the Airports Division of the Federal Aviation Administration of Alaska.

Just months after that stop in Medora, Theodore Roosevelt passed away at his Sagamore Hill mansion in January 1919. He died in his sleep at the age of sixty-one. He was a great leader for the country, a successful rancher, and a friend to the people of North Dakota and eastern Montana. He was also a special friend to two generations of the Kempton family.

Author's note: When I was growing up in Anchorage, Alaska, one of my father's coworkers told us that our dad knew a number of U.S. presidents from his trips to Washington, D.C., in his efforts to obtain federal funding for Alaska's airports. We did not believe it until we were stunned by an incident that occurred when President Dwight D. Eisenhower visited Elmendorf Air Force Base outside Anchorage in the summer of 1960.

From an open convertible in a downtown parade celebrating his visit, Eisenhower saw my father standing with us in the crowd. He called my dad by name, the parade stopped, and the president of the United States and my father exchanged greetings.

Dad was not fazed by this—he was friends with many people in high positions. He told us that even the mightiest still put on their pants one leg at a time. He said they were just normal folks like everyone else. Just normal folks in unusually high positions.

FLORIDA'S
CHRISTMAS GIFTS

No one on the Kempton Ranch knew his real name. In 1910, ranch hands didn't fill out personnel applications, and Social Security forms that required official names weren't even around until 1935. Cowboys simply signed on to work, and the ranch owner paid their wages in cash. Of course, everyone had a name they answered to, and his was the Florida Cowboy, shortened to Florida, from whence he came.

The Florida Cowboy with his horse, Miami.

The first winter Florida worked for Berney Kempton, he complained of the cold and bragged about the warm Florida sunshine, sandy beaches, and clear Gulf Coast waters. Nevertheless he grew to love the prairie, and in fact, he never left Montana. He was handsome, intelligent, and dependable, and as a ranch hand, he always did more than his share of the work. Martha Kempton sometimes asked Florida to help her prepare ranch meals, and on roundups, he cooked up delicious hearty fare from the back of the chuck wagon.

Florida, a young single cowboy, was sweet on a girl named Lynne, who lived with her family on a good-sized ranch not far from the town of Fallon, fourteen or so miles from the Kempton Ranch. Florida and Lynne first met in the spring, danced together at the Fourth of July celebration, and then Florida escorted her to church a time or two, but late fall was a busy time for ranch hands, so he hadn't seen much of her for more than a month. He hoped to remedy that real soon.

The annual Fallon Christmas Eve Dance was coming up, and Florida looked forward to the prospect of swinging Lynne around on the square dances and maybe getting real close on the slow ones. He thought he might even sneak a quick kiss in one of the dark corners of the Grange Hall. Everyone else on the Kempton Ranch planned to go to the dance in Terry, ten miles west of Fallon, so Florida knew he would have to make the ride to Fallon and back by himself.

About a week before the dance, Florida got a big dose of some good-natured ribbing when Berney brought the mail out to the bunkhouse. There was a pretty pink envelope addressed to Florida. Berney held it to his nose, closed his eyes in pleasure, and sniffed the perfume on the envelope before passing it around. Each ranch hand did the same until Florida grabbed the letter and took it outside to read in private.

It was from Lynne, and, yes, she planned to attend the Christmas dance and looked forward to seeing him there. She even signed the letter with an X and an O!

Days before the dance, the weather turned cold and a light snow fell. Florida knew his horse would be fine with her thick coat of winter hair.

"It's me I'm worried about," he said to the animal. "It's sure gonna be a cold ride just for a dance, but I'd willingly go all the way to the moon to dance with Lynne," he added as he patted the horse named Miami. Florida chuckled for the umpteenth time at the combination of their names—Miami and Florida. "Wish I was in Florida tonight, Miami. That wind coming down the draw is the coldest I've felt in a long time."

Florida hoped to get an early start the afternoon of the dance, but he couldn't get away until four. Still, he knew he could arrive with time to spare if he rode steady. In the bunkhouse, Florida pulled a low wooden chest from under his bed. It held special gifts he had bought for Lynne. There was a box of tiny, delicate French cakes ordered from the Terry Mercantile. The proprietor, Mr. Stith, called them something that sounded like "petty furs." There was also five yards of pink and blue-sprigged calico. The blue was the color of Lynne's eyes. The woman at the dry goods store who sold him the calico told him it would make a lovely frock, with fabric to spare. She chuckled kindly when Florida asked her if a frock was the same thing as a dress, but what cowboy knows much about female apparel?

Florida dressed for the cold ride with an extra pair of socks, long underwear under his jeans, and woolly chaps over them. He pulled on a long-sleeved top and two warm shirts and took his thickest jacket from the hook above his bed. He grabbed his sheepskin-lined gloves and a knitted cap to wear under his hat.

Martha Kempton was out in the barn when Florida saddled his horse and loaded the gifts in his saddlebags. She told him to take care and stay in Fallon if the weather got worse, then she handed him his pay envelope.

"Berney thought we should give this to you now, just in case you have to stay in Fallon because of the weather or if you want to take Lynne out to dinner."

"Thanks, ma'am. That's thoughtful of you," Florida said, blushing as he slipped the cash-filled envelope into his shirt pocket. "I'm sure I'll be back later tonight—there's work to be done tomorrow. Those cows won't know it's Christmas. Thanks again, ma'am, and merry Christmas!" he added as he swung into the saddle.

Usually when Florida went to Fallon, he drove a team and stayed on the main road, but that night he took a shorter back way. He'd heard a number of new farming families had moved in along this side road. The ranchers called them "honyockers," a mocking term that originated in Montana in the 1890s to describe new settlers and homesteaders who fenced their land and farmed. Most ranchers and cowboys didn't have much love for these newcomers, since their way of life made it more difficult to run cattle on the open range. Florida knew that Martha and Berney sometimes helped these new families and readily shared information about ninety-day corn and quick-growing wheat, but Florida had little use for honyockers.

Florida rode silently for an hour with no sign of life before hearing the distinctive whack of an ax on wood. "Now who in the world would be out cutting wood on Christmas Eve and in this weather besides?" he said aloud. "Sounds like their swing's pretty weak and puny."

In the distance, he could see the outline of a cabin and a barn close by. A lantern burned brightly in the window and another outside near the barn. As he got closer, he made out the figure of a woman in a long skirt and jacket lifting an ax. She must have heard him coming because she turned, then began to back away toward the house.

Sensing her fear, Florida called out a friendly greeting as he approached, "Merry Christmas, ma'am. What're you doing out on a night like this chopping wood? Why, it's Christmas Eve."

The woman relaxed some and responded, "Yes sir, it may be Christmas Eve in some parts, but it ain't Christmas 'round here. Not this year, I'm afeard. And if I don't get some wood chopped, we'll run out before mornin'," she added.

Florida dismounted, walked closer, and said, "Don't you have a man around who can do this for you?"

"My husband's inside sleeping. Been sick for two weeks and just now starting to turn the corner, but he's still too weak. Why, he can barely stand, let alone chop wood."

As they talked, the cabin door opened and a young face peeped out. "Ma, I heard you talking to someone. You all right?" a girl of about seven asked with concern.

"Yeah, Mary. Just fine. Now you go back in and shut the door afor all the warmth gets out. I'm good, child. Thanks."

"Nice girl you got there, ma'am," Florida said. "It's good she cares about her ma."

"Thanks, mister. She's a good young'un, but not old enough to be much help around here. I've got another girl too, but she's even younger, and a little boy whose gonna be just like his daddy," she added with pride.

Florida looked at the scene before him and pondered some. He could simply bid the woman good night and be on his way to the dance, but what kind of man would he be if he did that? Riding away was not an option for him. This woman needed help, and he could provide it.

He dismounted, tied Miami to a nearby fence, and said, "Ma'am, you go on inside and let me finish chopping this load. I can do it in a short time, and I'd be glad to. I'll let you know when I'm done."

She hesitated and then said, "I'd be mighty beholding to you, mister. I thank you very much. I am a mite weary."

She handed Florida the ax, pulled her jacket closed, and turned to go inside. "You sure?" she asked from the doorstep.

"Yeah, I'm sure," he called back as he swung the ax. In a short time, he had split and stacked more than enough wood to last the family several days or more.

Florida walked to the porch, knocked, and waited. The woman opened the door and asked him to come in. She motioned to a place at the table, set with a steaming bowl of stew and thick fresh-baked bread. "You must be hungry after all that work," she said quietly, introducing herself and asking his name.

Florida knew time was passing, but he was hungry and could hardly refuse this kind hospitality. He sat down and ate while the woman took a chair across from him and picked up the mending she had been working on. She told Florida that the family had been doing okay until her husband took sick. Even sick, he had continued the work that needed doing until he had collapsed in the barn one night milking the cows.

She half carried him inside and later sent for the doctor, who advised complete bed rest for at least a fortnight.

"He's gettin' better but still sleeps most of the time," the woman said. "It's just mighty hard now, and I don't know how we're ever gonna pay that doctor, but I'm just beholdin' that he came all the way out here."

When he finished the stew, Florida looked around the small cabin lit by the fire in the fireplace and a lantern on the table. "You got a Christmas tree I can bring in for you?" he asked. "You know it's Christmas Eve tonight."

"No, not this year," the woman said quietly. "No tree this year. It's just been too hard with my man so ill. We'll skip Christmas this year."

"But with little ones, you can't just skip Christmas," Florida replied, thinking of his own childhood and the excitement he felt seeing the tree on Christmas morning. "You know, I saw a little pine not far back that would make a perfect Christmas tree. How 'bout if I go back and cut it for you?"

"Well, it would look purdy in the corner over there, and I got a bunch of fancy buttons I could hang on it," the woman replied, with a hint of hope in her voice.

"I'll be right back," Florida said as he grabbed his jacket and gloves and headed out again.

Seeing Florida, Miami snuffled as if to say she wanted to get going. "Okay, girl, I'm gonna put you in the barn for just a while. Why, that dance probably hasn't even started yet, and we got lots of time."

Florida walked back to the little tree, cut it easily with the ax, hoisted it onto his shoulder, and started back to the cabin. He brought the tree inside and put it in a bucket of water the woman had set in the corner. It was a beautiful tree, and it filled the cabin with the clean scent of pine and the cold outdoors. The woman had already strung a few buttons and began hanging them from the branches.

"What about presents for your youngsters?" asked Florida. "Every tree should have a few presents under it. Little ones want a Christmas surprise, don't ya think?"

"Like I said, mister, there's nothin' this year. We're just hoping to make it 'til our first crop. There's nothin' for Christmas," she said as she sat back heavily in the rocker.

"Momma," came a tiny wail as a wee child pulled back the curtain that separated the sleeping area from the living space and peered out. "No Christmas? But I want Christmas. Please, Momma. I been good, and I be good more." This plaintive plea came from a little girl with dark curly hair, who looked very much like her mother. She rubbed her eyes, and Florida saw a tear slide down her cheek.

He took a couple of steps toward the child, knelt to her level, and said, "Now, if you go right back to sleep who knows what you might find under the Christmas tree tomorrow morning. Okay? Will you do that?"

The little girl smiled shyly, nodded, looked at her mother, and went back to bed.

"Ah, mister, that ain't right. Please don't tell her things that just ain't possible," the woman said with a tired sigh.

"Oh, no, ma'am. I wouldn't ever do that," Florida said as he donned his coat again. "You know how to sew clothes—like girls' dresses or skirts?" he asked.

"Course I do. That's the only way we're all clothed—from my sewing."

Without an explanation, Florida left the cabin and headed for the barn. He eased up to Miami and took the precious yards of pink and blue-sprigged calico meant for Lynne from his saddlebag and headed back to the cabin. Looking at the sky, he muttered, "Well, the need here is greater, and ain't that what Christmas is all about?"

He handed the folded calico to the woman. When she looked up with a question in her eyes, he asked if she could make up some pretty dresses for her girls that night while he whittled the figure of a cow for her little boy.

She unfolded the calico slowly and smoothed her hand over the length.

"Dresses would take too long, but I sure could make up a couple nice skirts with flouncy ruffles, and they already got some blouses." With a smile, she began to unfold the goods. "Why, there's plenty here with a good deal left over. My lands, this is purdy stuff."

"Good. You can use the rest for a dress for yourself someday," Florida said as he sat down near the light of the fire, took out his knife, and began to carve a nice chunk of clear pine that he took from the stack of firewood. The blade of his knife glinted in the firelight as he shaped the wood. The only noise was the fire popping, the sound of the knife on wood, and the scissors snipping out the skirts for the little girls. Minutes passed as they each worked on their special gifts in silence.

Florida wondered how late it was getting, but he wasn't the kind of man who carried a pocket watch, and there was no clock in the poor cabin. He figured he still had time to get to the Fallon Grange Hall and dance some with Lynne.

More time passed as Florida whittled the figure of a cow. He held it up in the firelight and thought it was quite good, just needed a bit of smoothing. The next time he looked up with his completed wooden carving, he saw the skirts were finished and spread across the woman's lap. She had fallen asleep with her needle still in the hem of the larger ruffled skirt. Florida gently took the needle from her fingers and put it on the table beside her. Then he picked up the woman's shawl from the floor where it had fallen and draped it over her shoulders. He put enough logs on the fire to last well into morning.

Carefully he knelt and placed the skirts and the wooden animal under the Christmas tree. They looked nice, but there was nothing for the woman and her husband. Without really thinking about it, Florida made another trip to the barn, pulled the box of French cakes from his other saddlebag, and returned to the cabin. The box was done up with a fancy bow. He pulled off the card that said it was for Lynne and gently put the box of "petty furs" under the tree.

That was nice, but there was no gift for the husband. Florida thought about the envelope of cash he had with him. He knew he had money in the bank and another paycheck coming in a month. He had a great, secure job he loved, plenty of food, and a place to stay.

"I can certainly spare a paycheck to help these folks," he whispered to himself as he reached inside his jacket and pulled the pay envelope from his pocket. He hesitated only once, then he took a pencil from the table and wrote, "Merry Christmas and good luck in the New Year!" on the envelope and placed it under the Christmas tree beside the other gifts. "Now that's the way Christmas should be. There's something for everyone," he said quietly.

Florida glanced once more at the tree decorated with buttons and pieces of the flower-sprigged calico and the five gifts beneath. Then he quietly left the sleeping family. Outside, he walked to the barn where Miami greeted him with a whinny as he led her out. He settled himself in the saddle and turned around, noticing how the saddlebags that had bulged earlier in the evening now lay flat. But he felt satisfied and not the least bit sorry for giving away the French cakes and calico meant for Lynne. Had Lynne been with him, he thought she would have done the same.

Miami and Florida rode away from the cabin toward the party in Fallon. It occurred to Florida that his unkind thoughts and prejudice against honyockers stemmed from his own ignorance, and he regretted them. Now he knew a brave mother, careworn but still trying to do her work in addition to her husband's, three little children who dreamed of Christmas, and their father, ill and struggling to once again head his household. These folks were not honyockers—they were courageous people trying their darndest to make a go of it.

As he drew closer to Fallon, his thoughts turned to Lynne. Even though he now had nothing to give, it would be wonderful to just see her and hold her in his arms for a dance or two. She might well be the girl for him, and he caught himself thinking about having his own ranch with Lynne by his side and a couple of kids at their feet. It was a nice picture in his mind, and he hoped it would someday come true.

Florida rode over the last hill and finally saw the Fallon Grange Hall in the distance, all lit up. Ah, glory be! He wasn't too late after all, but as he looked closer, he saw wagons and buggies lit by small lanterns heading away from the hall. Then the gaslights in the hall went out one by one except for a single light in the back. With a sinking heart, Florida realized he was too late. The dance was over, and Lynne and all the others had gone home.

Florida rode into the empty yard. Through the hall windows, he saw a lone man and woman still inside cleaning up and putting chairs away. He dismounted, climbed the porch steps, and went inside.

"Guess I'm too late, huh?" he said.

"Yeah, you sure as tooting are! Way too late," the man answered. "This shindig finished a while ago, and a great time it was. You can help yourself to cookies over there and get warm," he added as he paused in his work.

"Let me ask you something," Florida said. "Was there by chance a girl here with long, brown curly hair and blue eyes, about this tall?"

"Well, there was plenty of girls here tonight and your description matches a number of 'em," the man replied.

The woman, overhearing the conversation, cocked her head thoughtfully and said, "Yes, there was one young lady who fit your description who had such a sad expression on her face. Why, she kept going out on the porch, kinda like she was looking for somebody. Such an unhappy look on such a pretty face. Was she, by chance, looking for you, cowboy?" the woman added with a sympathetic smile.

"Could be," Florida sighed. "Maybe so, ma'am."

He didn't know what more he could say to the couple. "Well, then, merry Christmas to you both. Can I lend you a hand cleaning up?"

"How far you got to go yet tonight?" the man asked Florida.

"Kempton Ranch over near Terry."

"You came all that way and plan to ride on home tonight too?" the woman exclaimed.

"Yep, gotta get back for work tomorrow, but it'll be fine," Florida answered.

"You best get going and take a bunch of those cookies with you now. And merry Christmas back to you!" the man said.

Florida filled his hand with cookies, tipped his hat in thanks, and went outside to his horse.

"Well, Miami, we missed her. Guess we stayed too long helping those folks. But you know, girl, that family truly needed some Christmas, especially this year. I guess doing that good deed will have to be enough for me. Merry Christmas, girl," Florida said as he patted his horse's neck and fed her a cookie.

As he mounted his horse, Florida suddenly felt tired from his full day and long night. He leaned down to share another cookie, and they started for home at a walk.

An hour later, as horse and rider topped a rise, the wide night sky spread out before and above them. The glittering stars seemed unusually bright and close to earth. Florida thought of a starry night long ago when the Christ child was born to two poor folks in Bethlehem. Just regular folks caught up in the timeless history of the world. He remembered the kind innkeeper who offered his stable where the baby who was king of all mankind was born. *Helpers,* Florida thought. *That's what the world needs—helpers, folks who take the time to make things better.* He was glad he had been that kind of person, and the thought eased his sadness.

Then the Florida Cowboy sat up straight in the saddle, threw back his head, and began singing Christmas carols at the top of his voice. The words of "Silent Night" rang across the quiet landscape, and he was surprised to find he remembered all the verses his mother had taught him long ago. The coyotes howled in answer, and Florida laughed at the star-lit prairie concert. Florida and Miami traveled the cold, nighttime miles back to the Kempton Ranch in high spirits.

Christmas on the Kempton Ranch and around the world came and went. Soon folks welcomed the new year of 1911. Florida wrote to Lynne, telling her he was sorry he missed the dance. He said he was delayed but gave no other details except that he looked forward to seeing her again. Florida told no one about his Christmas Eve. Even when the other cowhands asked him about the dance, he just said it was an evening to remember.

When Florida heard the other ranch hands talking about the generous $30 bonus Berney and Martha included in their pay envelopes, his heart dropped, and he gulped. *Oh well,* he thought to himself. *It's just money. It'll be well-used by those folks, and there's more where it came from for me.*

The Florida Cowboy from the Kempton Ranch had no idea that word would get around to folks in Fallon and Terry about a selfless man who chopped wood, cut a Christmas tree, gave gifts, and left money for a family who would have had no Christmas if he hadn't come along.

The week following Christmas, the woman rode into Fallon and paid the surprised doctor in cash. When the kind doctor hesitated to accept it because he knew cash was in short supply for her family, she told him about her Christmas Eve visitor by the name of Florida. Since there was only one cowboy with that unique name in all of Prairie County, the account of his kindness circled around and eventually got back to the Kempton Ranch. Berney gave Florida a nice raise, and Martha made him a Florida lime pound cake with key lime icing. Lynne soon heard, but in case she hadn't, Martha decided she would make sure the girl knew what a thoughtful and generous man Florida was, just in case there was a future marriage proposal.

When Lynne and Florida met just a few weeks later, she asked him about his Christmas Eve. He merely shrugged and mumbled something about being delayed by some unusual circumstances. Knowing what really happened, Lynne loved him all the more for his humility. Not too many months later, there was indeed a marriage proposal and a glad acceptance. Soon a joyous wedding took place, and success followed this good man, although he never changed from the plain old, everyday, down-to-earth, kind Florida Cowboy.

Every year at Christmas, Lynne told her children and her grandchildren this story about a compassionate cowboy who brought Christmas to a family who never dreamed such a thing could happen. Then she would put her arms around her husband, Florida, and tell him how much she loved him.

All these folks are now gone from the earth, and the story of that night is just a memory, but may the telling of this tale inspire us to be like the Florida Cowboy of 1910, filled with the selfless spirit of giving at Christmastime and always.

Author's note: The term honyocker probably came from the German word *honigjager,* which means "honey-chaser," referring to a sweet pursuit in which the pursuer unfortunately gets stung by unanticipated yet predictable consequences. This was eventually the case in Montana where poor agricultural practices and a failure to apply dryland farming methods to prevent land erosion, plus years of drought, caused many early farmers to fail. Although their first years looked promising with sweet results, the native prairie grassland, when broken by the plow, became unstable.

TWELVE CARLOADS
OF CATTLE

*B*erney Kempton was home from an afternoon meeting of the Range Riders Association, a group of Prairie County ranchers who met regularly to talk about cattle, horses, fences, and other such topics. He had just sat down in his favorite chair and picked up *The Daily Miles City Yellowstone Journal* when Jerry came looking for him.

"Hey, Dad, I found a bunch of old papers in a box in the attic. Looks like some kind of court case with Northern Pacific and Grandpa JB."

The Range Riders Association in 1925,
Berney kneeling in suit and tie.

"The attic, huh, son? You been poking around up there again?" Berney asked with an indulgent smile. He folded his newspaper, put it down beside his chair, and gave full attention to his son.

"It's keen up there," Jerry said excitedly. "I find neat things, and I put everything back."

"Yeah, I know you do. Sounds like you found papers from when your grandpa sued the Northern Pacific.

Jerry's attic explorations often turned up treasure troves of long-forgotten memories. Just a year or so before, he and Pansy found a trunk full of memorabilia and old show outfits that Berney wore when he was a young star rider and roper with Doctor Carver's Wild West Show. That revelation was the first the Kempton children knew of their father's famous past. Although Berney had put all that far from his present life, even he enjoyed reliving the memories.

Holding up some papers, Jerry said, "I think it's about cattle that died. How'd they die and when?"

"Yep, it sounds like that court case. As I remember," Berney said, "it began in 1899 when I was away with the Wild West Show, and it didn't end until 1904 when a court clear in California finally decided in our favor."

"Why'd it take so long?" Jerry asked.

"Well, the case first went to District Court in Helena in 1902, almost three years to the day of the event," Berney said. "And the jury didn't take long to agree that Northern Pacific should pay JB $3,000 for the cattle that died because the railway had been negligent. That should've ended it, but it didn't."

"Why didn't they just pay up? They had plenty of money," asked Jerry.

"Well, the railway thought it would set a precedent if they gave in."

"A precedent?"

"Yeah, they thought if they gave in, they'd be more likely to have to pay damages every time cattle were hurt in transit, so they appealed to a higher court. It finally went to the United States Circuit Court of Appeals."

"What's a court of appeals?" asked Jerry. "I got another question too."

"Let me think now," said Berney. "A court of appeals looks at lower court decisions to see if the law was applied correctly. I believe there are three judges and no jury. NP's first appeal was denied, and they appealed again, and finally the court in San Francisco agreed to hear the case. Now, what's your other question?"

"Did your pa ask 'em for too much money?"

"No," Berney said with a shake of his head. "He asked for $3,000 dollars in damages, but his loss soon amounted to far more because all the cattle suffered. Those that didn't die on the train or during the first week here were still in bad shape. Even with the best of care, they never thrived."

"So our family's case went that far, all the way to court in California?"

"Yep, the U.S. Circuit Court of Appeals in San Francisco heard the case. The only court higher than that one is the U.S. Supreme Court in Washington, D.C."

"Golly, that's real keen!" exclaimed Jerry.

"I can't remember all the details of the case. Let's take a look at the papers you found," Berney said.

Jerry gave him the bundle of pages bound with a leather strap.

"Let's see what you got," Berney said as he unbuckled the leather strap and spread the pages. A few photographs fell from the bunch, and Berney turned them right side up. "Hm, I wonder if we have time for this right now," he said as he looked at the mantle clock to see how close it was to dinnertime.

"As I remember, your granddad JB purchased twelve carloads of cattle in Minnesota in the spring of 1899. Since I was away with the Wild West Show, your Uncle Asa went with him. JB relied on Asa a lot during those years. I felt guilty that I wasn't around to help, but I made it up to both of them," said Berney thoughtfully. "I recall they went to various ranches to choose the best breeds that could stand our harsh Montana winters. After the horrible winter of 1887, when most of his cattle died from the cold, winter hardiness was a major consideration."

"Was that the year he said he lost 110 percent of his cattle?" Jerry asked, remembering the stories of that killer season.

"Yeah, he told everyone he lost 100 percent to the cold and spent another 10 percent just trying to find where they all went. He joked, but it broke the cattlemen's hearts to see their stock die day after day from the cold and be powerless to save them. After that winter, JB experimented with breeding shorthorns, Herefords, and polled Angus to get good beef that adapted well to our range conditions."

Berney scanned the first pages of the court document. "Here, look here. This tells where the cattle came from: Joseph Asken in Winnipeg, Minnesota; McDonald Brothers in Detroit, Minnesota; William McDonald in Wadena, then from Ulm, then more from a rancher named Mott. Oh, and more at Twin Valley from O. I. Crasguard. We still do business with some of these men even today," Berney added.

"Winnipeg, Minnesota? Isn't Winnipeg in Canada?" Jerry asked. "And isn't Detroit in Michigan?"

"No, this was Detroit, Minnesota, and Winnipeg Junction was also in Minnesota. The railroad went right through it. Not much of a place, even then, but they had stockyards and loading ramps for the railcars. The railroad changed their route, and now it's a ghost town."

Berney continued, "I remember the first problem came when our cars full of cattle were added to an already long, slow freight train that stopped frequently, sometimes for half a day or night. Those jerky stops threw down the cattle and jammed 'em against each other. Then a snowstorm delayed the train, and more cattle, already weakened, died from exposure. When they were finally unloaded at Fallon, the ones still alive were in bad shape. It was real hard on the old man, I tell you. You know, it's too bad JB died before you were born. You would have loved him, and of course he would have loved you too, all you boys. He was a good man, well respected in his day," Berney said proudly.

"He died of ammonia, didn't he?" Jerry asked.

"Pneumonia, it's called, and he had it real bad. Your grandmother Maria did all she could for him, and so did Doc Bennett, but there was little hope. Maria herself was ill with cancer then, and I think she gave up when JB died because she went just a few months after that. He died in late August of 1910, and she was gone by November. It was too bad because they both had good years left."

Berney got up, walked to a side table, and rummaged around in the drawer. He found a picture, showed it to Jerry, and explained, "Here's one of the last photos of them together."

"Gee whiz! She was really big, wasn't she?" Jerry exclaimed.

"Yes, she was! You know she was part Sioux, and some say her Indian name was Big Woman. She was a good mother, kind to all of us, and well-respected in Prairie County," Berney added. "A lot of folks mourned the deaths of those two."

"Too bad I never knew 'em," said Jerry, patting his father's hand.

Berney cleared his throat, pulled himself back to the present, and said, "Let's see, where were we? Oh, yeah. Well, the stock loss on that trip was very hard on JB 'cause he loved his cattle. It wasn't just a herd of animals to that man—he really cared about 'em. Sometimes out on the range, you could hear him talking to the beasts, almost like he was visiting with them, like you would a neighbor. Course, all ranch hands talk some to the cows, but not like JB. He talked like he expected 'em to answer back."

"Why'd Grandpa hafta go to court? Why not just ask the railroad to pay for the dead cows?"

"He sure tried, but they refused," explained Berney. "You know, Jer, our family's always believed in the law of the land and the power of the courts to settle disputes when they're hard to put to rest. This wasn't the first time we took someone to court. JB also took a weasel of a small-time rancher to court over cattle rustlin', but that's another story. We don't go after bad guys with a six-gun and a rope!"

Jerry laughed as Berney continued. "That type of frontier justice was more for early cowboy stories than real life, at least around these parts. First we go to 'em, man-to-man, and if that won't work, we turn to the courts.

"Look at the attorney's name on this page," Berney said, holding the paper up to Jerry. "We still use that same lawyer in Miles City—George W. Farr. He's honest and even-handed, and there's talk he may become a judge. The courts have been fair to us, though sometimes justice is a long time comin'. That water rights suit I told you about is still going on, and it began in 1895. Here it is 1920, and it's still not settled." (This suit by Northern Pacific over rights to water on the Kempton land was finally decided in 1935, in favor of the Kemptons.)

"Tell me more about this in plain English," Jerry said as he picked up a few pages. "This stuff doesn't make much sense."

"Yeah, that's legal language, but the gist of it was the railroad blamed most of the loss on the blizzard, but that wasn't true. It was late May, and there was a blizzard, but four passenger trains, going both directions, got through the snow there, so it wasn't that difficult.

"I remember a funny story from the first trial in Helena," Berney chuckled. "The high-priced Northern Pacific attorney asked JB to tell the jury who he was. The old man introduced himself as a rancher, saying he'd been buying, raising, and selling cattle for forty years. The attorney asked him when he was born. JB replied 1843. Doing some arithmetic, the railroad attorney smugly told the court that it wasn't possible that JB had been raising cattle that long because he'd have been only seventeen years old at the start of those forty years. Some jurors laughed, dismissing JB as an ignorant rancher from the backcountry.

"Then JB paused, stood up tall, and in his commanding voice told the jury that he'd been looking after cattle since he was a boy. He told 'em he was sent out to look for strays by himself on his horse, with a gun and a little food, alone for days on the prairie, in all kinds of weather, with wolves, snakes, and other dangers, when he was just ten years old. 'Cause of that, he said, by the time he was seventeen, he was very experienced at handling cattle. Then he added he now owned one of the largest horse and cattle ranches in the West, and ran up to 4,000 horses and near that many cattle! He said he also started the first church and the first bank in his community and began the efforts to build a high school. Then he said he was also part owner of the Ranchman's Supply Company that did mighty good business in eastern Montana. After that, he nodded to the jury and quietly sat down.

"The court was absolutely silent for a moment, then the jurors began to chortle, and finally the judge asked the railroad lawyer if he'd heard enough! JB sure showed those high-priced railroad attorneys in their expensive suits! They were totally out of touch with the life of Montana ranchers. They had no idea how hard it was for kids like JB who grew up fast to become exceedingly skilled, good men," Berney added. "That pompous railroad attorney accidentally showed JB to be the successful, intelligent man that he was."

"Good for Gramps! He showed 'em!" Jerry said with pride. Then with a look of concern, he asked, "But, Dad, did you hafta go out all by yourself when you were that young too?"

"Nah, Grandpa and Grandma made sure things were a little easier on us kids, and I'm doing the same for you boys too. That's what good fathers do. Try to teach their kids skills and independence yet give 'em a better life than they had," Berney said as he reached over and hugged Jerry's shoulders.

Both father and son went back to looking at the pages of legal testimony. Berney didn't see Jerry pause and look over at him with love.

A few minutes later, Jerry spoke. "There's stuff in here from both JB and Uncle Asa. Did both of 'em hafta be there for the trials?"

"Yeah, they did," Berney answered, "because they were the ones who saw what happened. Asa worked really hard on that trip. He rode with the cattle, trying to keep them on their feet. They stood up while the train moved, but when it stopped, some lay down and when it started again, they got trampled."

"What was JB doing on the train ride?" Jerry asked.

"Probably tearing his hair out at every stop and working with the railroad personnel to get the train moving. Once he even got off in a small town to talk to the NP manager, and the railroad blamed that long delay on him. He said he was only gone ten minutes trying to get things moving. He sure had some very interesting conversations with the train workers. The Northern Pacific attorneys sure didn't want all that used in court."

"Why not? Did they swear?"

"Ha! I imagine there was plenty of that too, but these were the crew's opinions about the delays and rough handling," said Berney.

"What'd they say?"

"Well, one conductor told JB that someone up front must have the 'jim-jams' to be makin' all those rough starts and stops." Berney and Jerry laughed, and Berney began leafing through the pages again. "You know, son, your Uncle Asa's comin' to the ranch real soon, and we can ask him about it. I'll bet he remembers the whole story."

"When's he comin'? 'Cause I wanna know what happened."

"As early as tomorrow afternoon," Berney said. "Let's put all this away 'til then, and he can help us make heads and tails out of this legal stuff. Hey, I'll bet your ma's got dinner almost on the table right now," Berney suggested.

"Sure smells good," Jerry said with a sniff as they went into the dining room.

Asa Kempton, Berney's younger brother, arrived the next day. The first words out of Jerry's mouth, after greeting his uncle, were, "Can you tell us about the cattle that died on that railroad trip? I wanna know what happened."

That night Asa and Berney sat chatting about family, cattle prices, ranching, and the weather.

Soon Jerry joined them and asked, "Can we talk 'bout the cattle now, Dad?"

Berney looked at Asa, who said, "So, Jer, you wanna know about that court case between your granddad and Northern Pacific? That right?" Asa asked.

"Yes, sir. Dad remembered some, but said you knew it all."

"Well," said Asa with a laugh, "Maybe I knew it back then, but that don't mean I know all the details now! But I'll try."

"That's good enough for us," Berney said with a smile.

"You know, Jer," Asa began. "Your own dad didn't go on that trip 'cause he was gallivanting fancy free all around Europe—or was it Asia?—with Doc Carver and his bunch."

"JB was lucky you went with him, Asa," Berney responded.

"He sure was," said Asa as he furrowed his brow in thought and then continued, "As I remember, we spent 'bout a week buying top-notch cattle from ranchers along the railroad line. It was late May of 1899 when we arranged for shipping then loaded 'em all into twelve cars."

"Sorry to interrupt, but how big is a cattle car?" Jerry asked. "And how many cows can go in each one?"

"Usually they're about thirty-six feet long," said Asa, "and we loaded 582 cows. I remember one car was seven short, so that's about forty-eight in a car, which was less than the standard load, but JB was always careful not to crowd his cattle." Asa continued, "JB shipped cattle many times before, but this time things didn't go well."

"Why not?" asked Jerry.

"Well, first of all, when JB shipped cattle, if he had at least ten cars full, he was given an engine all to himself. He never had his cars put onto another train. He did good shipping from Colorado, Oregon, the Midwest, Idaho, and Montana to Fallon and Terry, from both the East and West Coasts. He shipped cattle without a problem to markets in Chicago, St. Paul, and Omaha from 1885 to 1899."

Berney spoke up. "I'll read your exact testimony about that, Asa: 'We started out and the run to Fargo was about usual. The conductor told JB that he would get his own train at Fargo, but that didn't happen. JB didn't like that but finally said it would be OK as long as he got a good run, but we stayed at Fargo. JB asked the superintendent when the train would leave and was told that it would be just as soon as possible—within thirty minutes. It was two or three more hours before we got going.'"

"Then there was another delay of about four hours," Asa said. "And between Fargo and Mandan, it seemed that train stopped on every siding. They sided us every twenty miles or oftener and switched us every time we went on a siding. We didn't know why, but JB got madder and madder with the long delays."

"That's hard on cows," Berney said.

"Yeah," Asa explained. "Cattle do fine on a long run, as long as cars are moving, and we don't care much about the speed, which is usually about twenty miles per hour. But when the train stops, the cattle lie down and get trampled by the others."

Jerry interjected a question. "Why do they lie down? Do they think it's night?"

"Ah, who knows what cows think?" said Berney.

Asa continued. "I rode mostly in the cattle cars, going from one car to another. I walked among the animals, getting them off the top of others so the ones down could get up. There were a number of hard jerks then stops. One jerk was so hard that I came darn close to falling."

"Here's JB's own words," Berney said as he read from the legal brief. "'We had rough usage, stopping sudden and starting sudden—jerky. A sudden stop will jam the cattle up in one end, and a sudden start piles them all up in a heap the other way. This cripples them.'"

"Yeah, it was bad," Asa continued. "When we finally got to Mandan, some were in bad shape, with broken legs. We had to drag 'em out of the car 'cause they couldn't get up on their own. The rest moved like they had a hard deal. We fed and watered 'em at Mandan and loaded as soon as that was done. We left twelve dead there, and that was just the beginning."

"JB asked again for his own engine at Mandan," Asa said, "and was told that Number Fifty-Three wasn't made up yet. He said he didn't care about Fifty-Three being ready or not, but he wanted an engine."

"I was getting riled at that point too," explained Asa, "but the conductor said they couldn't get going 'til they got more power. Finally an engine came from the west, but she couldn't hitch onto us for some reason. There were three or four telegrams back and forth, and finally they said we would get our own power. It took hours more, but at last we got our own train of twelve cars, an engine and caboose, but soon we were side tracked again for a passenger train.

"Then that engine started havin' trouble pulling the cars. Even the conductor was at his wit's end when he said, 'Whoever was in charge shouldn't have sent out that dummy because it didn't have enough power for the train!'"

"Huh? He called the engineer a dummy?" Jerry asked.

"Nah, 'dummy' referred to the engine, but now even the train crew thought NP was at fault for the delays. Here, I'll read from the legal papers," Asa said, paging through the court documents. "Ah, here it is: 'The run was very slow and JB asked the conductor for the reason. He said, 'Why don't you get over the road?' and the conductor replied, 'I can't get anywhere with this dummy. They should have known better than to send it out in this kind of weather.'

"Then I remember the train stopped nearly fifty miles from Mandan. Even though JB complained and repeatedly told 'em about the danger to the stock, we stayed there for eleven or more hours," Asa added.

"That trip was particularly hard on JB," Asa explained, "because his rheumatism was acting up. I took care of the cattle, so he mostly stayed in the caboose, fretted, and tried to convince the train people to get us moving. He got off our train as a last effort and went westward on a passenger train headed to Glendive to talk to NP Superintendent Kline. When he got there, a trainman who knew JB said, 'You now have your chance to get some revenge.' Those were his exact words. Then the trainman pointed out the superintendent's car and urged JB to go in and talk to him directly. So he walked right in and complained about the delays and urged the man to get things going. The superintendent asked him who he was. JB introduced himself and said the train was making mighty poor time, and he wanted to get his cattle over the road. Superintendent Kline told JB that he, himself, had just as much interest in those cattle as JB did. The old man told him if that was true, he would get them going. Then he suggested the engine was underpowered to haul the train, but Superintendent Kline said the engine was sufficient for twelve cars.

The superintendent's train began moving, so JB left and caught our stock train, and we all went on."

"Then didn't a broken knuckle cause another delay?" said Berney.

"What's a knuckle?" Jerry asked.

"It's the coupling between the cars," Berney answered.

"Yeah, and when it broke," said Asa, "the train parted and brakes on every car were thrown to stop 'em. I was taking a little snooze in the cupola of the caboose and ended up on the floor. That stop jarred the stock considerably, probably threw them down, but we knew it was an accident, with no one at fault, but it still added to our problems."

"Was that about the time of the blizzard?" asked Berney.

"Yeah, I think it came on full force somewhere along there," answered Asa. "But we should've been through there before it hit. The cold did in more cattle 'cause they were in such bad shape by then."

"Here's more," said Berney, reading from the court report. "This says the train was also stopped by a steel gang near Crystal Springs, and then a wreck with a steam shovel delayed it again soon after."

"Yeah," Asa responded, "and during the blizzard, a switch plate broke and had to be repaired before we could go again. We were stuck on that siding for another ten or more hours."

Martha Kempton came into the living room carrying a tray loaded with coffee and apple pie. She set it on a side table, and Berney, Asa, and Jerry eyed the dessert with interest. No one could resist Martha's apple pie.

"Are you still talking about the cattle JB lost on the train?" Martha asked. "And didn't he put the survivors in the pasture down here by the house where there's always plenty of water and good grass?" she added.

"He did just that, but even with special treatment, those cows never did good. He lost money when he sold 'em," said Asa.

"As I heard it, the cattle could hardly get off the train," added Martha. "It must've been a terrible sight."

"That's right," said Asa. "Then another problem was the shipping pens at Fallon were so wet we couldn't use 'em and had to put the cattle out on the prairie. Most of the stock didn't have the energy to walk or even eat. I had to hire a man to help me take water out to 'em and another man to care for the ones we had to leave at Fallon. We couldn't even drive 'em. They'd get up and fall down. We tried to trail the rest to the ranch, and it took two days for 'em to go just eight or so miles 'cause they couldn't go any faster. They were worn out, and half to two-thirds were lame at that point.

"That was mighty hard for the old man to abide," Asa said. "He loved his stock and kept 'em in top shape. He was a humane master long before most ranchers even thought about that. Ya know, I still miss him and Maria too, even though they've been gone for years."

"Yes, we all miss them. We all do," said Martha as she leaned down and gave Asa a quick hug before she handed around slices of pie, cups of coffee, and milk for Jerry.

After a few bites, Asa began again. "The count at Fallon was damn disheartening. Those animals were in great shape when we loaded the 586 of 'em at Winnipeg Junction, but 63 died in shipment, 59 were gone when we got to Fallon or soon after, and the rest of the 464 suffered damage. Old JB truly grieved."

"Did any recover?" asked Jerry.

"Nope, not even with the best care," said Asa. "They weighed an average of 1,000 to 1,100 pounds each when we left Winnipeg, and when we sold them a few months later, their average was less than 800 pounds each."

"Golly, that's a big difference," piped up Jerry.

"Yeah," said Berney. "JB was sorry he hadn't waited longer before determining the damages, 'cause $3,000 was far too little to cover all his losses."

"When JB put in a claim, the Northern Pacific said they sincerely regretted the loss and wished they could help bear part of it but it wasn't possible cause their stock rates were so low," said Asa.

"The old man was furious when he got that letter. Really furious!" said Berney. "He stormed around the house hollering and damning the NP all to hell. Finally, Maria told him to pipe down or go outside.

We couldn't tell him that, but Maria sure could. And he minded what she said! They were a great pair."

Martha spoke up again. "Wasn't there a blizzard during the trip? Didn't the railway call it an act of God and say they weren't responsible?"

"Yeah. Here's what the Northern Pacific said about the blizzard," Berney muttered as he handed pages to Martha, who sat down and began to read.

"Now remember that if we hadn't had delays and problems before that, we'd have been through that area long before the storm broke," said Asa.

"And don't forget four passenger trains got through just fine going both directions during that storm," Berney added.

Berney said, "I remember when JB cooled off from their letter refusing to pay, he wrote back that he wouldn't let it drop without resorting to the courts. Here's their answer: 'I beg to advise you that this matter has been thoroughly investigated by our division superintendent, also our general superintendent, and they both advise that the trouble was mainly due to the condition of the weather at the time the stock was being transported.'"

"That really frosted JB more, and he wouldn't let the matter drop," said Asa.

"You know," said Martha, holding up the pages she was reading, "when I read this, I almost feel sorry for the railroad. All that snow and cold, the engine bucking snow from the tracks, the broken switch, and all those poor men out shoveling in the cold. But of course, this was written by NP attorneys specifically to elicit sympathy. The 'proof of the pudding' is what you said about passenger trains getting through on time going both ways. That's the most telling detail of all, Asa," Martha concluded.

Asa finished his pie, looked at the pie plate, and thought about another slice, then said, "Both JB and I went to Helena for the first trial, and eventually we had to go to court in San Francisco. I admit it was intimidating, dealing with all those attorneys and the judge. I'm more comfortable around here talking with ranchers, but we did okay. In fact, we did good!" he added as he accepted another slice of pie from Martha.

Berney spoke up. "I remember the lawyers for Northern Pacific argued that JB hadn't reported the dead cattle directly to the stationmaster in Fallon when the cattle got there. They said that voided any contract and damage claims. JB told them he didn't report the loss at Fallon 'cause there was no stationmaster at Fallon at the time nor had there ever been, and that was why he reported it to the stationmaster in Terry. That made those lawyers look like saps!"

"Then the Northern Pacific asked the judge to set aside the first decision," said Asa, "'cause there wasn't enough evidence to show they were careless. Eventually the U.S. Circuit Court of Appeals for the Ninth District in San Francisco agreed to hear the case. In the spring of '04, JB and I had to show up for court, this time in California."

"It sure dragged on, huh?" said Jerry.

"Yeah, justice moves slow, I'm afraid," said Asa, "and it hung over our heads for a long time."

"Here's a picture we bought that shows the court in San Francisco," said Asa as he lifted a photo from the pile and showed it around. "It's a really pretty building, and that city was nice, but we didn't know our way around. We stayed at the Palace Hotel on Market Street, took a streetcar up to Van Ness Avenue, and walked from there to the court. The people were nice enough, but, you know, we were real glad to get back home. Jer, your pa is the only Kempton who's seen the world much. We all travel some, but he's our world traveler," joked Asa.

"Maybe," responded Berney. "But since I left the show, I haven't done much traveling. I'd like to see Seattle and maybe New York, but I love our prairies." Berney added as he looked out the window at the clouds gathering on the western horizon. Night was coming.

"It would've saved time and trouble if they'd just paid that first amount," Martha said as she returned to the living room after taking the dessert tray to the kitchen.

"Yeah, and they were probably sorry they didn't do that 'cause they paid JB a lot more in the end," Berney said.

"So what did the court in San Francisco decide, Uncle Asa?" Jerry asked, wide-eyed.

Berney, looking over at the mantle clock, interrupted, "Look how late it is. How 'bout if we wait 'til tomorrow for the rest of the story?" he suggested.

"Aw, Dad, no, that's not fair. I really wanna know how it all turned out."

Martha spoke up. "Son, it's way past your bedtime and your brothers are all asleep. Tomorrow will be soon enough. No arguments. On your way now!" she added.

"Dang! I wanna know how it all comes out," complained Jerry as he dutifully picked himself up, slowly walked out of the room, and plodded up the stairs to bed.

"He's some boy, that one," said Asa. "Of all the youngsters, he's the only one who's interested in family affairs, isn't he? Maybe he'll become the Kempton historian, do you think?"

"It's likely," said Martha with a laugh.

The three adults headed to bed themselves, but after Berney and Martha closed their bedroom door, Asa quietly walked back to Jerry's room and knocked softly. Jerry opened the door and Asa stepped inside.

Courtroom at the U.S. Ninth Circuit Court of Appeals in San Francisco.
PHOTOGRAPH BY CAROL HIGHSMITH, LIBRARY OF CONGRESS, LC-DIG-HIGHSM-10518.

"Ah, Jer, I just had to tell you how it turned out. I didn't want you staying up all night wondering."

"Thanks, Uncle Asa! I really wanna know what happened?"

"Well," Asa began in a quiet voice, "the court in San Francisco agreed with the first verdict that the railway was at fault, and the money they paid JB was increased to $10,000!"

"Gee whiz," Jerry whispered excitedly. "That's great!"

"Now tomorrow when we talk about this again, you gotta act surprised when you hear what happened," Asa said in a conspiratorial whisper. "I just couldn't leave you hanging all night not knowing," he added as he tousled his nephew's hair.

"Golly, thanks, Uncle Asa. You're the greatest! Night, now," Jerry whispered as his uncle left the room.

The next morning, after breakfast, Berney brought out a thin stack of papers and put them on the kitchen table. Breakfast dishes were cleared, and Jerry's brothers were off doing other things, but Jerry stayed at the table. No one saw the sly smile and quick wink that passed between the boy and his uncle.

"Now before I tell the final outcome of all this," Berney said slowly, "I want to read what the judges of the U.S. Circuit Court of Appeals said. I looked this over late last night. It's really good, and you should hear it."

Berney began to read from the pages. "'The usual running time for stock trains is from fifteen to twenty-five miles an hour. At that rate of fifteen miles an hour, the train should have made the distance in some thirty-six hours, including five consecutive hours for rest, water and feeding. . . . The time actually consumed in transporting the cattle to their destination was seventy hours.'

"Here's more," he added as he began reading again. "'And if such train had proceeded with reasonable speed, it would have arrived at the town of Fallon before the snowstorm or before it had prevailed a sufficient length of time to cause any injury to the cattle.'"

There was a murmur around the table, and then Berney paused for dramatic effect, raised his voice, and continued, "'Finding no error in the records, the judgment of the Circuit Court is affirmed.'"

Returning from a party on the Kempton Ranch.

Asa laughed and said, "That's a fancy way of saying that the first verdict was upheld! JB won and the damages were increased to $10,000!"

Jerry put on a surprised face and said, "We won! We really won, and by golly, the railroad deserved to pay. It was worth all your trouble, Uncle Asa, wasn't it?" he added.

"Yeah, it sure was, and when JB heard the news," Asa began, "he decided to celebrate by throwing a big party for all the folks in Prairie County right after we got home. It was quite a shindig. Even the Northern Pacific stationmaster at Terry came to tell JB he hoped there were no hard feelings. JB gave a rousing speech about the laws of our country and the justice of our court system. I wrote it down and still have it somewhere," he added.

"Yes, it was quite a party!" added Martha. "I remember baking at least thirty pies, and not one was left."

"Yeah, that and a lot of beef and chicken and even some of the best moonshine in the county, as I remember," said Asa with a chuckle.

All the adults laughed. Berney turned to his son and said, "So now you know all about what's in those old court papers, don't you, Jer?"

"Yeah, Dad, I sure do. It's a keen story, but next time I find something like that in the attic, maybe the explanation won't be quite as long. But it was really interesting," Jerry joked as he ran outdoors to join his brothers in a baseball game.

"Like you said, Asa—he's some kid," Berney said proudly as they watched Jerry go.

FOUR GENERATIONS
OF FROSTBITE

*G*enerations of Kemptons, myself included, lived in cold climates
where frostbite was a common winter concern and exposure to
frigid temperatures could prove fatal. Joseph Kempton, my great-great
grandfather; JB Kempton, my great-grandfather; Berney Kempton, my
grandfather; Jerry Kempton, my father; and I have all faced intense cold
in Colorado, Montana, and Alaska.

I first heard these family stories of frostbite when I was growing up in
Anchorage, Alaska, where I was born and raised. It was 1955, the "Winter
of the Big Snow," when some 132.6 inches fell, which was very unusual
for this northern town on the water, warmed by the Japanese current.
I had been skating on a backyard neighborhood rink when numb feet
finally forced me to quit. This was before the days of insulated footwear,
and the several pairs of socks I wore inside my skates did little good. This
was not unusual, as we often skated until our toes went beyond cold and
into numb, forcing us to hobble home on feet with little feeling.

Both Mom and Dad lectured us about the potential for severe frostbite, but we never believed it could happen to us. After all, the rink was
close, and we were sure we could always make the block-long walk up
the alley to the warmth of home.

Once home, I took off layers of mittens, scarves, jackets, snow pants,
and sweaters, ran a few inches of water in the tub, and sat on the edge
with my feet in the warm bath. As feeling came back into the numb tissue,
the pain was excruciating, and I remember crying while rocking back
and forth. After a gentle I-told-you-so lecture, one of my parents often sat
with me and told stories to take my mind off the pain. I believe these were
meant to be "cautionary tales," but I just thought they were interesting.

The first story Dad told was about the time he became lost in a snow-storm outside a small Alaskan village. I don't remember the name of the place, but it was somewhere on Alaska's north coast. As chief of the Alaska Airport's Division of the Federal Aviation Administration (then called the Civil Aeronautical Authority), Dad arranged for the building of hundreds of small civilian airports around Alaska. He sometimes complained that the government officials "outside" (*outside* to Alaskans means the more southern forty-nine states) just didn't understand the challenges of building airports in Alaska. Consequently, on his frequent trips back to Washington, D.C., Dad's aim was to make them more aware of the difficulties.

In Alaska, Dad usually flew out to towns and villages in a small plane with an FAA pilot. Once there, he met with townspeople to discuss potential airport sites. Sometimes the only suitable location for a landing strip that could handle larger planes included the level spot where generations of villagers were buried—the graveyard. In some small communities, the mountains practically met the sea, and level land was scarce.

Dad took many photos of potential airports, airports under construction, and finished airports. In fact, he was known for his pictures of airports. One snapshot I especially remember showed a bulldozer uncovering human skulls and leg bones as it leveled a former graveyard. Dad said the remains were gathered and carefully reburied in another spot, and the villagers were glad to move the graves in exchange for a larger airstrip that would become their link to the outside world.

The day Dad flew into that particular village, the landing was not easy. The existing runway was short, and the only approach was from the ice-locked sea. Wind gusts shook the plane like a dog shaking a toy, and the landing was difficult. Thankfully, the pilot was skilled, and they made it. Dad had experienced numerous such "rough landings," which he usually made light of, but he knew that many early Alaskan pilots and their passengers died in similar circumstances.

Before Anchorage International Airport was remodeled, some twenty large oil paintings of Alaskan bush pilots lined one wall of the original terminal. One afternoon while we were waiting for Grandma Kempton's plane to land for her annual visit, Dad pointed out the pilots he knew. Most of them were no longer alive, and Dad told us how each had met his demise.

"He crashed in Rainy Pass during a snowstorm," dad said, pointing to one portrait and then another. "His plane was never found. He went down when his wings iced. He crash-landed at Kotzebue. He went down out of Nome and wasn't found for two weeks."

I remember praying my dad wouldn't join the men on that infamous wall of paintings. Fortunately, he never did.

Dad said the flying fatalities per capita in Alaska were twenty times higher than the national rate, but Alaskans accepted it because aviation was essential to their lives. With very few roads, it was the only way remote villages received mail and supplies. It was the way villagers, hunters, and miners got out for medical care, and how fishing lodges brought in their visitors. Even today, without small airplanes, modern life would be impossible across much of Alaska.

After they landed at the village, Dad, the pilot, and the village elders went to see the proposed location for their airport. It was winter, and they were dressed for the weather, but while they looked over the landing site, snow began to fall and temperatures dropped. The villagers suggested they start back, but Dad wanted one more look to make sure the length of the area was sufficient. It was snowing hard as Dad and the pilot paced off the terrain as best they could and then started back to the settlement. They thought it would be simple to just go down the slope since the graveyard was higher than the houses of the village.

After almost an hour of struggling through the blinding snow, they knew they had gone wrong somewhere and tried to retrace their steps. The pilot began stumbling and suggested they stop to rest. Dad knew any stop in that weather might be their final resting place, so he urged him on. Finally, above the sound of the wind, they heard the villagers

Jerry Kempton in a traditional parka.

hollering their names, searching for them. They had wandered far afield and were glad to be led back to warmth and shelter. Both men were okay, with only very slight frostbite on the tips of their noses, but Dad said that brush with cold exposure taught him a strong lesson in winter caution.

Back at the village, they found that the elders had planned a special dinner to celebrate the first steps in building their airport. The men sang to the lively whack of the walrus-skin drums while the women, dressed in beautiful beaded parkas, danced gracefully.

The headman gave a speech, and the priest talked about the benefits of an airport able to handle larger planes and how grateful they were to my father for his role in this project. Dad was their honored guest.

The village elders placed a specially prepared delicacy in front of Dad. It was chunks of blubber, oily and black. The layer of fat that insulates whales from icy waters can be from one to eleven inches thick, and the people of the north country consider it a delicacy. This blubber was from a bowhead whale killed in a recent subsistence hunt. That one whale would last the village most of the winter, and they would use all parts of the mammal, but they especially favored the blubber.

All eyes were on my father as chunks of blubber swimming in oil were offered to him. He did not want to offend these good men and women, so he gamely took a piece and put it in his mouth. He planned to swallow it as quickly as possible but said that it just seemed to get bigger and bigger the longer he chewed. Had he not been the center of attention, he surely would have spit it out. Somehow he swallowed, took a long drink of some fermented liquid, and politely declined any further culinary treats as he talked with the people.

When he and the pilot landed in Fairbanks later that night, the first thing they did was have a beer and a thick beefsteak. They were both famished. That was Dad's first and last taste of blubber, and that was also the end of this particular story.

"Dad," I begged, "I don't want to practically freeze my feet again just to get another story. Will you please tell me one more tomorrow night?"

"Well, I guess I could tell you about your great-grandfather JB's frostbite and the turnip treatment."

"Turnip treatment? Do you mean the vegetable turnip?" I asked.

"Yes, but you'll have to wait for the rest of the story," Dad said as he tucked me in bed.

True to his word, the following night Dad told this story, but he warned me it had sad parts.

"It began when a young boy took a shortcut during a snowstorm and never came home," Dad said. "It was late winter, almost spring, when the weather suddenly turned cold one afternoon and an icy wind blew the snow almost sideways. The storm came on suddenly after school was dismissed. If the snow had started just a half hour earlier, the teacher would certainly have kept the children inside until their families came for them, but she had no way of knowing the fierceness of the coming storm and the unfortunate choice a child would make."

"Which child?" I asked. "Was it you?"

"No, the boy in this story would have been the age of my father, a generation before me, although I made a lot of bad choices and got into more scrapes than most kids. I don't know quite why, but I did," Dad admitted.

Dad continued, "Usually the kids of Prairie County—actually it was called Custer County then—left school in a group on horses and peeled off at the roads to their homes. One of the youngsters, nine-year-old William King, was with his brothers when he decided to take a shortcut. He wanted to beat them home to warmth and food. His older brother tried to convince William to stay with the group and thought he had been successful, but when he looked back a few minutes later, William was gone. William's twin, Walter, reported that William took off across the field, saying he would be home before them. Both Walter and the oldest boy felt it was their fault that they didn't force William to stay with them, but of course, the only fault lay with William, and the price he paid with his death was a great sadness to his family. In those days, one bad choice, one misstep, one simple illness could prove fatal. Many children didn't make it to adulthood, and many adults didn't get to be old folks."

"But everyone in your family, all the kids and your parents, lived really long lives, didn't they?" I asked.

"Well, no. My grandfather, JB, died just a year after his own father in 1910 from pneumonia, and he was only sixty-seven, with many good years left. Some of my cousins didn't survive, but most of us did pretty well. But let's get back to the story," Dad said.

"When the King children reached home, they found that William wasn't there and neither was his horse," Dad continued. "They ran inside and told their mother about William leaving the group. Quickly Mr. King and their ranch hands mounted up and set out to hunt for the lost boy. Word was also sent to neighboring ranches, and others joined the search. Among the searchers was JB Kempton, your great-grandfather. He was the father himself of six sons and two daughters, and one of those sons was my father. Raising six active boys, JB knew that kids, especially boys, often get themselves into dangerous situations."

"Like you did, huh, Dad?" I said.

"Well, yeah, but I always seemed to make it through. Unfortunately, William didn't," Dad answered.

"JB and the Kempton ranch hands dressed warmly and mounted up. As was their practice in such poor conditions, they carried handguns to signal if they were lost in bad weather. Several times, JB mused that maybe that would be a good safety procedure for his own boys, but then he remembered how often they got to horsing around and weren't always careful with firearms."

"Did you ever carry a gun, Dad?" I asked in awe.

"Not regularly, although we sometimes did when we went out on the range by ourselves without our dad or a cowhand," Dad answered.

"Did you ever shoot anything?" I asked.

"Yeah, some old bottles, and I always missed," Dad replied. "But my brothers often shot prairie dogs or rabbits."

"Did you shoot them too, Dad?" I asked.

"Nah, I didn't like guns much, and I liked killing even less."

Dad continued, "After several hours of searching in the cold, JB was chilled to the bone and about worn out. If the child had been found by another searcher, he would have heard two shots as a signal of success. He heard nothing and was about to head in when he saw the outline of one of King's distinctive horseshoes near a tree. The shelter of the dense bare branches must have given the hoofprint some protection since it was not covered by snow. It looked like the print of a small horse or pony, about the size William would ride. JB dismounted to study the single print to see which direction the rider went. Then he spent a futile hour on foot, leading his horse and just trying to find another hoofprint or any sign of the lost boy. He knew he should give up and that he was far too cold, but each time he started back, he wanted to give it one more try. Finally he headed his horse to the King Ranch."

"What happened to the boy?" I asked.

"I'll get to that soon," Dad replied. "Just be patient. But remember, this particular story didn't end happily. JB was one of the last people to come in from the search, and his own men were beginning to worry about him. When he rode into the King Ranch, JB didn't realize how numb his feet were until he dismounted and couldn't stand. He had no feeling in his feet. Several ranch hands and Doctor Abernathy, Doc Bennett's predecessor, helped JB to a chair. When JB got up to tell King about the hoofprint he found, several men had to help him, one on each side. Doctor Abernathy just shook his head.

"Mr. King told the group about the hoofprint, but he was still forced to call off the search that night because it was just too dangerous to be out there in the dark and the cold. Sadly, he recognized there was little chance of finding William in the darkness. He thanked the searchers and said he hoped they would assist him again at first light. Many of them decided to simply sleep in his house or bunkhouse to be close by when the sun came up. They didn't want to lose any time in continuing their search.

"Mrs. King and their oldest daughter ladled hot soup and buttered bread, and they both made a point to thank each person who came to help. The searchers all knew that if roles were reversed, King would be helping them find their lost loved one. It was just what neighbors did to care for one another," Dad said quietly.

"So they just left the boy out there all night in the cold?" I asked.

"They didn't have much choice. They didn't want to risk more lives, and besides, whether they spoke the words or not, they all knew that any hope of finding the youngster alive was almost futile. But still they planned to resume the search as soon as it was light.

"Doctor Abernathy told JB he had no business staying around any longer, and he was concerned about the frostbite in his feet. Under protest, ranch hands loaded JB into Doc's buggy and headed back to the Kempton Ranch.

"In the warm ranch kitchen, Doctor Abernathy removed JB's boots and socks to find his feet were red and swollen. JB repeatedly dismissed his concern and said that he'd be fine in the morning. The doctor just frowned when Maria asked how bad it was and then told her he wanted JB to go to a doctor in Miles City the following day for another opinion. As the ranch hands left the kitchen and went to the bunkhouse, they thought it looked mighty grim. They had seen other cases of frostbite but none as bad as this. The doctor gave JB something to help with pain, and the household finally got some sleep. Doctor Abernathy stayed with them that night. Sadly, word came the next morning that young William King's body had been found at first light."

"He was dead?" I asked.

"Yes, but it took awhile to find him because first his horse had wandered into the ranch at dawn without William. The snow had stopped,

The Kempton Ranch in winter.

and Mr. King and his ranch hands followed the hoofprints back across the prairie until they found the boy's body. Somehow, he must have dismounted or fallen from his horse, wandered around, and lost his sense of direction in the snowstorm. In the end, he simply lay down in the open and just never awakened. The only consolation for King was that his son's passing would have been peaceful. We all knew that a cold weather death was painless, just like going to sleep, except that the victim never arose to another dawn—at least not an earthly dawn."

"How sad," I said.

"Yes, it was really rough," Dad answered, hugging me.

"Keep on with the story," I said, fighting back tears. "I want to know what happened to Great-Grandpa."

Dad continued, "The next morning, JB had trouble just getting out of bed and was remarkably docile when he agreed to be taken to see doctors in Miles City. One of the ranch hands hitched up the buggy for Maria, and the three of them headed for Miles City. The day was clear and bright, with a warm feeling in the air. What a difference from the freezing temperatures and blowing snow the previous afternoon.

"Just as Doctor Abernathy suspected, doctors in Miles City soberly told JB that immediate amputation of both feet was the only way to save his life. JB furiously replied they might as well kill him as cut off his legs and that he would not have anything amputated. Not anything! Not ever! He loudly demanded to be taken back to the ranch.

"They took JB home the next day, brought him in, and helped him to his favorite chair. An old 'darkie' woman happened to be there collecting JB's mother's washing that afternoon since Joseph and Eliza Kempton were visiting from their home in Loveland, Colorado."

"Darkie?" I asked. "Do you mean a black woman?"

"Yes, in those days, they were called 'darkies,'" Dad explained. "The term meant no disrespect—that's just what they were called back then. The old woman glanced at JB's swollen, frostbitten feet. The skin on parts of his toes was dark now. She looked again and then quietly told Maria she thought his feet could be saved. She said she had seen even worse frostbite cured. Maria paused and thought about it for a few minutes. What did they have to lose when the alternative was the double amputation of an active, vital man's feet? Maria said it was worth a try and JB agreed, but he was skeptical.

"My dad, Berney, the oldest child, was standing in the kitchen watching all of this when the old woman asked Maria if they had any turnips in the root cellar.

"'Turnips? Do you mean turnips from the garden?' Maria had asked. 'Plain, everyday turnips?'

"'Yes, regular turnips,' the old woman had responded. 'Please bring them at once.'

"Your granddad ran outside, opened the door to the cold root cellar, and looked for turnips among the vegetables that were kept there all winter. He found some, brought them inside, and gave them to the old woman. Thank goodness they had a hefty store of these root vegetables because the turnip treatment the woman planned would use almost all they had. No one in the family bemoaned a shortage of turnips because they were certainly not a favorite vegetable!"

"Plain, everyday, old turnips?" I asked, incredulous.

"Yep, plain, everyday turnips," Dad answered. "The old woman told Maria to bake the turnips and then mash them into a poultice."

"Dad, sorry to interrupt, but what's a poultice?" I asked.

"It's a soft, wet mass of plant material applied for medicinal purposes. It's usually held in place with a cloth. This poultice would be applied to JB's feet just as hot as he could stand without further injuring the tissue. She said the poultice had to be renewed at least three to four times during the first five days."

"Yuck, that doesn't sound very good to me," I said.

"No, it wasn't! The place smelled of cooked turnips, and JB was in a foul humor, snapping at anyone who came close. The old woman told Maria that JB's feet would take in the moisture from the poultice for five days, but after that no more would be absorbed. She added that Mr. Kempton must stay off his feet completely during that time. JB overheard those instructions and hollered, 'Damn, woman, I can't stay off my feet, I have things to do. I can't just lie here all day!'

"Now, my grandmother, Maria Gerry Kempton, was a quiet but well-respected woman in the county. She was said to be very intelligent, and I think she was, and few knew that she could neither read nor write, although JB was well-educated and their children were also schooled. JB was the undisputed head of the house, the one who made most decisions. But right then, Maria rose up to her full, imposing height, stomped toward JB with her hands on her hips, and said, 'James Berney, you will do exactly what you are told or I will haul you to those doctors in Miles City and tell them to cut off both your legs and maybe an arm to boot! Now which one will it be? Do you want to give this woman's cure a good try or shall I hitch up the buggy and we'll head for Miles City?' She had steel in her voice, which was unusual for this kind, mild-mannered woman. JB was stunned but listened quietly.

"JB's parents agreed to extend their stay, and now they stood in the doorway listening intently to all this. Joseph walked to JB's bedside and said, 'Son, I have heard of this treatment. It is not easy, but I have seen it work and the victim was cured. You have a choice, and both your mother and I pray you make the right one and do everything you are told to do.'

"Then Maria ushered everyone from the bedroom and said to JB, 'I will leave you to think and will come back for your answer.' Then she shut the door. Even with the door closed, JB's hollering and loud curses could be heard throughout the ranch house.

"In the kitchen, the old woman and Maria began washing more turnips, cutting them into pieces and putting them in the oven to bake. The woman put a gnarled hand on Maria's shoulder and softly told her that the procedure would work. She had seen its success many times. It would not be easy, but if followed, it could restore health to JB's feet. Maria smiled, took the woman's hand, and pressed several silver dollars into her palm. She thanked her and whispered there would be more when the treatment was complete.

"When Maria went back to JB's bedside, he was quiet. 'I would be no man without my feet,' he whispered. 'I could not live that way. I would rather die. If this is a way to possibly save my feet and legs, I ask that we try it. I will make a strong attempt to be a good patient.' Then he took Maria's hand, and pulled her close. She saw tears in his eyes and he in hers.

"And so it began. The turnip treatment! It was decided the old woman would stay at the ranch for the first weeks to supervise the treatments. There was no time to be lost. The first batch of baked turnips were mashed with a bit of water. The hot poultice was carried upstairs and applied to JB's feet and lower legs. The boys in the room, standing back near the door, saw JB grit his teeth, grimace, and then groan as the hot poultice was applied to his feet. The smell of turnip poultice and rotting flesh filled the house, and those odors were most unpleasant.

"When the old poultice was changed and a new one applied, JB again cursed loudly. It was hard to bear—the smell of mashed turnips mixed with the increasingly foul smell of JB's feet as the skin continued to decompose and blacken. The girls went to stay with neighboring families, and the boys took to sleeping in the bunkhouse and even the barn. Although it was cold in the barn and the animals were noisy, it was far more pleasant that being inside the ranch house."

"That must have been really bad," I said.

"Yes," Dad said. "At first the boys often went into the room to see their father, but soon the door to JB's room was kept closed. Doctor Abernathy came often and gave JB more laudanum for the pain. The doctor was dubious about this nonmedicinal folk treatment and told Maria he hoped she knew what she was doing because he didn't want to lose a friend like JB.

"JB's father and mother stayed on at the ranch, helping both inside and outside the house. JB's mother read endlessly to him during the day, and his father took a turn watching him the first few nights until they deemed he was out of danger.

"Finally, after about five days, JB's feet had absorbed all the moisture they were going to from the poultices. Now they just had to wait. The wait was hard for an active man like JB. He had the ranch handyman make him a set of crutches so he could get around a bit but spent most of his time in bed. He was not easy to live with during that time, and the intense smell became even more nauseating.

"Mr. King, the father of the boy who perished in the snowstorm when JB frostbit his feet, came to call several times. He said he felt partly responsible for Kempton's hard time, but JB reassured him that had the tables been turned King would have done the same to look for a missing Kempton child.

"Other friends and neighbors came with books for JB to read, with sweets and food. They told him many prayers were being sent up on his behalf. Unfortunately JB was not at all that cordial with visitors, and soon the smell kept all but the hardiest away.

"About eighteen days later, the dead, blackened skin of both feet slipped off entirely, just like a thin, leather moccasin. Underneath, JB's feet were bright, puffy, red, and very sensitive. The old woman said JB could now wear tight slippers or boots to keep the inflamed tissue from swelling. Then she dusted his feet with a medicinal powder, and he endured the pain as Maria laced up a new pair of boots. When he tried to stand, he said it felt like his feet would burst. He spent another few weeks off his feet, mostly in bed, but at least he could take a couple of steps. Doctor Abernathy still came out to the ranch, but now he was encouraged. In fact, he could see amazing progress when he examined JB's feet.

"Gradually the fiery-red skin began to crack down to the soles of his feet, but it was apparent that new tissue was forming. Eventually new skin grew back completely, and JB was finally on the road to recovery. His feet were still very sensitive. He walked carefully and complained for many months, but he admitted that he was glad to still have feet. The old woman was rewarded, and things soon got back to normal.

"JB healed completely and led a full and active life for years until he came down with a sudden and severe case of pneumonia that took his life. Townspeople and ranchers were stunned by his death because they had seen him in town so recently, hale and hearty.

"So that's the story about JB's frostbite and the turnip treatment that saved his feet," Dad said. Then he turned to me and added, "So now, Trude, you know about our family's experiences with the cold. I trust you'll be more careful so those incidents don't continue into your generation!"

"Yeah, Dad," I said, then asked, "Did you ever hear of anyone else using turnips for frostbite?"

"No, I didn't. Perhaps those in Prairie County learned to be more cautious. No one wanted to go through what JB had endured!" With his story ended, Dad said, "You go right to sleep now, okay, Trude?"

Trudy Kempton Dana as a child in Anchorage, Alaska.

I wasn't sure how quickly sleep would come after all those hideous images, but I guess it did.

I admit my respect for cold temperatures and what they can do to the human body made me more cautious. One severe frostbite and the turnip treatment for a Kempton family member was more than enough for all our generations.

Author's note: Using turnips as a treatment for frostbite is a well-known folk remedy. It is used in India, and early American slaves swore by it. The North Carolina State University Cooperative Extension also advises boiling turnips and using that water for medicinal baths.

DECISION IN
A SNOWSTORM

The winter of 1923 was nearly over in Prairie County. Daffodils, lovingly planted years before in sheltered spots near the Kempton ranch house, were pushing up green shoots. The calendar showed that spring was just around the corner, but you'd never know it by the weather. An unusually nasty cold front moved into eastern Montana— temperatures plunged and snow fell. It was still calving season, however, and the mother cows would give birth to their young regardless of what the calendar or the thermometer read.

Usually this phenomenon of new birth took its course naturally, and a calf or occasionally twins were born. Sometimes ranchers had to help a birthing mother, but generally all went well, just as nature planned.

For the previous three years, Jerry had asked to help with calving but was repeatedly told he wasn't old enough. This year would be different, and his help would be crucial. He would do a man's work and be forced to make a man's decisions. This calving season was a turning point in Jerry's life and would determine his future, even though he was only eleven years old.

It was about three in the morning, and Jerry, tucked under warm covers, was in the middle of a good dream when his father shook him awake.

"Son, get up," Berney said urgently. "We need you. We got problems with the cows. Dress warm 'cause it's freezing out, and get some breakfast. Hurry, Jer."

Jerry stumbled out of bed, rubbed his eyes, and pulled back the curtains. There was snow on the windowsill, and the yard below was covered in white.

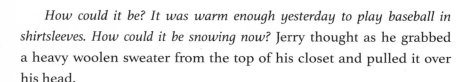

How could it be? It was warm enough yesterday to play baseball in shirtsleeves. How could it be snowing now? Jerry thought as he grabbed a heavy woolen sweater from the top of his closet and pulled it over his head.

He was still groggy when he entered the kitchen downstairs and found his father and the ranch hands eating flapjacks, bacon, and eggs and downing cups of hot coffee. His mother and the Florida Cowboy, one of the ranch hands who often helped cook, were working hard to keep up with the hungry men.

Jerry thought about his three younger brothers, John, Ed, and Berney Jr., probably still in their warm beds. They were too young for the job at hand. His older brother Jim was away, staying with Uncle Asa and his family. Of the five boys, Jerry was the only one who could help.

"Dad, it's still dark outside," Jerry moaned. "Why're we all up this early?"

"The cows are calving, son, and the weather changed," Berney said between mouthfuls of breakfast. "It's been snowing since before midnight and looks like it's gonna keep on. Unless we get those mothers into shelter, we could lose a whole lot of calves."

Just then, Jeff Dixon, the ranch foreman, burst in the kitchen door. His cheeks were red, and his jacket was dusted with snow. He nodded to Berney, looked at the ranch hands still around the table, and said, "You ready? We got lots of work ahead. It's getting worse, and I can hear those cows bawling. Let's go!"

Martha thrust a plate of flapjacks and bacon into Jerry's hand and advised him to eat fast. Berney, turning to leave, told him to come out to the barn as soon as he could. In the past, it had sounded like fun to help with calving, but it was cold outside, and Jerry was tired. A warm bed seemed like a better idea right then, but he didn't want to let his father down.

With his mouth still full, Jerry grabbed his heavy jacket, gloves, and hat and headed for the barn. The cold caught him as he opened the door, and he was again stunned to see the change in weather. Yesterday felt like spring, but now everything was covered with snow, and thick flakes whirled.

"Blasted Montana weather," Jerry muttered.

As he pulled open the barn door, his father nodded to him and said, "Thanks, Jer. We can really use your help today."

Then Berney turned to the group of men and began giving instructions. "We've gotta bring the expecting mothers down to the barns or at least to the lower corrals where we can keep an eye on 'em. If they've already dropped their calves, they'll be a challenge. Save as many calves as you can and leave the dead ones. We can get that meat as soon as the weather's better—it'll be fine in this cold. Put down any mothers that can't be saved. End their misery and leave those carcasses too."

"Dad, is it that bad?" Jerry asked.

"Yeah, and it's getting worse," his father answered, handing Jerry a revolver and holster.

Turning back to the group, Berney said, "Try to keep your bearings, but if you get lost in this whiteout, signal with three shots. Remember, we wanna save cows today, not cowboys, so good luck and stay safe."

As the ranch hands mounted up and headed out, Jerry realized he was deep in a situation beyond his ability to handle. He didn't want anything to do with taking the lives of cows or calves. Of course, animals were killed for meat or out of necessity on the ranch, but he hadn't been involved in any of that directly and had tried to keep his distance. His brother Jim often killed chickens needed for a meal. Once, Jerry overheard some older boys at school laugh and say that Jim "just lined 'em up real neat and straight and chopped off their heads, real quick. One at a time." When he heard that, Jerry shuddered and decided to stay clear of Jim when he was near the hen house.

Jerry was relieved when Jeff said, "You'll be with me, Jer. We'll work together."

"Jeff, will we really have to kill cows or calves?" Jerry asked.

"We hope not, but we may have to put some animals down. Remember, a quick death's kinder than leaving 'em to die slow."

Jerry and Jeff rode in silence toward the high pastures. Their horses followed a trail broken by the first group of ranch hands who had already found some cows.

"No babies yet," one of the men hollered. "We'll get 'em down 'afore they drop calves," he added as the men slowly herded the animals toward the corrals.

After getting a group of cows to safety, the men started back up the hill for others. Jeff and Jerry made a few of these round trips, and then Jeff suggested they head back up to a particular canyon. He had seen cows struggling through the snow in that direction. The poor beasts probably thought they might find shelter there.

At the canyon's entrance, Jerry saw what looked like a pile of snow. Then the pile moved as a snow-covered mother cow struggled to her feet then collapsed again. The small pile of snow beside her, tinged with blood, was still.

"Okay, Jer," Jeff said solemnly, "we gotta put this one down. Her calf's already dead."

They both dismounted, and Jerry walked over to the mother cow and stroked her behind the ears. Most of the Herefords were docile creatures.

"Jer, stand back now and cover your ears," Jeff said gently.

"Isn't there any other way?"

"No, Jer, this is a kindness to her. She's half dead already."

Jerry stepped away and put his hands over his ears. The sound of Jeff's gun echoed from the canyon walls. Blood spattered the snow, and the cow died instantly. Jerry turned away and gagged. Even though he knew this death was necessary, he still hated the killing.

The two rode farther up the canyon until Jeff spotted another mother and calf. The calf was still but suddenly struggled to stand. It was alive but wouldn't be for long.

"It's one of your pa's prize Herefords. Let's see if we can save it," Jeff said. "We'll put the little one over the saddle in front of you, Jer. Try to cover it with the tails of your jacket and maybe it'll be okay."

Both Jeff and Jerry dismounted and waded through the snow. Jeff picked up the newly born calf as Jerry remounted his horse. Jeff heaved the calf onto the saddle in front of Jerry, who opened his jacket and tried to cover the newborn. The calf struggled briefly and then was quiet. Jeff prodded the mother to her feet, and she walked slowly downhill toward the shelter of the barn. The snow was coming down faster and turning to sleet.

"This sleet'll be even harder on 'em, and we may lose a bunch of these animals," Jeff called to Jerry.

When they reached the barn, Jeff pushed the exhausted mother into a stall and lifted the baby from Jerry's saddle. Jerry noticed the front of his sweater was bloody from the calf's recent birth but knew it couldn't be helped. He buttoned his jacket and hoped his mother could get them both clean in the wash. The calf bellowed then moved to its mother, which roused when the little one nuzzled and started sucking.

"Well, we saved this pair. Now let's go out and get more," Jeff said to Jerry.

Back and forth they went all morning, herding cows into the lower corrals and bringing half-dead mothers and calves into the barn, where most of them revived. Jeff and Jerry had worked hard since before sunup and were famished.

"Let's see if we can get some food," Jeff said. "Your ma told me they'd bring stew out to the barn, and I think I can smell it now. Come on, Jer."

They tied their horses and walked toward the barn. Inside, Martha ladled hot, delicious stew into bowls. It was just what they needed. Everyone was exhausted, but they knew there was more work ahead.

A little later, Martha refilled their bowls and gave Jerry a pat on the back.

Jeff looked up at her and said, "He's doing fine, ma'am. Really fine."

Martha wanted to hug her son but knew this was not the time or place. Jerry was doing a man's work, so she would treat him like a man, not a boy. "Stay safe," she whispered to Jerry, who nodded, his mouth full of stew. After two bowls of stew, bread, and coffee, Jeff suggested he and Jerry return to the canyon and search for more cattle.

Kempton cattle endure winter.

The cold hit them again as they left the barn and headed back up. Jerry wondered when he would ever get back to a warm house, a bath, and clean clothes. It seemed like a day ago when his father awakened him. Those thoughts ended as they came around a corner near the canyon's end and saw a cow heaving in distress as she tried to give birth. The unborn calf seemed to be stuck.

"Another Hereford. Let's see if we can help her," Jeff said as he got off his horse, took off his gloves, and knelt by the mother.

The calf's little hooves protruded from its mother's birth canal.

"Sometimes we can help nature along when the mother's having a hard time giving birth," Jeff said as he grabbed the unborn calf's hooves and pulled steadily. As the baby came out, the mother's blood stained the snow.

"Is she supposed to bleed that much, Jeff?" Jerry asked.

"No, that's too much. Something's not right," Jeff said as he stood close to the cow and bent over the animal to get a better look.

"She's in trouble, Jer."

Suddenly, as Jeff leaned close to her, the cow gave an unexpectedly strong kick that caught Jeff's lower arm. He staggered back and fell, groaning and holding his arm against his chest.

"Jeff! Jeff, are you okay?" Jerry hollered as he ran to him.

"No! Oh, damn," Jeff groaned through clenched teeth as he tried to stand. "It's broke! My arm's broken, Jerry!"

The cow bellowed, got to its feet, and staggered a few steps, leaving a trail of blood on the snow. The poor beast fell over, and her warm blood pooled beside her.

"Jerry, help me up," Jeff yelled in severe pain.

As Jerry went to him, Jeff tried to stand but slipped, went down to his knees, and cried out as he fell on his injured arm. Jerry helped him sit then pushed him up to a standing position, and the two moved to Jeff's horse.

Jeff leaned against the horse, looked back at the mother cow, and said, "I can't do it, Jer. You're gonna have to put her down. The little one's gone."

"No, Jeff, you do it," answered Jerry, almost frantically.

"Jer, I can't shoot her! I can't even get my gun outta the holster. I can't shoot like this, and we can't just leave her."

"No!" Jerry answered, his face white with fear.

"We can't leave her like this. We gotta end her suffering. It's up to you, Jer."

"I don't think I can do it," Jerry said, his voice high and almost hysterical.

"Come on, Jer, you know it's best. Do it now! Now! Kill her now! You saw me do it. You know how. Do it now!" Jeff said as he struggled to stay upright.

Jerry cried as he stood over the cow and finally pulled the trigger. The gunshot was muffled by the deep snow in the small canyon, and the cow lay quiet.

"You did it," Jeff said, mumbling with pain.

Jerry turned away from the bloody scene, began retching, and then vomited in the snow. When he straightened up, he wiped his mouth with a handful of clean snow and brushed the tears off his face.

"You did it, Jerry! You did what you had to do," Jeff said, holding his arm and now staggering.

Jerry looked away from the cow and quickly pulled himself together. He knew Jeff was badly hurt. The foreman's face was white, and he was shaking. Jerry knew it was up to him to get Jeff to safety as quickly as possible.

"Jeff, hold on. We're gonna get you down to the ranch!" Jerry said.

As he tried to help Jeff up onto his horse, the injured man gasped with pain and looked like he was going to pass out. Jerry knew he couldn't lift Jeff's dead weight, and the seriousness of the situation sobered him. He had to take charge. There was no one else to help.

"Come on, Jeff, you gotta get up there. Pull yourself together! You can do it. I know you can," Jerry encouraged.

Jeff remembered thinking through his haze of pain that the tables were suddenly turned. Now Jerry was in the adult role, and he was the one who needed strong support.

"You can do it. I know you can. Just try harder," Jerry heaved, pushing Jeff up and into the saddle. "We'll get you down to the ranch and have someone ride for Doc Bennett. You'll be okay."

When they finally got down the hill to the ranch, Jeff was slumped over the front of his saddle, groaning with every breath. Jerry knew he was in bad shape.

"Help! Someone help! Jeff's hurt!" Jerry shouted.

Almost at once, the Florida Cowboy and Martha ran out of the barn. Together the three of them got Jeff off his horse and inside the ranch house. Martha told Florida to ride into town for Doc Bennett.

Martha and Jerry put Jeff on the bed in the spare room off the kitchen and gently pulled off his coat. He cried out and lost consciousness. When

Jerry saw the white arm bone protruding from Jeff's sleeve, he gagged for the third time and could feel the bile rising in his throat. He knew he had to help his mother, so he focused on that and tried not to look at Jeff's arm. They covered Jeff, sat nearby, and awaited the doctor's arrival.

Several hours later, after Doc Bennett examined Jeff and bandaged his arm, he talked to Jerry and Martha.

"It's a bad break, and Jeff will be out of commission for a while, but he'll be okay. I've bandaged his arm and given him something for the pain, but I can't set the bone for a few days until the swelling goes down." Doc Bennett looked at Martha and added, "You can be very proud of Jerry for getting Jeff down the hill and to help quickly. He wouldn't have lasted long injured and in that cold."

Jeff called from the room, and Martha and Jerry went in to see what he needed. He motioned for them to come closer to his bed, then said in a slurred voice, "Jerry did real good. He worked like a man and handled it all. I think he saved my life!" He lay back on the pillow and fell into a deep slumber. Jeff said nothing about the killing of the cow injured in birthing her calf, and Jerry didn't want to talk about the incident at all, although Jeff later told Martha and Berney what happened.

That difficult April snowstorm was a turning point for Jerry. Although he was still young and had a number of years ahead of him before he left the ranch, he clearly knew that ranching was not for him. He could not stomach the killing. True to his conviction, he went to college and became a civil engineer. Although he always held a fondness for the ranch in eastern Montana, he never lived there again and never questioned his resolution. The Kempton Ranch was not for him.

Thirty years later, when Jerry looked at a snapshot of the ranch's frozen artesian springs and cattle nearby, he said it brought back sharp, uncomfortable memories of that cold day in the spring of 1923 when he had made a life decision in a snowstorm.

Frozen artesian springs on the ranch.

Author's note: As Jerry's daughter growing up in Anchorage, Alaska, I noticed that most of my friends' fathers, and even their brothers, often talked about hunting. They went on hunting trips and brought back ducks, moose, caribou, and even bear. But not my father. He was not interested in hunting. Dad said he wanted no part of that killing. Once had been enough for him.

FAMILY LORE
ON A MIDNIGHT RIDE

erney Kempton's younger brothers, Asa and Sanford (known as Sant), were spending a week at the home ranch in Terry to meet with the family attorney about testifying in a long-running lawsuit. The Northern Pacific Railway was suing the Kemptons over rights to the artesian springs near the ranch house. This expensive, frustrating, and seemingly endless suit began in 1895, and it was now 1923.

Asa and Sant grew up on the Kempton Ranch but now owned their own spreads in Montana and South Dakota. The brothers all had the thick, black, curly Kempton hair and dark complexion of their Sioux ancestors. Of these brothers, Sant was the scholarly one, and even as a child, he seemed mature. He wasn't as physically active as his siblings, and he took far fewer risks. In contrast, Asa was more slapdash and casual about life.

Although the three brothers got along well, it hadn't always been that way. In the past, both Sant and Asa held some hostility toward Berney because of the nearly two years he had been away with the

Left to right, Asa, Sanford, and Berney Kempton.

Wild West Show. They stayed home and did all the hard work on the ranch, compensating for their eldest brother's absence. This wound deepened after Berney returned and soon took over the ranch. In the end, Asa and Sant's animosity eased as they became successful ranchers and landowners in their own rights.

One evening after dinner, the three brothers were relaxing over a game of poker when a ranch hand, returning from trailing cattle, reported his stock refused to drink at a spring-fed waterhole at the northeast corner of the ranch. Berney needed to find out why the cattle refused that water because those springs were good and reliable, even in the dry months. Since most of the ranch hands were helping with branding at the nearby Patterson Ranch and foreman Jeff Dixon was also away, Berney knew he would have to check the spring himself. Both Sant and Asa volunteered to ride along to keep him company. Eleven-year-old Jerry also asked to go. Berney agreed, thinking this would be a good opportunity for his son to get to know his uncles better. He regretted that his other boys were away in Spokane with their mother and would miss this chance.

The four planned to ride most of the night, sleep out on the prairie, check the waterhole in the morning, and be back the next afternoon. It was two hours shy of midnight and the sky was clear when they set out from the ranch.

"I remember how JB used to say there's just something about sitting on a horse and riding together under the stars that gets the old-timers to talking. I guess that means I'm getting to be an old-timer now," Berney said as the four began their ride on that mild summer night. A halfmoon lit the prairie and the sky was full of stars.

"Yeah, Berney, you're the oldest Kempton around here, so I guess you qualify as the old-timer," teased Sant.

"Come on, Dad, if you have trouble talking and riding at the same time, I can lead your horse for you," joked Jerry.

"I can out-ride and out-talk any of you, any day, any time!" Berney said, puffing out his chest.

"Oh, I don't know about that," said Asa, winking at Jerry. "Maybe we'll have to have a contest so you can show us."

This good-natured banter went on for several minutes.

On the flat just above the ranch, the horses went around a large depression.

"Do you know why the ground's lower there, Jerry?" asked Asa as he looked out over the prairie.

"Isn't the land just that way?" Jerry answered.

"Nope. This area and that depression over there are old buffalo wallows where the beasts rolled in the deep dust. Their dust baths probably helped with the flies that bedeviled them in the summer. Why, I tell you, at the turn of the century, these wallows could hide a hundred head of horses! They've filled in a lot over the years."

"Jeepers, that must've been really something," Jerry said.

Sant said, "Yeah, there's a lot of evidence of the past out here. Once, when we were boys, we found old wagon trails that wound across the prairie. We thought the tracks were ancient when we found them, and that was probably more than thirty years ago. You remember that, Berney?"

"Yeah," Berney replied. "You were the one to spot those tracks, weren't you, Sant?"

"Yep," Asa interjected. "That's 'cause he was always poking around and asking questions. Not much got by him, as I remember."

"Well, someone had to ask questions and find out about things since none of you knew what was going on," Sant retorted.

"No, Sant wouldn't take any wooden nickels," Berney added, and they all laughed.

"Dad, what are your other brothers' names? I haven't met all of them, have I?" asked Jerry.

"No, you haven't seen all of 'em. There's Joe, Henry, and Jim, besides these two right here. And don't forget, I have some sisters, too—

Marie and Sarah. You know, maybe we should have a family get-together, while we're all still walking the earth," suggested Berney.

"Good idea," agreed Sant.

"We'd all come," added Asa.

"That gets me to thinking, Jer. It's too bad you never knew your grandma and grandpa, JB and Maria. Both of 'em died in 1910, and you came along in 1912," said Berney.

"I've heard about Grandpa, Dad. Didn't he start the Bank of Terry? Miss Phillips once told the class that he raised money to build some of the schools in Prairie County, too."

"Yeah, he did. Education was very important to that man, and he passed his love of learning down to all of us. You know, during the early years when we lived far from any school, he hired tutors for us."

"Yeah, Berney, I remember some of the tricks you played on those poor, unsuspecting tutors," said Sant.

"What'd you do, Dad?" asked Jerry, tickled to learn about his father's boyhood antics.

"Oh, nothing real bad," said Berney. "I'll tell you another time 'cause I can't quite remember."

"Oh yeah, I'll bet those tutors sure remembered!" said Asa, with a laugh. "How could they forget?"

Wanting to change the subject, Berney said, "JB also started the Ranchman's Supply Company in Terry, which still does a great deal of business in Prairie County and beyond. JB was what you'd call a 'town father,'" he added proudly.

"Yeah, that man had a vision, all right, and the town was better because of it," said Sant.

The group came to the Yellowstone River, and their mounts easily waded across single file at a wide ford. Berney stopped to fill his canteen and said he would catch up. Jerry and his uncles went on, then waited for Berney at the crest of the next hill.

"You need help, old man?" Sant called back to Berney.

The Ranchman's Supply Company in Terry, Montana,
was started by JB Kempton.

"Nope, I'm coming," Berney replied. As he caught up to the group, he said, "You know Sant, you'll be pushing 'old man status' soon, yourself."

"Yep. All too soon," Sant agreed. "All too soon."

The group rode in silence until Jerry asked, "Where was Grandpa born and when?"

"As I remember," Asa began, "your granddad was born somewhere in the mid-1800s in Jackson, Michigan. His father, Joseph Kempton, was from Hampden, Maine, clear out on the East Coast. He was the captain of a whaling ship that sailed out of Penobscot County, Maine, before he met your great-grandma, Eliza Sabrina Foote. The Footes were a well-known, wealthy family from New York who descended from someone famous named Nathaniel Foote. I think he was an early English immigrant who founded Wethersfield, Connecticut, the oldest settlement in that state. After Joseph and Eliza married, they moved first to Michigan and then to Fremont's Orchard, Colorado, where they were some of the first settlers in that area."

"You know a lot about them, Uncle Asa, don't you?" Jerry said.

"I guess I'm the family historian out of all us siblings."

"There are a couple of old pictures of Joseph and Eliza on the wall of my office," said Berney.

"You mean the ones of the really old man and woman who're frowning, Dad?"

Eliza Sabrina Foote Kempton,
1821–1901.

Joseph Kempton, 1817–1909.

"That's right. They all look somber because photographers back then didn't want their subjects to smile."

Asa, who had been moving around in his saddle trying to get comfortable, spoke up, "Hey, Berney, this saddle's too narrow through the seat."

"Nah, Asa, it's not too narrow. You've just gotten too wide through the seat," Berney joked.

As they all laughed, Jerry felt the deep camaraderie that existed between these siblings. He wondered if he and his brothers would have the same easy relationship when they were grown men.

The group stopped their horses and listened to a chorus of howls exchanged back and forth between the hills. The sounds were eerie in the darkness, and Jerry was glad he wasn't alone. Then he remembered

Asa Kempton's saddle.

both his father and grandfather had been on their own trailing cattle when they were just a little older than he was now. *How did they do it?* he wondered.

They heard more howls, and Asa said, "Sounds to me like that's more than just coyotes. I wonder if wolves are coming back again."

"I hope not," Berney answered, listening intently to the baying of the animals. "We don't need wolves around here."

Sant spoke up. "I've still got an old photo of you, Asa, on your horse with a long rope, leading a wolf you caught back to the ranch."

"Yeah, I remember they were really bad that year," Asa responded. "Do you recollect how the two of us would find a pack out on the prairie, then ride beside one of 'em to cut him off from the pack, and then rope him?" asked Asa.

Asa Kempton with a roped wolf.
PHOTOGRAPH BY EVELYN CAMERON, KEMPTON FAMILY COLLECTION.

"Yeah, that was pretty effective wolf control, I'd say," answered Sant.

They listened once more, but the calls had died down, and the night was again quiet.

"I remember some of the stories JB told us 'bout going west over the plains with a bull train," said Asa.

"What's a bull train, Uncle Asa?" asked Jerry.

"It's a bunch of freight wagons pulled by oxen before there were railroads. JB was little more than a big kid then, but he made a number of trips from St. Louis to Colorado, and somewhere in those years, he also served in the cavalry of the Union Army."

JB Kempton

"Gee, Grandpa fought in the Civil War?" Jerry asked.

Berney spoke up. "Yep, he was in Sherman's March to the Sea in 1864."

"Why, Berney, you're just a walking library. You know all those dates, don't you?" asked Sant.

"Yeah, well, I read a lot, and many of the books are about wars," Berney explained.

"Did Grandpa ever tell you about the war?" asked Jerry.

"Nope," Berney responded. "He only told us he lost a lot of friends in the battles and didn't like to talk about it. After the war, he came back west again and settled thirty-five miles below Greeley, and that's where he met and married your grandma, Maria Gerry, whose mother was a full-blood Sioux."

"It's funny how you always pronounce her name 'Mariah' instead of 'Maria,'" Jerry commented.

"I don't know where that came from 'cause it's spelled 'Maria,' but that's just how it always was," said Sant.

"And you know your Aunt Marie? Her name's spelled like 'Marie,' but we pronounced it 'Mary.' I don't know why that was in both cases," added Berney.

"Do you remember how Pa and Ma met, Asa?" asked Sant.

"Yeah," Asa began. "She was the daughter of a mountain man named Elbridge Gerry, who traded with the early trappers and Indians. Pa told us that Gerry bragged about buying buffalo hides by the hundreds and selling sugar by the cup."

"Really?" said Jerry.

"Yeah, and when we were kids, we saw an old letter written by a French fur trapper, describing Gerry. It said something about him not being much of a landsman, woodsman, or hunter but that he was a great, easygoing fellow, good-natured and honest," Asa said with a laugh.

"I think the fur trade fell off about then," said Sant, "and Gerry went to Fort Laramie in Wyoming, where he began trading with the Indians. That's where he met Maria. There were very few white men in Colorado at that time and even fewer white women. Because of that, it was common back then for white men to marry half- or full-blooded Indian women," he added.

The group had been riding for several hours, and Berney suggested they stop for a break. In the light of the half moon, the prairie looked dreamy and peaceful. Jerry got off his horse and spread his arms wide to catch the cool night breeze.

"What a country, huh?" Berney said to his son with a sigh. "I wouldn't want to live anywhere else but the prairies."

"I'll remind you of what you said, Dad, when it's winter and you're complaining 'bout the cold, snow, and blasted Montana weather," Jerry said with a smile as he poked his father's shoulder.

"You're right, son. This country gives both the good and the bad, but the good is so good that it makes the bad bearable." All four of them chuckled at this bit of homespun philosophy.

When they mounted up and continued on, Asa spoke up first. "Ah, let's see, where were we?" he asked. He thought for a second then said, "Oh yeah, after JB and Maria married, they built a fort at Fremont's Orchard."

"A fort? Why a fort?" asked Jerry.

"Well," Asa answered, "maybe it was more like a fortified trading post that was typical for the times, to protect them from Indian raids. There were two long buildings built parallel, with some distance between them, and a high stockade at both ends. At night, they drove the cattle and horses inside the open yard so they wouldn't be stolen. Your pa was born there, Jer, before the family came to Montana."

"Can we go back in the family a little?" asked Jerry. "Wasn't Elbridge Gerry the son of the man who signed the Declaration of Independence, Uncle Sant? Mom told me something about him."

"Yeah, the Colorado Elbridge Gerry descended from a man of the same name who signed the Declaration of Independence. He was probably the grandson of that famous patriot."

"That's keen," said Jerry.

"Yes, it is," continued Sant. "The Colorado Elbridge Gerry was born in Massachusetts and went to school there. When his father died, he went to sea briefly, and then he came west. Our pa told us that Gerry was one of the first white men to settle in this region and that he carried on trade with the Indians clear up the Powder River."

"There's a note in the Bible that says he had a whole lot of wives. A whole bunch!" Jerry said, with raised eyebrows. "Isn't that illegal?"

"Well, it's illegal now, but it wasn't back then. But I, for one, don't know how he did it. I have trouble keeping track of just one wife," said Sant jokingly.

"And I don't think I want one, not even one," exclaimed Jerry.

"Ha! Your pa'll remind you of that a few years from now when you get more interested in girls," Sant chuckled.

"I'll never be," said Jerry, unconvinced. "But really, why did he have so many wives?"

Their conversation was interrupted by a meteor shower, bright in the heavens.

"Hey! Look at that!" Jerry exclaimed as a shooting star streaked across the firmament.

"Criminy! That one even had a tail on it," added Asa.

"There's another!" said Jerry, pointing to the northern quadrant of the night sky. "They seem so close. Do they ever hit the earth?"

"Yeah, but not often," Berney said. "Down in Arizona there's a huge crater where one hit, probably millions of years ago. I saw it once when we were trailing cattle up from Mexico. It was like from here to there," Berney said, pointing to an outcropping of rock in the far distance. "But shooting stars aren't likely to hit the earth 'cause they usually burn out on the way down."

"It's really a night for them," said Sant as another shooting star crossed the sky, nearer the horizon. "Jeez, what a show!"

After watching the meteor shower for a few more minutes, Jerry wanted to get back to the topic of Elbridge Gerry.

"So how'd he have that many wives?" Jerry asked again.

"Now, here's where it gets complicated. Let's see if I can keep it straight," Asa chuckled. "As I said, back then it wasn't against the law, and there were some good reasons for a man to have more than one wife. You know, life in those days was real hard, and many women died in childbirth."

"Yeah, but I looked at the dates in the Bible, and he had a couple of wives at the same time," piped up Jerry.

"Well, there's also a custom where a white man who married an Indian woman was considered almost part of the tribe and expected to follow their tradition of having multiple wives," Berney explained.

"Let's see, I think he first married Molly Red Kettle, the daughter of Chief Red Kettle of the Sioux tribe. Your grandmother Maria was their second child. Then he married Molly's twin, Polly Red Kettle. Gerry was said to be the first white man to settle in Weld County, Colorado. Since his wives were related to strong tribes, not to mention they also were chief's daughters, he was immune from trouble with the Indians."

"That was a good plan in those days," said Sant.

Berney continued, "Then I believe he married two additional Sioux Indian twins, Minerva and Millicent Swift Bird, who were daughters of Swift Bird, a chief of the Oglala Sioux. There was also talk that Gerry married Big Woman, whose mother was a Cheyenne. It was said that he paid five ponies for her."

"Five ponies in those days was a big gift," Asa interjected.

"He wasn't a Mormon, so that wasn't his reason for having more than one wife," Berney said. "We don't know the whole story, but it was said he was good to his wives and loved by his children, and that's really saying something. You can still see his grave out on the prairie in Colorado. We saw it once as kids."

"How could he keep all those wives straight?" Jerry asked.

"I don't know, son, but it's all family lore. Your ancestors settled the West and were a part of history," Berney said.

"You know," said Asa, "there are some historians who say the Colorado Elbridge Gerry wasn't related to the man who signed the Declaration of Independence."

"That's right, but most agree we're related," answered Sant. "But you can certainly see why those upright, puritanical relatives back East might not want to claim Gerry, with the strange lifestyle he had. They looked down on all his Indian wives and preferred he not be included in their family tree."

"Do you know at one time Gerry actually was urged to leave his Indian wives and marry a white woman so he would be more accepted by Denver society? He was outraged and flatly refused, and that speaks well of the man," Berney said.

It was getting on toward one in the morning, and riders and horses alike were tired. They rode in silence for a while, either deep in their own thoughts or gazing at the prairie, dimly lit by moonlight. Berney broke the easy silence by telling them that they were over halfway to the waterhole. When he heard Jerry sigh and groan, he thought he better liven things up with more stories.

"Ha," Berney said, "here's a good story for you, Jer. I remember hearing that when your granddad hired a man, he first asked if he smoked or wore a belt."

"Why would that matter?"

"Well, he said he couldn't use a man who was either hitching up his pants or rolling a smoke because that left little time for work," Berney laughed.

"Hey, Berney, do you remember the black two- or three-year-olds the old man usually drove?" Sant said. "Those horses were half-wild and you could hear and see him coming for miles. No one else dared drive that team."

"But I remember a time, Sant, when you and Berney tried to drive those horses," teased Asa.

"We were sure dumb kids back then, weren't we?" Berney said.

"What happened, Dad?" Jerry asked.

"As I remember, we couldn't control the horses to begin with. Then to make it worse, Sant dropped the reins, so there was no hope of slowing or stopping them," Berney said.

"Whoa! We just hung on for dear life and let them horses run until they finally wore themselves out, didn't we?" said Sant.

"Yeah, what a wonder the buggy didn't turn over and we didn't break our necks. The horses finally stopped by themselves, and we both jumped out before they could start running again. Then we led them back home," said Berney with a laugh.

"I don't think Pa ever knew you took 'em, did he?" asked Asa.

"Nope, and we sure didn't tell him," Berney said, and they all laughed at the memory.

"That beats all," Jerry said.

They rode in silence until Jerry said, "Hold it, I think Buttons got a rock in his foot. Let me check."

Jerry stopped, dismounted, and picked the rock out of Buttons' hoof. The others took the opportunity to get off their horses, stretch, and drink from their canteens. Berney passed around some of Martha's Parker

House rolls, meat, and cheese. It had been awhile since dinner. They'd been riding for almost three hours, but the conversation and companionship made it go quicker. They knew they were almost there and were ready to continue.

Once on their way again, Jerry spoke up, "What brands did your dad use on horses and cattle back then?"

"Mostly the same as we still use now—the J Lazy J, the Flying O, and the J Up and J Down," Berney answered.

"I know what they call the Flying O," Jerry laughed.

"Yeah, the flying asshole, that's what it's called," Sant chuckled.

"Sant, you gotta be careful 'bout your language, especially when ladies are around," warned Berney.

"No ladies riding with us tonight," Sant said, looking around. "Nope, no ladies on this ride, so it's okay."

"Wasn't there some brand trouble at one time because it was so easy to alter the J Lazy J with a running iron?" asked Asa.

"Is a running iron that thing that can be heated, and the brand is drawn instead of stamped?" Jerry asked Asa.

"Yep, that's it. The JT brand was used on horses 'cause it couldn't be easily altered," Asa added.

"Hey! Do you two remember when Henry uncovered some horse rustling?" Berney asked.

"Didn't he go visit some neighbor and saw eight colts in his corral, and he don't own but two mares?" Asa said. "Then Henry spoke up and asked him where the colts came from, and the man couldn't look him in the eyes."

"Did they hang him as a horse thief?" Jerry asked, so wide-eyed that the whites of his eyes almost glowed in the moonlight.

"Uh, son?" Berney gulped. "No, it wasn't like that. In fact, I don't know of anyone suspected of cattle rustling ever being strung up in this county. Henry just reported it to the sheriff. I guess those 'neck tie' parties happened before we came along."

"I read a story about some of 'em once," Jerry said.

Maria Gerry Kempton.

"That's mainly what they probably were, just stories, at least around here," Berney added.

"What was Grandma Maria like?" asked Jerry.

"Well, she was a quiet woman but well-liked by ranchers and folks in Prairie County," Sant answered. "She mostly stayed on the ranch, raising all of us."

"Mother told me once that Maria didn't know how to read or write. Is that true?" asked Jerry.

"Yep, that's true, all right, but most folks never knew that 'cause she was so strong and capable. She was one of the most respected women in Prairie County," said Asa.

"Ya know, Jer, it's real nice that you call your ma 'Mother' instead of 'Ma,'" said Sant.

"Yeah, she likes that, but I call her, 'Mom,' too."

"Most of our boys wanna stay on her good side, and calling her mother seems to help," chuckled Berney. "Maybe I should try that when she's riled at me, too," he added.

"Aw," Asa laughed, "I remember a great story about Maria and JB. Pa was sometimes real absentminded, and one time after going into town, he forgot that Maria had come in with him. He set off for home, left Maria in Terry, and drove the team all the way back to the ranch. When he got home and couldn't find Maria, he finally remembered she was still in Terry. He turned around and drove the three miles back again to get her. I'll bet Ma was hopping mad, and I doubt that he ever did that again!"

Gradually there was less conversation and the four rode quietly, looking at the fantastic display of stars in the great open Montana sky.

Jerry never forgot the stars of that night, how close they seemed to earth, and the brilliance of the Milky Way as it spread across the dark arc of the heavens.

They reached the waterhole at about two in the morning, settled the horses, made a fire, and spread out their bedrolls for a few hours of sleep. Since there was little they could see of the waterhole in the dark, they planned to be up at first light to check it.

"Dad, I just wanna stay awake all night, listen to the coyotes howl to one another, and watch for more shooting stars," Jerry said quietly.

Berney put his hands on Jerry's shoulders and said, "Son, you can stay awake as long as you want." But Berney knew sleep would come quickly for the boy.

They all settled into their bedrolls and bid one another good night. "Goodnight, Uncle Asa. Goodnight, Uncle Sant. Goodnight, Dad."

There was a chorus of answers back from the three men, but soon Asa was snoring softly, Sanford was quiet, and Berney's breathing was slow and deep. And then Jerry himself was in a deep slumber. Sleep had finally come for these cowboys.

A watering hole on the Kempton Ranch.

In the light of morning, they made a quick breakfast and then checked the springs and surrounding waterhole. The area was muddy from thousands of hoofs, but after they drained off the muddy water, they watched as the water cleared. Then they brought rocks from a nearby hill and placed them close around the springs in hopes of keeping the water clearer. At last, they drank and filled their canteens for the trip home.

There was less conversation on the ride back to the ranch. Berney wondered if the light of day seemed to diminish the talk, or if it was because they were all thinking about the day's work that lay ahead. Whatever the reason, the magical spell of the previous night was broken.

When they were within sight of the ranch house, Jerry rode beside his father and said, "It was really keen learning about my relatives on the ride last night. Those were great stories. We're an amazing family, don't ya think, Dad?"

"Yep, those men and women all came up the hard way and lived the hard way too. They had a lot of common sense and integrity. They built the West," Berney responded.

"I'm real glad to have 'em in our family. I'm proud of where we came from."

"So am I, son, but we have to remember it doesn't matter where you came from. What matters most of all is where you're going. Don't forget that, Jer. Don't ever lose sight of that."

Author's note: The Flying O brand was eventually transferred and is still used by my cousin's cousin, Gary Kartevold, on his ranch out of Glendive, Montana.

THEY THOUGHT THEY HAD ME, BUT THEY WERE WRONG

"*U*sually it's the cowboy who's the hero in stories about trail drives, but in this one the real hero was the ranch owner, your granddad, JB Kempton," Berney Kempton began.

It was a quiet night on the Kempton Ranch in the fall of 1923. My father, Jerry, and his brothers cajoled their father into telling them a story after dinner. Usually there were things yet to be done, but this evening nothing was pressing. The family sat on the couches and floor of the spacious Kempton living room near the fireplace faced with petrified wood and fossil rocks.

The living room and stone fireplace at the Kempton Ranch.

"Now this is a long story, so I may need sustenance to keep up my strength. Another slice of your mother's pie might just be the ticket,"

Berney said, smacking his lips. Jerry and his younger brother Ed got up and headed to the kitchen.

"Who else wants pie?" Ed called back over his shoulder. Of course, every hand went up in unison in this large family of all boys, always hungry.

A few minutes later Ed and Jerry returned carrying trays of plates, forks, and two apple pies. Their mother, Martha, followed with a knife and pie server, ready to do business with these desserts.

After his last bite of pie, Berney began his story. "It happened in 1883, soon after JB established the Kempton Ranch."

"JB—James Berney! He's named for me, isn't he?" piped up the youngest Kempton son, Berney, Jr.

"No, he's named for me!" said Jim, the oldest boy.

"You're both wrong," interjected Berney. "You boys were named for him. He was around way before either of you were born. *You* carry *his* names, not the other way around.

"Anyway, when JB started this ranch in the early 1880s, he brought in longhorn cattle from Texas, as did most ranchers, but he also trailed herds of cattle from Oregon and Washington, and horses too. Those horses, with Morgan and Kentucky bloodlines, made this ranch famous. Sir Elmore, JB's prize stallion, is one of those, as are his offspring.

"JB also bought many of his horses in Idaho from the Nez Perce Indians, who were well known for their beautiful Appaloosas. Do you know even as far back as the time of Lewis and Clark's explorations the Nez Perce raised outstanding horses that were the source of their wealth? Why, on his return trip from the Pacific Ocean in 1806, Meriwether Lewis noted the Nez Perce had the largest horse herds on the continent. A rancher I know told me he once saw 10,000 head of prime Nez Perce horses in a meadow from where he stood on the slopes of Chief Joseph Canyon near the border of eastern Washington and Oregon. Those horses provided transportation for the Nez Perce to travel great distances to visit other tribes—they even came to this area during the time of the buffalo.

"You're all familiar with that framed photograph that hangs in the hall of our Appaloosa colts with their spotted hindquarters. Those two are some of our prime Nez Perce stock.

"When your granddad bought that herd in both Oregon and Washington to trail back here to the ranch, he

Kempton Appaloosas.

needed a crew. I'm not sure where he hired them—maybe it was Oregon, but he didn't know them beforehand. Now JB was pretty good at judging men just by talking to 'em awhile, but this time, something went wrong. Either he made bad choices or there just weren't many men to choose from. Either way, it was almost disastrous.

"About a third of the men he hired were Mexicans or blacks, and some were former slaves. JB didn't care about their skin color and was really 'color blind' in that regard. He was more interested in their ability, trustworthiness, and loyalty. He paid them all the same for what they did, plus extra for longtime service. One of the hands who proved steadfast in this story was a black man who had been with JB for about five years, even before he came to Montana from Colorado. He and another faithful ranch hand saved this cattle drive, but I don't want to get ahead of my story."

"But I thought most of the Kempton cattle were from Texas, not Oregon and Washington," Jerry said.

"You're right. The first herds JB brought in were longhorns from Texas in the early '80s, but later he favored cattle from eastern Washington, northeastern Oregon, and northern Idaho that were all called simply "Oregon cattle." The animals descended from the cattle of early American settlers who herded them along the Oregon Trail in the 1840s and '50s. They were basically English shorthorns developed by selective breeding in the late eighteenth and early nineteenth centuries. They were good milk cows, could withstand the cold, and produced excellent-quality beef, as opposed to longhorns, which were tough and stringy. Oregon cattle were easy to appreciate, and JB brought in at least two of these herds before he was forty years old.

"During this time, around 1882, the Northern Pacific Railway was being built across Montana. The land grants awarded to that railroad were incredible. I believe they got forty square miles of land to use, sell, or lease for every mile of track they laid— about 40 million acres in all. I admit much of the track was put through some real rough country, but the government sure paid a pretty penny for that line. NP finally got the track laid and had a big ceremony at Gold Creek, Montana, not far from Deer Lodge, when they joined the tracks coming from both east and west and drove in the last spike—the Golden Spike."

"Was it really a gold spike?" asked Ed. "Real gold?"

"I doubt if it was real gold, but it was still called the Golden Spike. It was said to actually be the same spike they drove when they began constructing the line in Minnesota about thirteen years earlier."

"Dad, how do you know all this?" asked Jerry, his raised eyebrows expressing skepticism.

"Son, from books. You know how much I read, and I favor U.S. history and books about wars. I guess I just retain a lot of the facts," Berney responded. (Jerry himself became a veritable library of historical facts, plus details about wars, from his own voracious reading.)

"Okay, Dad, but I don't see how the railroad figures in this story of JB driving cattle from Washington and Oregon to here," interjected Jim, the oldest son, who was often impatient to get things moving.

"Just wait, Jim. You'll find out what part that all played in my story. Hold your horses, son. Now you boys haven't been on any long cattle drives, since beef's now shipped mostly by railroad, so I'll tell you some about the men involved in a drive. In JB's day, the crew consisted of about

Keeping an eye on a cattle herd.

ten to fifteen men to herd around 3,000 head."

"One man was the trail boss, and that was JB. He scouted the route ahead, searched for water and good places to stop, and checked the terrain. Of course, there was a cook—a very important man to keep bellies full and muscles strong on the trip. The cook also doctored injuries, wrote letters for the cowboys, and sometimes even kept the money for the trail boss. He drove the chuck wagon, pulled by two to four horses. The one they used in those days is similar to the wagon we sometimes take when we spend a night or two on the prairie. It's an amazingly compact use of space—JB's cook wagon even had a folding table and a stove that could be set up on the prairie. I'm always surprised by the delicious meals a camp cook can produce from these small portable kitchens, sometimes even pies, but of course, the cooking your mother does in our kitchen here is unrivaled," Berney added, looking at his wife Martha who sat on a dining room chair crocheting a tablecloth. Martha looked up and smiled.

"Then there was the wrangler, who usually rode off to one side of the herd. He was often a young, inexperienced ranch hand in charge of feeding and watering the remuda. You've heard the term 'remuda' for the group of horses the cowboys rode. Each rider needed more than one mount for such intense work that went on for a period of weeks, sometimes even months. The wrangler also had to know which horses were ridden by which man and had to be on the lookout for injury to the animals.

"There were lead riders who stayed at the front of the herd. These were some of the most trusted men who could take responsibility on their own. If something happened while the trail boss wasn't with the herd and couldn't give orders, these experienced and capable men took over. Then came the swing riders, who were about a third of the way back in the herd, and the flankers, who rode from the middle to about two-thirds back. Last came the drag riders at the end of the pack. They had the worst job with all the dust kicked up by those thousands of hoofs. I sometimes saw 'em come back to camp at the end of the day covered with dust nearly a half inch thick. Their eyebrows and beards looked like fur. That was a hellish job, but someone had to be at the end.

"JB didn't allow no drinking, gambling, or grumbling from his crew, but as you'll hear, some of that went on with the new men. Although they all carried guns, JB discouraged indiscriminate firing, since a gunshot could stampede the herd.

"Besides herding during the day, two men were always needed at night on two-hour shifts to ride around the herd and make sure they stayed together. Those nightriders were constantly on the lookout for danger or things that could stampede the beasts. They also watched for human threats, like rustlers who wanted to take advantage of the cover of darkness.

"Often the night herders sang while they circled the herd, and I remember falling asleep to their songs when I was a young boy helping with a cattle drive. Some of 'em had great voices and some didn't, but those soothing tunes seemed to quiet the herds. When cows hear someone singing, no matter what the words or how good the voice, they seem to stay steady and calm."

"The ranch hands taught me some of their songs, Dad," said Ed.

"Well, I hope it was only the clean ones you learned, son. Sometimes your vocabulary is mighty colorful for a lad your age."

"Aw, Dad," whined Ed.

"I agree with your father," said Martha. "You need to be careful, Ed," she added, thinking of when she recently overheard her third son use phrases he picked up from the cowhands that were certainly not appropriate for a young boy from a good family. She made a mental note to ask the men to watch their language, especially around impressionable Ed.

Berney began again. "Cattle drives were dangerous for all involved, plus being extremely hard work. There was always the chance of falling sick, having an accident, or being thrown or even dragged by a horse. In earlier years, drives had to deal with angry armed settlers, who didn't want cattle crossing their land, and before that, there was the threat from hostile Indians. Rustlers also preyed on the herds. One time when JB brought cattle up from Texas, he lost a bunch of animals to rustlers who also killed one of his men. Those crooks thought taking our cows was a

Cattle at a waterhole on the Kempton Ranch.

good way to start their own herds. Moving beef on the hoof was just an all-around dangerous job.

"River crossings were another big concern, and there were multiple necessary crossings on any route. The current of a fast-flowing river could easily carry away a cow, a horse, and a rider. Even when rivers were low, the shallow bottoms sometimes hid quicksand or deep holes.

"Weather was a threat—the sun was relentless, wind was almost always present, plus a day could suddenly turn extremely cold. I recall an early snow that took us all by surprise in August. Thunderstorms were particularly dangerous out on the flat prairie. I remember one back when I was a boy. After a muggy day, dark clouds formed, thunder boomed, and lightning hit the ground all around us. Once, my hair even stood on end as a bolt struck real close. The noise was deafening.

"There were also varmints like wolves, coyotes, and even cougars that preyed on the weakest members of the herd. Rattlers were a concern, and those stupid cows sometimes ate poisonous weeds. Prairie and forest fires were also a threat, and you'll hear more about that later in this story.

"Most of the men who signed on for cattle drives were some of the best humans I ever knew. They endured months on the trail, and the work was both boring and dangerous. They sometimes stayed awake for days on end and slept in the open in all kinds of weather in just a bedroll. Their steady diet was mostly beans, biscuits, beef, and sometimes dried fruit. Camp coffee was their staple, grounds and all—really strong and awful by anyone's standards. On the trail, the men often talked about the good meals they would buy when the drive finished or the high times they planned after they collected their pay."

"Dad, is that why you always say coffee just isn't ready until the spoon stands upright in the cup all by itself?" Jerry asked jokingly.

"Yeah, Jer, that's where the phrase came from. That's exactly how JB's cook made the coffee, and we all drank it by the gallon."

"Thank goodness we do better than that with the coffee we serve in the hotel and out here," Martha said with a wink at her husband, who nodded his agreement.

"Water was sometimes scarce, and the rule was the herd watered first when we reached a source. One time I heard a man complain, 'I ain't griping, but I had to chew that water before I could swallow, and I rightly believe it was more mud than liquid.'"

"Yuck," the boys uttered, and even Martha made a face.

"The ever-present threat of a stampede was always a concern when herding cattle. Cows can begin running for almost no reason, and you don't wanna to be in the way of all those hoofs and heavy bodies. Longhorns were more prone to this, but those Oregon cows could also take off. Stampedes could start from anything unusual that scared the cows. Often it was just an innocent thing like a horse whinnying or shaking, a tumbleweed blowing into the herd, even the striking of a match during the quiet of night. Those dumb creatures spooked at the weirdest things, and when a stampede started, it was extremely dangerous and hard to stop. Anyone not on a moving horse in the path of those cattle was like a sitting duck. Galloping at top speed, the cowboys attempted to get to the front of the herd and turn it into itself, like in a big circle. We called it 'milling.' Sometimes they just let 'em run until they were done in and then rounded 'em back up, but a stampede could end miles from camp. And when they stampeded in the dark, each man just hoped he would live to see sunrise. Unfortunately, some didn't. When you're running full out on a horse and neither of you can see the terrain, it's like suicide.

"I remember my first stampede when I was a boy. I heard a low rumble from the cows, and no one had to tell me what it was—I just knew immediately. Fortunately, I was already on my horse, and I rode like hell to get out of the way. I knew if I fell in front of the herd, that would be the end—there was no doubt. I came to an area of big rocks and small trees and the cows parted and went around. I took shelter there and remember feeling like a coward because I didn't help stop the animals, but hours later when JB found me, he grabbed me up and hugged the breath outta me. I could see tears streaking down the dust on his face. We lost a man during that stampede, and they wouldn't let me look at his body. One cowboy told me there wasn't much left except bloody pulp."

"Now, Berney, don't give the boys nightmares!" Martha said with concern.

"Nah, tell us more about it, Dad," Jim urged his father. "I wanna know more."

Berney noticed a warning glance from his wife and decided to temper his vivid descriptions and continue the story. He knew not to cross Martha when she wore that look.

"Enough about stampedes. Things went well at first. The weather was clear, and they made good time. But after some days, JB noticed several new men talking quietly in a group, glancing around to make sure no one else was listening. He tucked that fact away and kept watch for any other indications that things were not right. Several days later, the cook overheard some griping and suggested one of the drag riders seemed to be stirring up trouble.

"That man's name was Hugh Danvers. JB thought he was okay when he hired him, but as the days went on, Hugh showed he had a big chip on his shoulder. Whether it was wanting a larger portion of beans or the best spot to lay his bedroll, he seemed to think he was entitled to more. Now when a drive's in progress, the boss just can't ride to a nearby town and hire more men because there weren't any nearby towns, so JB hoped he could make it with Hugh.

"JB was a good man to work for. He paid well and was more than fair to his cowhands, but this group seemed to be strongly influenced by Hugh. At night when Hugh and another cowboy took their turns riding around the herd, JB noticed there was a lot of interaction when the two men's routes overlapped, but these chats ended abruptly when he came near. As time passed, JB could feel the growing tension, and decided to confront Hugh about it.

"One morning at sunup, JB took his coffee and went over to where Hugh was still bedded down. He shook the sleeping man awake and said they needed to talk. Hugh crawled out of his bedroll, stood and stretched, then followed JB a ways. The old man was a smart boss. By waking Hugh from a sound sleep, JB already had the upper hand in any conversation that would take place. He often used this same technique with us kids. We would wake up with JB sitting beside us on our beds, wanting to chat. To be roused from sleep with him parked beside you, alert and wide awake, while you're still groggy and half-asleep . . . why you might promise him almost anything.

"JB asked Hugh what was going on, why he seemed so hostile and was stirring up contention. At first, Hugh denied the accusations, but after more questioning, Hugh admitted he was sick and tired of riding drag and had not signed on to do that. JB retorted that he told the men when he hired them that this would be a hard, dirty job and that they might well find themselves eating the dust of the herd. Hugh responded they should get more money to do that. JB said he had clearly stated what he would pay before they agreed to work for him. Hugh looked at his boss with a shrug and said, 'Well, you just may want to reconsider.' Then he turned to walk back to camp. JB would have pushed him for more, but just then one of the horses in the remuda spooked and ran right into camp, knocking over the coffee pot and the Dutch oven, full of biscuits baking. All the men ran to help catch that crazy horse, so there was no further conversation, and Hugh stayed as far from JB as he could that day.

"The herd traveled about twelve miles a day, and they were now in the mountains of Idaho near Lolo Pass in some pretty rough country. JB noticed increasingly hostile stares and whispers and attempted to talk to the men, but they were a closed bunch. That night when they bedded down, JB slept near his two trusted men. He tucked his pistol under his bedroll and urged them to do the same.

"Long before daybreak, JB quietly got up and walked to the remuda. About half the men carried rifles on their saddles, and they all wore six-shooters. He quietly slipped their rifles from the saddle holders, carried them like cordwood, and carefully stashed them away behind a log. He kept his own rifle with him within easy reach when he returned to camp.

"When daylight came, the hostility was mighty oppressive, and JB knew something was about to happen. After eating biscuits and gravy and downing cups of coffee, the men stayed around camp, furtively looking toward Hugh. Slowly Hugh stood up, became the center of attention, and, in silence, walked toward JB. All eyes were on the two as this tableau unfolded.

"Hugh began, 'We been thinking about this and talking it over. You ain't paying us near enough for this work, and we aim to strike! We're all gonna leave you right here, JB, unless you increase our pay another $20 each. If you don't agree, we're taking one horse each and cutting outta here this morning. You don't got much choice as we see it, Mr. Kempton, if you wanna get this herd to Montana. I'm thinking we got you over a barrel this time, boss! We got you!' he said. There was a heavy silence.

"'Well, let me think on that,' JB said, just as cool as a running stream. Then he turned toward the chuck wagon, picked up his long gun and cocked it. The cook told me later he saw the burn creep up JB's neck until his face was bright scarlet, but his speech remained calm and measured. I won't repeat what that man said, but it was plenty strong and not too nice. He looked like he was gonna blow his stack."

"I'll bet I know what he told 'em," said Ed, "but I better not say it in front of Mom."

Martha's brow furrowed as she looked up from her work and stared at her middle child, once again concerned about his foul language. What were they going to do about Ed's swearing?

"Yeah, JB was rightfully furious. He slowly looked at each man in turn, holding his gaze, until most of 'em hung their heads low. Both his loyal fellows, the cook and the point man, moved closer to their boss, holding their pistols level and cocked. JB walked over to the chuck wagon, took a small key from a hook hidden behind a cupboard, and opened a locked drawer. He pulled out a thick wad of cash and said, 'I'm gonna pay off you sons of bitches right here and now, minus what you would've got for completing the drive. We'll also be taking your pistols, and I already have your rifles in case you were thinking of looking for 'em.'

"After that heated speech, JB's glance went from the men to Hugh's face, just waiting to see if any in the group dared draw their pistols while he and his two men had their weapons trained on them. It was a silent standoff with both sides exchanging angry glares. JB said he never forgot the bravery of his two men, standing beside him, ready to back him up should any shooting begin.

"The tension broke when the first man put up his hands in surrender then took his gun from the holster and handed it butt-first to the cook. The others saw they had no choice and followed. JB peeled off bills from his roll of money and thrust the cash at each man.

'If you ever get back this way again, you can pick up your firearms from the sheriff in Miles City. But I doubt you'll be back 'cause word spreads about traitors like you. Around here, we'll remember who you are, you damn vermin!'"

Martha looked up from her crocheting again and said, "Why Berney, the worst I ever heard your father say about a person he strongly disliked was that they were a poor excuse for a human being."

"Yeah, Martha, but this time was different, and he said a lot more, I can assure you! Then JB told them to clear out within five minutes or he would start shooting. He warned that if they came back or bedeviled the herd they would be shot on sight. A number of the group realized their miscalculation and would have gladly relented, but JB didn't give them the chance. He couldn't trust 'em, and within five minutes, the whole bunch slunk away, headed back west. JB was left that morning with just two men and about 3,000 head of cattle.

"JB just sat there, his head in his hands, assessing the situation and thinking about the route ahead. He well knew he could lose the entire herd. Finally, he said, 'You know, boys, if we three can drive 'em just another few miles, we'd be in that narrow pass. I think you'd have a good chance of holdin' 'em there while I ride into Missoula and hire more men. What'd you think?'

"His men agreed it might work and suggested the remuda of remaining horses would probably just follow the herd. One man said he got a glimpse of the pass in the distance the previous day and noticed there was a large forest fire burn ahead that was mostly out, but the ground was still smoking.

"The three decided holding the herd in the pass was their best chance to keep the animals together. Actually, it was their only option. Worried the disgruntled men might return, JB suggested they all carry both pistols and rifles, and keep a wary eye out for trouble. They knew they were facing several days without sleep, but they had done that before and would certainly do it again.

"'Those blasted skunks to leave us here. Maybe I should have shot 'em,' JB muttered to himself as he filled his canteen with camp coffee, took a few biscuits and dried beef, and shoved that in his saddlebag. He folded the remaining cash and put it in a leather pouch at the bottom of the other saddlebag. He thanked his two men, shook their hands, and promised there would be a big bonus at the end of the drive. JB was beholden to those good men who remained loyal to him. And you know what? They stayed with him for years and years, even beyond his death. They could have lived on the ranch all their lives, but when JB died in 1910, they lost heart and decided to move on."

"Was the black man 'Old William'?" asked Jerry. "I remember hearing about him."

"And I bet the other man was Toby, wasn't he?" said Jim. "I heard about him too."

"You're both right. Old William and Toby were first-rate men. Eventually, JB offered to set 'em up on their own places, but they wanted to work for him at the home ranch instead."

"I remember Toby also did a lot of the finish work when the hotel was built too," said Martha.

"Then what happened, Dad?" Jim asked. "Did JB get more men in Missoula to move the cows?"

"Yeah, he did, Jim. He rode hard the forty miles from Lolo Pass into Missoula, and when he got to town, he put out the word. There was no lack of men looking for work, so he quickly had his crew. He started back as soon as he could, worried how his men and the herd were faring."

"Did the bad guys try to come back while JB was gone?" asked Ed. "Did they ever have a big gunfight?"

"You know, son, gunfights are not good. They're not like in the books. In real life, someone almost always gets hurt or killed. Gunfights are to be avoided, but to answer your question, they might have tried to come back that first night. Toby said he heard noises when he stopped at the chuck wagon to make a pot of coffee after midnight. Remember, JB took guns from those men, and they probably presumed he had stashed them in the chuck wagon. Instead, he put them in the packs of several horses in the remuda, but when Toby got out the coffee, he noticed someone had been rummaging around in the chuck wagon and thought the noise he first heard was likely that person running off. He thought about emptying his six-shooter somewhere in that direction but knew the shots might spook the cattle. Almost certainly it was one of those men, but thankfully that was the only incident.

"When JB returned, he found the cows spread out across the forest fire burn but still pretty much contained in the pass by his two men alone. Many animals were footsore from the still-warm burn, but other than that, they were in good shape. After dinner, JB sat thinking of his next move.

"'That's it,' he said excitedly as he stood up and slapped his knee. 'We'll ship those cows on the train! Why can't we do just that?'

"One of the new men from Missoula said cattle hadn't yet been shipped, since the rail line was so new.

"'Well, then, Kempton cattle will be the first livestock to ride on the Northern Pacific. Yes, the first herd! We'll put those sore-footed beasts on the train at Missoula, ship 'em to Miles City, put 'em in a feedlot for a few days of rest, and then drive 'em the rest of the way to the ranch. Ha! Those damn scoundrels! They thought they had me.' Then the old man got a hard look in his eyes and repeated, 'But they were wrong! Yes, they were wrong!'

"So that's the story of how Kempton cattle had the distinction of being the very first herds ever shipped on the Northern Pacific Railway! Too bad we didn't take a snapshot of 'em loading onto makeshift ramps into the cars and coming off at Miles City, but we did take one when we finally got the herd to the ranch.

Kempton cattle.

"So that's how it all happened, boys!"

There was a chorus of "Tell us more. More!" from the children.

"Nope, that's all there is to tell. That's it," said Berney.

"Well, bravo!" Jerry and his brothers hooted as they stood cheering. "Bravo for JB Kempton!"

"Good story, dear! Good story, but I think it's time these young men were in bed," Martha suggested.

"Yeah, it is. You heard what your mother said. Off to bed, all of you. Now scoot, boys!"

Martha and Berney watched their sons climb the stairs to their rooms. Would any of these young men follow them into ranching? They were proud of their boys and wondered what the years ahead held for this new generation of the Kempton family. If the past was any indication of future success, their sons would do just fine in life.

THE WAGER FOR CLOVER

artha Kempton was a lucky woman. All her life—even from childhood—she could look at a patch of common clover and pick out a lucky one with four leaves. Even during the dark years after her parents died and she ended up in an orphanage in Norway, she still sometimes found lucky clover.

During those grim times, when good fortune wasn't evident, she figured she was building up a bank of good luck for some later time. She found that to be true when she immigrated to America, came to Montana, fell in love, and finally found happiness. As a co-owner of the largest horse and cattle ranch in eastern Montana as well as a popular hotel and restaurant in nearby Terry, she knew life had turned lucky.

Martha Kempton, my grandmother, always had a touch of magic. After Berney passed away in 1942, she often visited us in Alaska. In the summer, we watched in awe as she plucked out four-leaf clovers from the garden, smiling mysteriously.

"One leaf for faith," she told us, "one leaf for home. One is for love, and the last leaf is for luck," she added as she presented us with the lucky clover. "One of you grandchildren will someday inherit this magic," she promised us.

Four-leaf clover.
COURTESY OF JOE PAPP, CC BY-SA 3.0.

I was the lucky one to inherit her extraordinary ability. One summer soon after Grandma Kempton returned to Montana, while helping my father, Jerry, weed an overgrown raspberry patch behind our garage, I began to find one four-leaf clover after another. My father, weeding in that same spot, couldn't find any. That magical afternoon, I found forty-one four-leaf clovers, seven five-leaf clovers, and even one with six leaves. What an awesome discovery! I pressed them between pages of a heavy book and gave some to family and friends. I believe I still have a few from that auspicious day, but I can't remember which book they're in. Perhaps someone will open that volume someday, find the pressed clovers, and wonder where they came from.

My ten-year-old granddaughter, Annika, now seems to be next in line for her great-great-grandmother Kempton's magic, as she now finds lucky clovers on her school playground. She gives them to friends and classmates and presses them between her math papers.

During her lifetime, Martha Kempton's clover magic was usually reserved for friends and family, but one summer her special ability was put to the test when the Kempton Ranch was visited by an English earl.

The Kempton Ranch was well known for the variety of horses they trained for multiple uses. The U.S. Army bought hundreds as excellent warhorses for their cavalry. Percherons (large but gentle workhorses) were purchased by farmers for plowing before tractors were common. There were also Thoroughbreds sired by "Sir Elmore"—JB Kempton's famous horse—that were trained for the steeplechase and the racetrack.

The Kempton Ranch was also renowned for its excellent polo ponies. These horses were some of the best in the world, and gentry from the British Isles often traveled to Montana just to buy these special ponies. The horses were then shipped east by rail to steamship ports and loaded on ships bound for England.

Polo ponies required the ability to run close to other horses and be attentive, alert, nimble enough to make quick, tight turns, and of good temperament. Berney Kempton and some of the ranch hands broke suitable, gentle range horses and conducted extensive training, which took more

Ed Kempton with his trick pony.

than a year to complete. These animals were called ponies, not due to their size but because of their agility and good temperaments. The famous prairie photographer Evelyn Cameron and her husband, Ewen, good friends to two generations of the Kempton family, came to Prairie County hoping to raise polo ponies, and at one time there was even a polo club in Miles City. Both those ventures were short-lived, and Cameron was forced to turn to photography to support herself and her husband.

The wealthy English nobility who came to Montana to purchase polo ponies often stayed at the Kempton Hotel in Terry. Some opted to stay out at the Kempton Ranch, and a few even took part in ranch life for a change of pace.

One such man, the English Earl William of Chambers, was a favorite visitor who came to Montana almost every summer. Although the earl stood as tall as Berney, he carried more weight. He was a friendly person with a round, clean-shaven, sunburned face. Despite his tremendous wealth, the earl was a down-to-earth fellow in his late forties who loved ranch life. He wore a flat cap made of wool herringbone, more common in the English countryside than on the Montana prairie. Berney often offered him a cowboy hat that was better suited for the hot Montana sun, but he liked his flat cap.

The Earl of Chambers was a strong, excellent rider who even helped with roundups and brandings, all without a complaint, no matter how hard the work. In the evenings, he told the children stories about life on his country estate in England, the fox-hunting parties with the baying hounds running ahead, the antics of his nephews, and the grand dances his sister often arranged and expected him to attend.

"I do believe my sister's trying very hard to get me married. Why, this spring she even brought a friend of hers from London to stay several weeks on our estate. I knew very well exactly what my sister was doing. She hoped I would fall in love with this city-bred beauty. The woman was indeed beautiful and cultured, but when I took her out to the stable, she wrinkled up her nose at the smell of hay and horse manure. She didn't want to know anything about our horses, and then she stepped in a fresh pile, shrieked, and hobbled back to the house on one foot. I guess I should have been more of a gentleman and helped her clean off her little boot, but I was too busy laughing. That's not the kind of life partner I want, for sure! My sister just wants to clip my wings, so I'll settle down

Berney with Earl William of Chambers.

on the estate. Never! Life is just too much fun, and I'll always want to spend summers here in Montana," he stated, to the laughter of the family.

"Blimey, I should've been born a cowboy!" his voice boomed most mornings as he arose early and came downstairs for breakfast. "I do love your Montana prairies!" he added as Martha handed him his usual cup of tea. "I envy you this life, my dear."

Berney overheard this conversation and said, "Chambers, there are a few days, especially during winter storms, when I would easily trade places with you! Just come around then, when it's forty degrees below zero and the snow's blowing sideways, with no break in sight! We'll see if you still want to switch!"

One afternoon during his annual visit, the earl and Berney relaxed outdoors over a game of chess when the topic of luck came up.

"Talk about good fortune! Martha is one of the luckiest people in all Prairie County. I tell you, that woman can find four-leaf clover any time she's in the garden. She just reaches down and plucks them out."

"How can that be? Such good luck charms are rare. I haven't found one in all my years," the earl retorted.

"It's true, Martha finds them at will," Berney bragged. "All the time."

"Truly, she can? Oh, I doubt that," said the earl with a dubious look.

"I'll show you. Let's find Martha and put her to the test," Berney said with a hearty laugh.

The men searched the house and finally located Martha in the vegetable garden near the house, gathering carrots for the evening dinner.

"Martha, can you help us settle a disagreement about luck?" asked Berney.

Martha looked up with interest.

"Yes, your husband tells me you can find four-leaf clover anytime you want, and I don't believe that's possible," the earl said.

"Oh, do you mean like this?" Martha asked as she picked a four-leaf clover out of the weeds attached to the carrots that she had just pulled from the ground.

"Why, that takes the biscuit! I can't believe my eyes!" said the earl as he looked in disbelief at the clover Martha handed him. "One, two, three, four leaves. Indeed, a four-leaf clover it is. Indeed!"

"Yes, it is," said Berney proudly, putting his arm around his wife. Martha just smiled.

"Let me have a look at these," the earl said as he examined the remnants of clover plants pulled up with the carrots Martha was still holding. "None here." Then he looked at the weeds growing between the rows of vegetables and especially at the clover. "And none here either, but this is right in the spot where you found it."

"Yes, it is," Martha smiled and nodded. "I seem to have mystical abilities."

"Let me see," said Berney, kneeling over the plants and looking carefully. "Well, I don't see any either."

"Martha," the earl said, "I think it was just a fortuitous accident that you found that single lucky clover. In fact, I'll bet you $50 that you can't find another one like that in under a minute."

"You ought to raise that to $100 if she can find three in that time," Berney jokingly suggested.

"Why, I heartily concur," said the earl as he looked at Martha, who became more and more amused with her husband and their special guest.

"Oh, for goodness sake!" Martha laughed. "I'd be glad to find you a four-leaf clover for free anytime you want, sir."

"No, no, I insist on a wager. I will even time you for one minute," Chambers said, taking out his gold pocket watch.

By this time, the children and some of the ranch hands had gathered to see what was going on in the garden. They laughed about the wager because they knew from past experience that Martha had the gift.

Ranch foreman Jeff Dixon, who was bringing over a polo pony to show the earl how its training was coming, also got in on the debate. "I suggest she be held to finding four, at the least," he said jokingly with a smile at Martha, who nodded in agreement.

"Well, then, if you insist," Martha said, putting the carrots she was holding down on the lawn.

The earl looked at his watch, raised his arm in the air, and gave the signal.

First Martha looked down again at the clover growing between the radishes and said, "Oh, there's the first one, and another," as she quickly pulled out two lucky clovers. She moved closer to the row of carrots, bent, and said, "Now, here's number three and four, and one more for good measure."

To outdo herself, within the minute's allotted time, she found a fifth four-leaf clover and then a rare one with five leaves, to boot.

"Here are your clovers, sir," Martha said as she smiled, curtsied dramatically, and handed the lucky clovers to the earl, who stood dumbfounded. "I don't believe it, even though I saw it with my very own eyes!"

Then the earl walked to the rows of carrots, looked down, but found nothing but regular clover with three leaves. He moved to the row of radishes and stared at the greenery, combing through the plants and separating the leaves. No four-leaf clover.

Now even the children and ranch hands squatted and peered into the rows to see if they could find a lucky one.

After a few minutes of hunting, Jerry spoke up. "Mother, I think you got them all. It's no fair. You found all of them, so there's no chance for us now!"

"Oh, my poor Jerry, here, let me help you, dear one," said Martha with mock sympathy as she reached down and found two more four-leaf clovers right where Jerry just looked. "Here you go, son," she said, presenting them to Jerry, who threw up his hands in good-natured defeat. No one else found any lucky clover, although they looked carefully in the very same spots where Martha had found so many.

"Martha, my dear, how do you do it?" the earl asked, shaking his head.

"Why, sir, I think it must be a rare gift of magic I possess," said Martha with a mysterious smile, all the while thinking to herself that it was simply the ability to look at patterns and distinguish differences.

That evening, after he finished his second helping of a delicious chicken dinner with all the trimmings, Earl William of Chambers stood and with a flourish silenced the crowd.

He proposed a toast. "To our hostess, Mrs. Martha Kempton, the luckiest woman in all of Montana! Maybe even the luckiest in all of America."

Then he dramatically pulled a crisp $100 bill from his breast pocket and waved it around. As the diners applauded, Martha put down the pie she was serving and walked to the front of the room where the earl stood. "Oh, please, there's no need to pay me. It was my pleasure," she said graciously.

"No, no, I insist you take it," the earl declared, putting the bill in her hand. "It was a wager, fair and square." (At that time in the early 1920s, $100 was equivalent to more than $1,000 in today's cash.)

The Earl of Chambers stayed at the ranch for several more weeks, during which time he spent far more than the wager to purchase a number of choice polo ponies. He also bought several offspring from JB Kempton's own magnificent Thoroughbred stallion, Sir Elmore.

JB Kempton with Sir Elmore.

Although JB was no longer alive, Berney continued to breed and train these horses.

Toward summer's end, the earl decided he should return home to England. He wondered how many ladies his sister had lined up for him to escort to the fall series of dances and parties. Once Martha overheard the earl asking Berney if there were any eligible women in Prairie County who were smart, unattached, could ride a horse, and cook like Martha. Berney laughed and said he got the last of those uncommonly wonderful women when he married Martha.

When the earl and his horses finally boarded the train for the first leg of their trip to the East Coast, Berney, Martha, and Jerry saw him off at the station. As Berney shook hands with the earl, Martha happened to look at some weeds growing between the boards of the railroad platform. She bent down, picked a four-leaf clover, and showed it to the earl. Then she slipped it in the buttonhole of his lapel and patted him on the arm.

"To give you much good fortune on your trip home," Martha said with a smile. "And may you return soon."

"Martha, you are one lucky woman," boomed the earl as he stepped up into the first-class passenger car.

Oh, yes, I am a lucky woman," Martha answered, linking arms with her husband and her son. "Oh, yes, I am."

HOW BUTTONS
GOT HIS NAME

he Kempton Ranch was famous for its excellent horses, with herds numbering more than 5,000 at one time. In the 1880s, when JB Kempton first established the ranch near the small town of Terry in eastern Montana, he brought along a number of his horses from Colorado. Among them were early Morgans and Kentucky-bred animals, originally from Oregon. He later purchased Appaloosas from the Nez Perce tribe in Idaho and also imported fourteen Percheron studs from France and England.

Some of the horses on the ranch were originally wild mustangs running free on the prairie. The term "running free" sounds romantic,

Horses on the Kempton Ranch.
PHOTOGRAPH BY L. A. HUFFMAN, KEMPTON FAMILY COLLECTION.

but the reality for a wild horse on the Montana plains was far different—
it meant frequent starvation, thirst, the intense cold of winter, and the
constant threat of attack by cougars and wolves. Life for a wild horse was
not good, and most lived longer and fared far better on the ranch.

Feeding so many horses was challenging, and JB, the family patriarch, showed great foresight by being one of the first ranchers who also
farmed. He planted and harvested hay and other crops for his herds so
they didn't depend solely on prairie grass.

JB's oldest son (my grandfather), Berney Kempton, was known for
his special way with horses. It was said he "spoke their language," and
there wasn't a horse Berney couldn't soothe and ride within minutes.
When the famed Doctor Carver interviewed on the Standing Rock
Lakota Sioux Reservation for potential members for his Wild West
Show, Berney found a wild mustang and rode the animal bareback into
the saloon where Carver sat. Berney stopped directly in front of
the stunned man, turned
the horse, and rode back
out—without a word—to
the awe of the crowd. He
was hired on the spot and
became Doctor Carver's
star rider and roper. While
the show was in Russia,
Berney subdued a wild
Cossack horse from the
steppes that had thrown
off an entire regiment of
cavalry. When he suc-
cessfully rode this beast
into the ring, the Dow-
ager Empress of Russia
was amazed that this tall,

A Kempton Ranch cowboy on a bucking bronc.

lean cowboy from America had done what her trained riders could not do.

Another man who worked on the ranch, known as the Florida Cowboy, was also an expert at breaking and training the most difficult animals. Florida stayed for many years and was one of the favorite ranch hands. (The story of his special Christmas gifts starts on page 130.)

Berney Kempton and his father before him, along with their natural affinity for horses, also had a reputation for treating their stock humanely. Any ranch hand who was cruel or unnecessarily harsh with a horse or cow received but one warning. Any hint of further problems earned an immediate firing. Even during procedures like castration and branding, the animals were treated well.

Jerry was particularly fond of a photo of his father, neighboring ranchers, and cowhands standing around a horse that was down and trussed (perhaps for branding). One man gently cradled the horse's head.

When Jerry was just a boy, a special horse came into his life. That day, the cowhands had rounded up a bunch of wild horses from the hills that were near starvation. In this herd was a small palomino colt they said was the ugliest horse they had ever seen. Its eyes were two different colors, its coat a dirty tan. Its dingy mane was missing hair, and the little beast had a number of unhealed scabs on its stick-thin legs where other horses had kicked it. The little fellow was in extremely poor shape when he joined the Kempton herds.

When Jerry first saw this misfit, the colt was trying to escape from the corral that fenced the new horses. Although the others had quieted, this one was frantic to get out. He ran back and forth along the fence, trying to find a way out of the enclosure, and this riled the other horses. The ranch hands talked about letting the colt go back to the wild. They didn't think he was worth their effort to break and train.

Jerry, who often felt an affinity for the outcast or runt of a litter, spoke up for the colt. Recently, he had hand-fed the tiniest cat in a brood of ten kittens. That cat, now a family favorite, would not have survived without Jerry's attention. Now, seeing this unfortunate colt, the boy asked the ranch hands to keep the little animal. After some arguing, they finally agreed to let the horse stay, at least temporarily, just to humor Jerry.

After dinner that night, Jerry took a few sugar cubes and headed to the corral where the little horse stood by himself, apart from the others. Jerry stood quietly for a long time outside the fence, then slowly held out his hand, thinking he could understand what the little horse was thinking and how terrified he was.

Softly he said, "Come here little guy. Here's some sugar. Come on, easy, easy now. Bet you want this, but you're scared. Bad day for you, huh? Did they take you away from your ma?" Jerry murmured.

The horse ventured closer, then turned and galloped away.

Jerry didn't give up. "Hey, little fella, here's some sugar."

This time the colt sidled over, snatched the cube from Jerry's hand, then turned and ran. While he was close, Jerry could see the many open sores on his little legs.

"Hey, fella, we gotta get you outta there. You're gettin' hurt."

The colt whinnied and came closer to Jerry again.

"Now that's it. Come here. You're scared, but I won't hurt ya. In fact, I want you for my own."

The horse stood and looked at Jerry, almost as if he understood what the boy was saying.

The Florida Cowboy, one of Jerry's favorite ranch hands, came up to the fence, looked at the colt, and said, "That little guy's not doing good, if you ask me."

"Do you think we could put him somewhere safe, maybe in the barn? I really like him."

"Well, maybe," Florida drawled. "How 'bout you talk to Jeff 'bout that, son?"

A few minutes later, Jerry found the ranch foreman, Jeff Dixon, in the bunkhouse. After some pleading, Jerry convinced him to separate the colt from the other horses. Jeff didn't have much sympathy after all the trouble this animal had caused, but he loved Jerry like a son and saw how earnest he was with this request. Jeff agreed to have the cowboys separate the little horse in the morning and put him in a stall in the barn by himself. As he left, Jerry gave Jeff a quick hug, and Jeff found himself returning the hug and giving the boy a pat on the back.

Jeff had grown to love all the Kemptons, but it hadn't always been that way. He thought back to the time he first came to the Kempton Ranch. Until then, life had been very hard—he'd been in and out of trouble, and he didn't think he could ever trust or feel affection for anyone. Berney Kempton took a gamble when he offered Jeff a job as a ranch hand. Although Berney knew of Jeff's dubious history, he looked beyond that, seeing something worthwhile. His gamble paid off—Jeff was a dependable worker who soon became a top-notch foreman, trusted to be in charge of the ranch when Berney was away. Jeff knew all this happened because Berney gave him a chance.

The next morning, when the ranch hands tried to separate the colt from the others, things went bad. The little colt annoyed the other horses, who were now settled down and enjoying the abundant hay and water not available in the wild. When the little one was cornered, he ran into the middle of the herd, and it took several tries to get him into a stall in the barn. That horse was nothing but trouble. When Jerry came home from school that afternoon, several ranch hands told him they thought the horse was just no good.

Jerry knew the ranch existed because of the hundreds of horses rounded up, broke, trained, and sold. He knew how much intense year-round work this was for his father and the ranch hands, and there was little time to spend on just one horse. He decided he would train this horse himself and sought out his mother for advice.

"Mom, they still wanna let the horse go 'cause he's getting the others riled. Even Jeff sort of agrees with 'em, but I really wanna keep him. What should I do?"

"You're not sure what to do?" Martha questioned.

"Yeah, I think he'll be a good horse, even with the trouble he's caused, and I want him to stay."

"Well, son, there's your answer," said Martha, thinking to herself, *If I remember, it was the same when Jeff first came here. No other ranchers would give him a job, but Berney saw qualities in Jeff that others didn't recognize, and Berney gave him a chance. What a success that's been. Jeff's like a member of the family, and I don't know what we would do without him. Thank goodness Berney acted on his instinct.*

Turning back to Jerry, she said, "Gerald O'Meagher, now listen. If you really want to keep the horse, speak up and tell them firmly how important he is to you. You must see something in that little animal that others don't."

"I think he's worth it and wanna train him. I think he'll be good. But we gotta keep him away from the others. Okay, I'll tell 'em I want to keep him for sure! Thanks, Mother, you always know the right thing to say."

"Ah Jer, I think you knew what to do, and you would have done it, even without my help," said Martha as she handed her son a warm cinnamon roll spread with butter.

With renewed resolve, Jerry went to the barn to tell the men this horse would stay. Several of them shook their heads and grumbled but said they would go along with Jerry's request.

Jerry looked at the horse and then cautiously went into his stall to muck it out. He avoided getting in a position where the horse could kick him, but the animal made no move and seemed to like Jerry's company. Jerry kept up a running commentary about what he was doing, and the horse perked up his ears.

"Okay, boy, let's clean this place out," Jerry said in a quiet, even tone as he shoveled manure into a wheelbarrow. "I think you like having me here, don't ya? And I think you understand what I'm saying."

"Ya know, Jerry," said Florida, who was nearby in the barn, "I reckon that animal knows what you're saying. Horses ain't just dumb animals. That one perked up when you came near."

"Yeah, I think we kinda understand each other. Could that be?" Jerry asked.

"It sure could," said Florida. "You know the book your pa read to all of us the other night—the one L. A. Huffman gave him? Well, Huffman underlined a passage about horses and riders. I borrowed the book from your pa, and if you think you'll be okay here by yourself, I'll get it and read you some."

"Yeah, we're good here. I'd like to hear it," Jerry answered as Florida headed for the bunkhouse.

A few minutes later, Florida returned carrying a small book that looked well-read.

He thumbed through it then said, "Here it is. Did you know your pa and Huffman worked together on roundups and were good friends? Why, Berney often posed for his photographs."

"I didn't know that. Huffman was famous, wasn't he?" Jerry asked.

"Yes, indeed. And your pa was also a model for other early Montana artists. When you see a broom tail, it's probably your pa on the horse. Berney's a handsome cuss." (A "broom tail" is a horse tail cut straight across—like the bottom of a broom. Berney cut most of his horses' tails this way.)

Turning back to the book, Florida said, "Here's the part Huffman underlined for your pa. He also wrote that he remembered many good times they shared.

"Okay, son, here's what it says about a man, or you know, it could be a boy, and his horse:

> How close, how intimate is the comradeship between a man and his favourite horse. It is a silent, comprehensive friendship, an intercourse beyond the need of words. They drink at the same way-side springs, and sleep under the same guardian stars. They are conscious together of the subduing spell of nightfall and the quickening joy of daybreak. The master shares his meal with his hungry companion, and feels the soft, moist lips caressing the palm of his hand as they close over the morsel of bread. In the gray dawn he is roused from his bivouac by the

gentle stir of a warm, sweet breath over his sleeping face, and looks up into the eyes of his faithful fellow-traveller, ready and waiting for the toil of the day. Surely, unless he is a pagan and an unbeliever, by whatever name he calls upon his God, he will thank Him for this voiceless sympathy, this dumb affection, and his morning prayer will embrace a double blessing— God bless us both, and keep our feet from falling and our souls from death!

Jerry listened intently to the description of a human-equine relationship. "Jeepers, Florida, that's really nifty! Thanks!"

"Sure, son. That's what I feel with Miami. She's the best horse I've ever had, bar none."

After a few days in the stall with good food and time to heal, the little horse looked better. Part of the healthy look to his coat was from Jerry's brushing.

"You like that, don'cha, little fella?" Jerry said quietly, running the curry comb in circles along the horse's back. "And it makes you look so good."

The horse tossed its head and nickered.

"You know what I'm sayin', don't you?" Jerry asked with a grin. As he put away the comb, the horse nuzzled the boy to show he wanted more.

"Ah, I gotta go. Chores to do. You're not the only animal on this ranch, ya know," Jerry said. As he walked away, the horse continued to whinny.

Some of the ranch hands still teased Jerry about the horse.

"Hey, kid, that animal looks better, but he's still no beauty," Joe hollered one day as Jerry led the horse into the ring.

"I gotta admit, that little beast can't no longer hold the title of Ugliest Horse in Montana," teased Jeff.

That night Berney talked to his son about training the horse. "It's about time, son, but you gotta have a name for him, not just 'that little horse.'"

"Yeah, Dad, I know. I tried a few, but none fit. Maybe Oats, Peaches, Sunny-Side-Up, and we'll call him Sunny. How about Goldheart, Sunset,

Pal, or Buddy? Maybe Ghost, Arrow, Phantom? At least no one can call him ugly anymore."

"How about Ginger or maybe Blondie?" Berney suggested.

"Hm, maybe," Jerry said, thinking to himself that none of the suggestions sounded right.

Soon the training began. First Jerry slipped a halter over the colt's head as it ate an apple. The colt didn't seem to mind. Then he led the horse around the corral.

"Hey, not too bad, Jer," said the Florida Cowboy, leaning against the fence and watching. "Let's put a blanket on him and see if he tolerates that."

Florida also suggested Jerry get the horse used to having his feet picked up so he could be shod. Together they worked on that for several evenings until the little horse was comfortable with a bridle and blanket and having his hooves lifted.

The training progressed, and Jerry thought the little horse was actually trying to please him by doing what he asked. He knew horses were submissive herd animals, but he had never seen an animal so in tune with its rider. After training sessions, Jerry fed the horse an apple, and often the animal laid his head on Jerry's shoulder, looking eye to eye. Gazing into the depths of those big, dark eyes, sometimes Jerry wondered if he was peering directly into the horse's soul. Finally, when the equine head got too heavy, Jerry had to end the love session.

One evening, Jerry asked his dad to help him saddle the horse for the first time. As soon as the saddle was on and the animal felt the unaccustomed weight, it bucked and shied but soon quieted. Berney led him to the fence, and Jerry climbed on. The horse bucked again. Jerry wondered how long he could stay in the saddle, but after two bucks, the animal calmed, standing quietly with Jerry on his back.

Berney said, "Son, I'm impressed. That horse has come a long ways, but we can't just call him 'horse.' He needs a real name."

"Yeah, Dad, I'm working on that. I really am."

Horses in the Kempton Ranch corrals.

The colt's training continued during the next months. Sometimes when the ranch hands saw Jerry on the colt they still ribbed him, but they agreed the little horse looked decidedly better. In fact, they said he looked pretty good for such a hideous horse.

A season passed and the colt proved trustworthy and friendly. There was a special bond between the boy and his horse, and even the toughest ranch hands softened when they saw the growing colt put his head on Jerry's shoulder, standing eye to eye.

Jerry took the horse for short rides, but the animal's easy gait and good behavior showed he was ready for longer outings. Jerry's younger brother Ed planned to go with him one afternoon but came down with a fever and was confined to bed. Jerry decided to take the little horse out by himself.

The afternoon was clear and mild when they left the ranch. Since Jerry was in the middle of reading *Treasure Island,* he stowed the book in his saddlebag, hoping to have time to read.

All went well, and Jerry stopped midday when he was hungry. He tied the horse on a long lead so the animal could graze and then settled down to eat and read. He held up part of his sandwich, and the horse gently took it from him, reminding Jerry of the description Florida had read about a horse's soft lips gently taking a morsel of bread from an outstretched palm. Like the rider in that story, he really did love this horse and thought the affection was returned.

Some time later, when he was in an exciting part of the story, Jerry noticed the sun had moved behind the hills. He was unsure of the time but knew he should be heading home. He untied the horse, but instead of putting the book in his saddlebag, he decided to read as he rode. He knew this wasn't a wise idea but couldn't bear to quit reading.

The little horse was perfectly behaved, and his smooth walk made it easy for Jerry to read in the saddle. He finished the exciting part of the book but was still reading when the path entered a stand of black cottonwood trees by the Yellowstone River. Jerry easily cleared the low branches, but he was so engrossed in his book he didn't see a large, partially broken limb hanging down. It caught him on the head, knocking him from the horse. Jerry saw stars as he landed. He lay there for a minute, stunned. When he finally sat up, he felt something wet on his head, brushed his hand across his forehead, and saw blood.

The horse stopped, walked back to Jerry, nickered softly, and stood close. Jerry mopped his head with his bandana. He felt lightheaded but wasn't sure if it was from the blow or the sight of blood. He had trouble standing, held onto the horse, and finally pulled himself up and climbed into the saddle. He remembered hearing that scalp cuts bleed profusely. He felt dizzy and tried to hold onto the horse's neck and stay in the saddle. He gently squeezed with his legs to signal the horse to go but did nothing else to direct the animal as it headed home at a slow walk.

At one point on the trip back to the ranch, Jerry felt woozy, and his vision got dark. He leaned to the side of the saddle, almost falling from the horse. He felt the animal slow its steps and try to offset the imbalance. Jerry struggled to sit upright but ended up slumped over the front of the saddle on the horse's neck. He gripped the mane as the horse slowly continued home.

The ranch hands, working in the corral, saw Jerry and his horse return. Florida immediately knew something was wrong, saw the blood, and ran to help Jerry off the horse.

"Be careful now. Let's get him inside to Mrs. K.," he said to the others.

They cautiously lifted Jerry from the saddle and carried him into the kitchen. When Martha took one look, she told Florida to ride for Doc Bennett.

As she cleaned blood off his face, Jerry groaned, "I was reading and caught a branch. I think I dropped the book back there."

"Don't worry about the book, son, I'm just glad the horse brought you home."

"My head hurts bad. Did the horse really bring me home?" moaned Jerry.

"Yes, he did," answered his mother. "Bless that little animal!"

By this time, several of the men came in the house to see if they could help.

"Where's my horse?" Jerry groaned.

"We put him in the barn with an extra measure of grain," one of the ranch hands answered, wincing when he saw the cut on Jerry's scalp. "He's one good horse," he added.

Doc Bennett came and looked Jerry over. It took six stitches to close the cut, but he didn't think Jerry even had a concussion. He said the boy had a hard head and pronounced him okay but advised bed rest for the remainder of the day.

When Berney and Jeff returned home that evening from Glendive, they heard the story of Jerry's injury and amazing trip back to the ranch.

As they looked in on the patient to find out the details, Jeff quipped, "I knew all along that horse was a good one. I'm glad I suggested we keep him!"

Berney added, "Yes, Jer, we foresaw that animal's true value the minute we laid eyes on him. We knew he was a 'keeper.' But son, you gotta give him a name."

Jerry started to shake his head and remind the two men they had favored releasing the horse because they thought he was so ugly, but it hurt when he moved his head.

Instead, he muttered, "Yeah, I'll find him a good name."

The next week, while Jerry trained the horse in the ring, Martha came out to watch. She stood by the fence, looking at the horse and her young son. *What a nice match they are,* she thought. *It's good Jerry spoke up for that little horse.*

Jerry rode over to her and said, "He's a pretty good horse, don'cha think?"

"Yes, son, he looks almost handsome."

Jerry looked at his mother thoughtfully and said, "Remember that story you used to read us when we were little 'bout the ugly duckling that became a beautiful swan? I think that's kinda like what happened here—he grew from ugly to beautiful."

Martha laughed and said, "Well, Jerry, when you believe in someone or even an animal and look for the best, you usually find it, even though it may be hidden from others."

"Yeah, I knew he'd be good."

"You had faith in him from the beginning, and it paid off. You worked hard to bring out his good qualities," she said. "He's a good one, and we'll always be grateful he brought you home after that fall."

"Yeah, but now I gotta find him a good name," Jerry said, dismounting and leading the horse closer to Martha.

The horse whinnied gently and turned toward the boy, nuzzling his chest and pulling at the buttons on his shirt pocket for the sugar cubes Jerry usually kept there.

"Aha!" laughed Martha. "That's why I've been sewing so many of your buttons lately. The horse is pulling them off!"

"Yeah, oh, golly, that's it!" exclaimed Jerry. "Let's call him Buttons. Yeah, Buttons!"

"Good choice," Martha chuckled. "Yes, Buttons is perfect. But I'll have to teach you to sew on your own buttons if he keeps pulling them off." They laughed.

Martha hugged her son and patted Buttons' neck. Smiling, she walked back to the house. *Life is good. Yes, it is good,* she thought.

Author's note: Of the 5,000 horses on the Kempton Ranch, some became polo ponies, others were trained for the steeplechase, and still others became racehorses. Many mounts were sold to both the U.S. and British armies during World War I and the Boer War. Large Percherons were raised as workhorses. Of all those horses, however, this golden palomino, which had such a rough start, was my father's favorite, and when Dad talked about his childhood on the ranch, he often mentioned Buttons and how he got his name.

ENCOUNTERS
WITH RATTLESNAKES

*I*n eastern Montana, the locals knew to be wary of rattlesnakes. Jerry, Pansy, and Gray Hawk were especially careful since all of them had previously suffered unpleasant encounters with these dangerous, slithery creatures.

Pansy was the first to notice a rattlesnake coiled in the corner of the school cloakroom, right under her coat hook. When she hung up her coat after lunch, she saw something on the floor. She was about to kick it aside, thinking it was a brown boot, when it moved! The little kids shrieked and cowered, and the older students offered to kill the creature, but Miss Susan Phillips, their teacher, bravely dispatched it with a long-handled shovel.

Then there was the night Gray Hawk slept out on the prairie with his uncles. He was tired after a long day of hunting and neglected to shake out his bedroll. When he crawled in, he found he was sharing his blankets with a snake. Fortunately, the rattlesnake was just as surprised to find it had a sleeping partner, and it slithered off quickly without incident. Gray Hawk never forgot to check again, and sometimes he even looked two or three times before turning in—just for good measure.

Jerry's own encounter happened when he and his brother Ed were climbing the rimrocks, racing to see who could get to the top first. Jerry was just about to put his hand on a ledge above his head to pull himself up when Ed, who was higher on the rocks, looked back to see if Jerry was gaining on him. Ed saw a large rattler basking in the sun on the rock Jerry was about to grab as a handhold. Ed hollered, *"Snake!"* and Jerry froze with his hand in midair, then carefully backed down the rocks. From then on, no matter what the hurry, Jerry always looked before putting his hand down.

The bite from a large rattler could be fatal since antitoxin to rattlesnake venom was not yet available, but most snakebite victims still lived to tell about it. One of the favorite Kempton ranch hands, the Florida Cowboy, was working alone when a rattler bit him on the wrist. He was tugging a rotten fencepost out of a large clump of grass and didn't see the snake coiled there until it was too late. Usually, snakebite victims should move as little as possible, but Florida had to get on his horse and ride back to the ranch for help. He was in bad shape when he got there, and the poor man came close to dying. Staying still was not always an option in eastern Montana in the 1920s, where people often worked alone and long distances from help.

Together, Jerry, Pansy, and Gray Hawk had a very serious incident with a rattler that actually began two weeks before the afternoon of the event. That summer, Berney's brother Asa and his young sons Harold and Allen stayed for several weeks at the home ranch outside Terry. Neither of the young boys got on well with the other kids—Harold was a bully, and Allen, a nice kid, usually hung out with Harold.

The only thing Jerry and Harold had in common was an interest in collecting arrowheads. Harold even brought his collection to the ranch so he could compare it to Jerry's. It turned out Jerry had more arrowheads. During Harold's visit, however, four of the choicest points somehow disappeared.

Jerry complained to his mother, but it did little good.

"You know, son, I found your collection scattered all over in a corner of the living room," she said. "It could be some of it just got lost."

"No, Mom, I put it all away later that night. It was just out for a while. I think Harold took some of 'em," Jerry said, exasperated.

"I know it hasn't been easy having the boys here, but we can't go around accusing someone of taking something without proof."

"But I'm pretty sure," Jerry argued. "Four of my best arrowheads are gone. Besides, Jim even saw Harold looking around in my closet when I wasn't home."

"Perhaps, but we don't know for sure. Remember Harold is part of the family. How about if you put your collection in the bottom of my closet, under my shoes, for a week or so? It should be safe there."

"Yeah, maybe I better put all my stuff there, huh?" Jerry mumbled as he left the room.

The next day, Harold showed Jerry a handful of snake rattles. "Look how many I got. My pa killed a snake yesterday and gave me this big one," he added as he held up a large rattle with bloody skin still attached.

"Gee whiz, that's a really huge one," Jerry admitted.

"Yeah, but look here," Harold said, pulling a piece of black velvet from his pocket and spreading it on the grass.

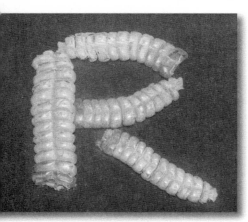

Rattles spell R.

"See how these four rattles make the letter R? I'm gonna get a bunch more so I can spell out the whole word, R-A-T-T-L-E-S-N-A-K-E. I might just kill 'em myself . . . maybe."

"Better be careful," Jerry said, thinking it was far safer to collect arrowheads or agates.

While the boys talked, they noticed Pansy walking toward the reservoir. She sat under the shade of a small tree, facing away from the water, opened a book, and began to write. Jerry recognized the book as her diary.

With a wicked smile, Harold said, "Hey, watch! I got an idea that'll make Pansy jump. It'll be so funny."

"Whatcha gonna do?" Jerry asked. Harold was known to often play tricks that exceeded the bounds of humor.

"Just watch," Harold replied as he pulled the rattles from his pocket.

"You're not gonna hurt her, are you?" asked Jerry.

"Naw, 'course not," Harold sneered. "Why? Is she your girlfriend?"

"No, just a friend. Actually more like a sister," Jerry replied defensively.

"Okay, whatever you say," Harold scoffed, walking toward Pansy.

Before Jerry realized what was happening, Harold said, "Pansy! There's a big rattlesnake moving toward you from the side. Don't look, 'cause he's kind of behind you. Just stand up, and back away!" Harold started shaking the rattles in his hand.

Pansy immediately stood up and stepped backward, toward the muddy edge of the reservoir, her face pale with fear. She backed away several more steps from where she thought the snake was. On the fifth step, she tripped over a muddy branch and fell backward into the mire with a splat. Still thinking there was a snake coming toward her, she pushed with her feet to get farther away from the threat, going deeper into the mud. Her backside and legs were covered in sticky brown goo, and it had splashed on her shirt and face.

Harold hooted with laughter. "Ha ha, Pansy, I got ya! It's a joke. Just a joke! Look here," he said, holding up the rattles and shaking them.

Pansy looked so funny sitting in the mud that both Allen and Jerry laughed too, even though they knew this had been a dirty trick, in more ways than one. Jerry quickly stifled his laughter and went to help Pansy up.

Pansy burst into tears and pushed Jerry's hand away. Now furious, she pulled herself up and waded out of the muck. Then, unexpectedly, she reached down, grabbed the branch she tripped on, and whacked Harold with it. She hit him a good one, then aimed for Jerry and Allen, who both quickly moved out of reach.

"Whoa, Pansy. Don't hit me! I told him not to," Jerry said. "I'm sorry I laughed, but you looked so funny."

Both Harold and Allen took off running. Jerry reached down, picked up Pansy's mud-covered diary, and handed it to her.

"Come on, I'll help clean you off," he offered.

Pansy, with tears running down her dirty cheeks, rebuffed Jerry's offer of help and stomped off toward the house. Jerry went after her, but she avoided him and said, "Don't you dare come near me. I hate you, Jerry. I hate Harold and Allen, and I'm gonna tell on all of you."

Not surprisingly, a few minutes later Martha stormed out of the house straight for Jerry, who was still wiping mud off Pansy's diary.

"Where are your cousins, young man? You find them right now and come back here, and if there's any delay, it'll be worse for all of you."

Jerry saw fire in his mother's eyes and knew this was no time for explanations. He turned and headed to the barn to find Harold and Allen.

Soon the three boys came back, heads down.

"They did it, Aunt Martha," Harold said, pointing to his younger brother and Jerry. Allen spoke up. "No, Harold was the one."

Jerry thought it best to keep quiet.

"Well, you'll all three be punished. What a terrible thing to do to poor Pansy! I'm ashamed of all of you, especially you, Jerry," Martha said, her hands on her hips. "You three get out to the barn and start mucking out stalls, every single stall. Your fathers will be out later to deal with you. Now go!"

About a half hour later, Berney and Asa came out to the barn. Berney's face was dark with anger, but Jerry knew any physical punishment wouldn't equal the regret he felt for not stopping Harold's dirty trick.

"Gerald," his father began, ominously using Jerry's given name. "Pansy told me you and Allen were not directly involved in this mean trick of Harold's, but you might have stopped it, and you certainly did not have to laugh at your friend."

"I know that, Dad, and I'm sorry," Jerry replied.

All three boys were punished. Harold and Allen apologized to Pansy that evening, and Jerry talked to her as soon as he went back in the house. Pansy realized Jerry actually had little to do with this incident and forgave him.

Harold and Allen left the ranch a week later to return home, but the memory of that mean joke still stung Pansy.

Several weeks later, Jerry, Gray Hawk, and Pansy decided to hunt for arrowheads at the Powder River. The morning they started out, the ranch foreman, Jeff Dixon, cinched their saddles tight and warned them,

"Now, be watchful. Rattlers are particularly aggressive 'bout now 'cause they've just given birth to live young."

"Don't worry," said Gray Hawk. "I'm bringing my slingshot along. I'm getting pretty good with my aim."

"Nah, you kids just stay away from any snakes, you hear me?" Jeff said sternly.

As they left the corral, Tucker, the family dog, ran from the house barking excitedly, eager to go with them.

"Maybe you should take him along," suggested Jeff.

"Nah, he just digs wherever we're looking, and we can't find anything after he's messed stuff up," answered Jerry.

"You stay home, boy," Pansy said. "I'll throw a stick for you when we get back."

Tucker woofed in response.

"Okay, Tucker," Jeff said, grabbing the dog's collar and leading him into the barn. "You come with me. Good boy."

When the children reached the nearby Powder River, they dismounted, left their horses to graze, and walked toward the river's edge.

"My father once told me this is where our people lived for many summers," said Gray Hawk. "They camped by the river and hunted animals that came to drink," he added, glancing at the large old cottonwoods growing at the shallow river's edge. "It was a place of peace and plenty."

"Yeah, I wouldn't mind living here all summer, either," said Jerry.

Pansy looked at the river and said, "Let's ask if we could camp here sometime. That'd be fun."

"Yeah, it would be, but how about now? Where should we start looking today?" Jerry asked.

"Your dad said to check the front side of a bend 'cause that's where arrowheads might settle," Pansy said.

"Okay, let's look over there," suggested Jerry, pointing toward a promising bend in the river.

Pansy found the first arrowhead, and then Gray Hawk discovered two nice ones. Jerry came across one made of agate that still had its sharp point. The children unearthed a few more, then for the next hour they found nothing.

"I think we got 'em all," Gray Hawk said.

"How 'bout if we pry up that flat rock over there?" said Jerry. "Maybe there's more under it."

Pansy wrinkled her nose and said, "Yuck! What else lives under there? Scorpions, spiders, snakes, centipedes?"

"You don't hafta help, but we're gonna try," said Gray Hawk.

The boys found a thick branch by the river's edge and dragged it back to use as a lever. They put one end under the rock and heaved.

"Eesh, look at that!" Pansy hollered as a seven-inch centipede darted out to seek other shelter. "It has a thousand legs. Yuck!"

They stood back to allow other displaced creatures to escape, then tried again. Finally, after multiple attempts, the large rock flipped and settled. They waited a minute and then poked in the damp sand for arrowheads. They found a treasure trove of good ones and congratulated themselves on moving the rock.

As they carefully wrapped their arrowheads in soft cotton to put in their packs, Jerry saw a flash of black, heard a bark, and was practically bowled over when Tucker jumped on him, licking his face.

"Tucker! How'd you get out here? Did you follow us, boy?" Jerry asked as he scratched the dog's ears.

"How'd he know we were here?" Pansy asked.

"Dogs have a great sense of smell. He probably got away from Jeff and followed our scent all the way here," Jerry explained. "Good dog, you can stay."

Tucker wagged his tail, woofed, and went to Pansy and Gray Hawk for more petting.

They had been at the river for several hours, and now the sun was directly overhead.

"I'm gettin' hot. Let's find some shade and eat," Pansy suggested.

They sat beside a pile of large upright rocks that afforded some shade and unpacked the food. As they ate, they threw bites of bread to Tucker, who gratefully gobbled down the scraps. Then the dog lay down in the shade to rest.

The children usually showed their finds to Jerry's dad when they got home since Berney knew a lot about the ancient people who once roamed the prairies. He told them most of the arrowheads found in their part of Montana were from the late prehistoric era, before the early plains Indians had horses. Once he showed them how to make arrowheads by chipping off pieces of rock to create a sharp edge.

The previous summer, Berney took his sons, Pansy, and Gray Hawk to the site of an ancient buffalo jump, where they found numerous arrowheads mixed in with very old buffalo bones. Berney explained how early Indian hunters had herded buffalo on the plateau above toward the cliff's edge, where the hapless animals jumped and died. Then the tribes harvested the meat and hides from the dead animals at the bottom of the steep rock face. They used arrows fitted with sharpened rock arrowheads or spears to finish off any animals still alive. Berney told them some of the arrowheads these early Indians left behind were beautifully shaped works of agate, flint, volcanic obsidian, or chert.

While they were eating, Gray Hawk pointed to a large, upended rock covered with ancient petroglyphs. "Look at that rock," he said. "It's got lots of stuff on it."

"Golly, I can see a snake and an antelope," said Jerry. "But what are those things?"

"It looks like an eagle, a person, and another snake," suggested Pansy as she squinted at the petroglyphs.

"I wonder what the people were like who lived here and did that," Jerry said.

"Probably they were here before white men came to America," suggested Gray Hawk.

"Gee whiz, that stuff is really old," said Jerry. Looking at the river, he added, "You wanna look for more arrowheads?"

Pansy, sitting with her back against a large upright boulder, yawned and said, "Not me. I'm tired of looking. I wanna rest before we go back."

"I'll help you, Jer. Let's keep on," Gray Hawk said.

"Okay, Pansy, wait for us right here," Jerry said. "We'll take Tucker."

But when they called for the dog, he didn't come, and he was nowhere to be seen.

"That's okay," said Jerry. "He's probably out exploring somewhere, and he'll be back."

Pansy stretched, yawned, and soon fell asleep while the boys continued to search for arrowheads. After a fruitless half hour, they agreed to settle for what they had, picked up their arrowheads, and walked back to Pansy, speculating about how much money they could make if they sold them to the Mercantile. Mr. Stith, the proprietor, often bought arrowheads and then sold them to visitors who wanted an authentic souvenir.

As they came back in sight of Pansy, Jerry grabbed Gray Hawk's arm and pointed. "Oh jeez! Look!" he said, his voice trembling.

Right above the sleeping girl, a large rattlesnake crawled over the rock to a flat place, just a few feet above Pansy's head. She snoozed away unaware of this threat, and the snake took little notice of her as it slithered closer.

"What'll we do?" asked Jerry.

"If we holler and she wakes up, the snake might bite her," said Gray Hawk.

"What're we gonna do?" whispered Jerry.

"I know!" said Gray Hawk, remembering the small slingshot he carried in one of his pockets.

He pulled out this rawhide and wood weapon, reached down for a handful of pebbles, fitted one in place, pulled back, and let the rock fly. The first one hit harmlessly above the snake. Gray Hawk quickly shot another rock that found a mark closer, dislodging a shower of little

A prairie rattlesnake.
PHOTO BY BETH WATERBURY.

pebbles onto the snake and Pansy below. The snake quickly retreated out of sight.

Pansy awoke to find her friends pelting her with rocks from a sling-shot. Then, because they didn't know where the snake had gone, the boys grabbed Pansy and roughly pulled her down from the rock onto the sand.

Pansy was furious. "What're you doing? Why'd you pull me down? Why'd you throw rocks! We're not supposed to throw rocks and you know it!"

"Pansy, there was a snake right by you!" Jerry said, pointing to the place where the snake had been.

"Snake? There's no snake! Is this another trick? You promised you wouldn't do that again, Jerry. You promised!"

"No, Pansy, there really was a snake, a big rattler," said Gray Hawk.

"Oh, yeah? You're just foolin'. Where's the snake now, if there ever was one?" Pansy retorted as she brushed sand off her pants.

The rattlesnake was nowhere to be seen, and there was no evidence it had ever been there.

"Pansy, there really was a snake," said Jerry sincerely. "Really and truly! I'll swear on a Bible."

"I don't believe you," Pansy scoffed. "You're makin' it up."

"Pansy, there truly was a snake, and Gray Hawk probably saved your life. You gotta believe us," Jerry pleaded.

"Liar, liar, pants on fire! I don't believe either of you, and I'm going home. I think it was just another trick," Pansy fumed, stalking to her horse. "I'm leaving, right now."

"Will she be okay alone?" Gray Hawk asked, looking at Pansy's retreating figure.

"Yeah, she'll be fine. She knows the way," Jerry said. "But I hate that she doesn't believe us. How can we convince her?"

The boys sat silently for a few minutes, mulling over the situation. Finally, Jerry spoke up. "I got an idea. How 'bout if we get the snake outta his hole, kill him, and take him home to show Pansy?" he suggested with a bravado he didn't really feel.

"Yeah, well, we could," Gray Hawk said. "Then maybe she'll believe us, but, uh, Jer, have you ever really killed a snake before?"

"Uh, not exactly, but I've seen Dad and Jeff kill lots of them. I don't think it's too hard. I wouldn't mind killing a snake 'cause they're kinda like horse flies—nobody cares 'bout ending their lives. But we gotta use a long stick so the snake can't get us," Jerry said.

"My people use a forked stick to hold down the snake and another to kill it," said Gray Hawk.

"Okay, let's look for somethin' like that," Jerry agreed.

The boys walked down the bank to the Powder looking for the sticks they needed. They easily found a long, thick limb, then saw a forked branch on a sandbar in the river.

Jerry took off his clothes and waded in. "It feels really good after being so hot. Come on in."

The boys swam around and waded out to get the long, forked stick. Tucker, finally back from his explorations, joined them in the water. The dog paddled around, barked, and chased bubbles. When the boys waded ashore, Tucker followed, shaking his wet coat all over them.

They intended to put their clothes back on once they were out of the river, but before they had a chance, Gray Hawk saw the snake had come out of his hiding place and was again slithering across the rocks.

"Quick, let's get him now, Jer! He's outta the rocks."

They grabbed the sticks and crept quietly toward the rock pile, climbing closer to the resting snake. When they got into position, Jerry aimed his forked branch, intending to pin down the snake, so Gray Hawk could kill it with his stick.

The snake somehow sensed danger and quickly slithered back between the rocks.

"Aw, we lost him!" Jerry moaned. "How'd he know we were here?"

"Maybe he saw our shadows," suggested Gray Hawk.

"For cryin' out loud, now he's gone again!" said Jerry.

"Maybe not," replied Gray Hawk. "Maybe we can still get him." He shoved his pole into the hole where the snake disappeared. Jerry did the same.

Seconds later, Tucker barked and ran toward them, climbing the rocks, growling frantically.

"Back! Get outta here, Tucker!" Jerry hollered. "You'll scare it!"

But Tucker wouldn't back away, and when Jerry looked down where the dog was focused, he saw the snake, right there, near their bare feet, coiled and ready to strike! The rattler must have crawled out the back door of his den to escape. As Tucker continued to bark and lunge at the snake, the boys backed down the rocks to safety. They hollered for Tucker to come, but the dog continued to face off with the snake, barking and snarling.

Gray Hawk ran for his clothes, pulled the slingshot out of his pants, grabbed a handful of rocks, and aimed for the snake. Luckily, the first rock hit the rattler's triangular head, stunning the creature. The boys continued hitting the creature, finally finishing it off, although it still moved for a time, even after it was dead.

Tucker bounded toward the boys, yipping and wagging his tail. Jerry hugged him and said, "Tucker, you probably saved our lives!"

"That's one brave dog," Gray Hawk laughed as Tucker licked his face and rolled over on his back wanting his stomach scratched.

"Let's get outta here," Jerry said, putting on his clothes, socks, and boots.

"What're we gonna put the snake in to take him home?" Gray Hawk asked. "He's kinda bloody."

"I got a burlap sack we can use, but let's make sure he's dead before we shove him in," advised Jerry.

The boys dragged the dead snake down to the river, swishing him around to clean off the blood. Then they stuffed his body in the burlap sack, and Jerry tied it on the back of his saddle.

"We better get home," Jerry said, looking at the lowering sun. He whistled for Tucker, and the three started off. They arrived back at the ranch just before sunset.

"Maybe we shouldn't show the snake to any of the grownups 'cause they'll just worry how we killed it," suggested Jerry.

"Yeah, it sure worried me," replied Gray Hawk. "Let's just show it to Pansy and then dump it up in the hills somewhere after dark. I don't want to save the rattle. That's disgusting."

The boys found Pansy making cookies with her mother. Mrs. McMillan smiled and handed the boys each several cookies, still warm from the oven. Pansy just glared at them.

"Pansy, we got something we wanna show you," Jerry told her quietly.

"Don't want to see it," she answered in a low voice so her mother wouldn't hear.

"Pansy," whispered Gray Hawk between bites of cookie, "you gotta come 'cause it's the snake we told you about."

"The snake?" Pansy asked, motioning for the boys to come out on the porch, away from her mother's hearing.

Outside, Jerry said, "Yeah, we got the snake that almost got you. We killed him, and he's out back of the barn in a bag."

"Yeah, come look," said Gray Hawk.

Pansy was now curious.

"You really killed that rattlesnake?" she asked. "Really?"

"Yeah! Come see for yourself," Jerry said as he stepped off the porch and walked toward the barn.

Gray Hawk followed. Pansy took off her apron and hollered to tell her mother she would be back in a minute.

"That's fine, dear, you run along and play," Mrs. McMillan called.

Jerry led the way to the shed behind the barn, went inside, and came out with a bulging burlap sack. He held the bag open and said, "This is it! It's the snake we told you about," he said, dumping it out on the shed floor.

"Yeah, the one you said wasn't there," added Gray Hawk, looking at the bloody body.

Pansy stepped closer, cautiously peered at the dead snake, and stammered, "You guys? There really was a snake coming for me? And you went back after I left and killed it?" she asked with a shudder.

"Yeah, how else could we get you to believe us? Gosh, we tried everything," said Jerry, putting on a hurt look to elicit sympathy from Pansy.

"So it really was true. I thought it was a trick," Pansy said in a small voice, her eyes downcast.

"Don't you remember? When Harold played that mean trick, I promised you I wouldn't ever do anything like that," Jerry reminded her. "You didn't believe me, did you?"

"We even offered to swear on the Bible," added Gray Hawk.

Pansy looked at the boys and said, "I'm sorry. I should've believed you. If that snake got you, it woulda been partly my fault."

"Nah, I wouldn't say that, Pansy, 'cause we didn't have to go after it. Oh, and we decided it's better not to tell any grownups 'bout this 'cause they'd just worry," Jerry added.

"I won't say a thing," Pansy said. "I hope we can be friends again." She looked at the boys imploringly and began to cry.

"Aw, Pansy, we didn't mean to make you cry. We just wanted you to see the snake," said Gray Hawk.

"Yeah," Jerry echoed. "Don't cry, Pansy. Let's just go inside and forget about all this. Maybe we can sneak some cookies before dinner. Okay?"

"Okay," Pansy replied.

"You bet," Gray Hawk chimed in.

The three friends went back to the kitchen and soon came out with their hands full of cookies. All was forgiven.

Tucker ran up to the kids, who fed him bites of cookie when he showed off his tricks.

"One trick we won't let him show again is how he protects people from snakes!" Jerry exclaimed. The three kids laughed and wrestled with Tucker, who wagged his tail and tried to lick their faces.

BABBY AND THE COYOTE TAILS

*A*sa Kempton, a younger brother of ranch owner Berney Kempton, was staying on the home ranch that summer with his wife, two boys, a little girl, and an infant daughter. Their newborn came earlier than expected, and doctors thought she would have a better chance at life if the family temporarily moved from their isolated ranch near Morristown, South Dakota, to be closer to medical care. Asa, Effie, and their children stayed in one of the houses beyond the reservoir and ate meals in the ranch house with the rest of the Kemptons and the ranch hands.

Their little girl, Barbara, nicknamed "Babby," just six years old, was tiny and thin but very bright for her age. She often played with Pansy, who was four years older, and sometimes with Jerry. Her own brothers, Harold, who was twelve, and Allen, a ten-year-old, rarely included her in their activities unless they needed her for something or wanted to play a trick on her. Even so, Babby adored her big brothers and rarely tattled on them. Fortunately, Allen, the younger boy, was protective of Babby, and he often talked Harold out of situations that might have harmed her. Neither Harold nor Allen got along well with the other children on the ranch and kept mostly to themselves. As long as they were home for dinner, their parents didn't question their activities, many of which were mischievous, and some downright bad.

About this time, the Montana Wildlife agent in Miles City put out the word that the coyote bounty had been increased to $1 per animal. To claim the bounty, ranchers had only to bring in the animal's tail as proof of its death.

Most ranchers favored reduction of coyotes because these predators were one of the primary causes of death of their young stock. The only thing that claimed more foals, calves, and lambs was harsh weather. Coyotes killed to eat, killed to teach their pups how to hunt, and also sometimes wantonly killed seemingly just for the pleasure. Ranchers agreed the only good coyote was a dead one.

Coyote.
PHOTOGRAPH BY JACOB W. FRANK, NATIONAL PARK SERVICE.

The Kempton boys—Berney, Asa, Sanford, Joe, Jim, and Henry— now adult men with children of their own, remembered how in past years they had often roped coyotes, and sometimes wolves, on the prairie and led them home to be killed and skinned. They would then tan the pelts. Coyotes were so hated, most ranchers simply destroyed them and left the carcasses where they fell, thinking the pelts were not worth the trouble.

After dinner one evening, Allen and Harold overheard the men discussing the recent bounty increase on coyotes. This was exciting news because only a few days earlier, the boys found a coyote den up in the rocks, not far from the ranch. That day, they watched the mother and her eight little kits play in the grass before she took them back inside the den and then left to go hunting. Harold suggested they take the kits and sell them, but the large rocks forming the den entrance were too close together. They could hear the pups inside, squeaking and whining, but couldn't reach them. They finally gave up, but the bigger bounty renewed their resolve. It also made the job far easier since they could just kill the animals, keep their tails, and collect the reward. They had to find a way into that den. Eight whole dollars was a lot of money!

Coyote pups.

Harold came up with the idea.

"Let's bring Babby up there. She's small enough we can push her in the hole. She can grab the pups and hand 'em out," he said, pleased with his plan.

"Nah, she might get hurt or get stuck in there," said Allen.

"Aw, jeez, Allen, you worry too much. She won't get hurt, and it's plenty big enough for her. We'll just wait 'til the mother's gone hunting and push Babby in. She'll be fine."

"It's not a good idea," said Allen nervously.

"Come on, Allen. She won't get hurt, and you know she loves doin' things with us. It'll be fun for her to come, and she'll be fine."

"Um, I dunno 'bout that," Allen said, still not convinced.

"It'll be easy," said Harold, "and we'll make good dough from each one." With a gleam in his eyes, he continued, "We'll tell Babby we're getting 'em out so she can choose one to keep—you know, kinda like a dog."

"She'd really go for that," Allen said, considering the money and beginning to warm to the plan.

"Yeah," said Harold, thinking ahead. "When we get 'em out, we'll put 'em in a burlap bag and bring 'em down here. We'll knock 'em off when Babby's not around. Remember, all we gotta have for that bounty is just the tail."

"What if she asks what happened to 'em?" Allen asked.

"Easy. Are you stupid? Just tell her they got out and ran away."

"You sure it'll be okay and Babby won't get hurt?"

"Yeah, no one's gonna get hurt—well, except those coyotes. Ha ha! Okay, let's offer to play with Babby tomorrow to get her outta Ma's hair, and then we'll take her up to the den. Okay?"

It was agreed.

The next afternoon, Harold and Allen told their mother they'd take Babby for a ride in the wagon. Effie was surprised they wanted to spend time with their little sister, but being glad for the break, she didn't ask many questions. The boys hitched up the wagon and found a burlap sack and a big stick. They put it all in the back of the wagon along with several large rocks in case the stick wasn't sufficiently lethal.

They found Babby playing dolls with Pansy McMillan near the ranch house. Pansy asked to come along, but the boys knew she would see what was afoot, so they said she could come another day.

"Babby," began Harold in a sweet voice, "we found a coyote den in the rimrocks and wanna show you. Maybe, honey, you can help us get the pups out so you can see 'em."

"Oh, can I have one for a pet?" Babby asked, remembering the pet coyotes she had seen recently when she, her mother, and Martha Kempton had called on Lady Evelyn Cameron, the famed Montana photographer.

Cameron, a neighbor and friend, kept several young coyotes as pets at her ranch. During their visit, she showed them to the little girl. Babby was enchanted and had been asking her mother if she could have one too. Effie's response was always a resounding, "No!"

"Now I'll get one all my own to play with and take care of," Babby said with a giggle.

"We'll see. Now, don't tell Ma about this," Harold advised. "She's so busy with the baby, we don't wanna bother her. Besides, if she finds out, she might not let you have one. Now go in the house and change into overalls," Harold added.

Babby jumped up and down with glee and ran into the house to change, pulling off her dress as she went, all the while imagining cute little coyote pups. As she came out and started around the corner, she heard Harold say, "Yeah, we'll just hit 'em over the head."

What? she thought as she stopped short before the boys saw her. *Why would they want to hit the baby coyotes over the head? That's not nice.*

She quickly stepped back out of sight and stood for a second, thinking. Then she heard the boys calling her, and she went around the house the other way to where they were waiting with the wagon.

"Come on, sweetheart. I'll help you up," Allen said, lifting Babby into the wagon.

As they started off, Babby again thought, *Why would they do that to the coyotes? Maybe I didn't hear right. Maybe they were talking about something else. Harold's being really nice to me today, so probably he just wants to show me the baby coyotes.*

When the three of them reached the rimrocks, they left the wagon on the flat and climbed up to the den. Allen helped his little sister and then held her on his lap as they sat quietly some distance from the den, watching for the mother to leave and go hunting. When she did, they waited a few more minutes and then went closer.

"I can hear 'em in there," Babby said excitedly. "Oh, I wanna see 'em! Bring one out here."

"We're gonna need your help to get 'em out. See, we're too big to get in there," Harold said as he tried to crawl into the den. "But you're just the right size to get 'em." He lifted Babby and put her at the opening.

"I'll just push you in the hole, arms first, okay? When you're all the way in, grab a pup in each hand, then kick your foot as a signal, and we'll pull you out. It'll be easy."

Babby looked at the entrance to the den and said, "I have to go in there? All the way in there?"

"Come on, don't be dumb. Be a big girl," said Harold sternly.

"But—but, I don't like the—the dark," Babby stammered and began to cry. "I don't wanna go in there. I wanna go home! I want my mama!"

At this point, Allen nearly backed out.

"She doesn't want to, Harold," he whispered. "Let's not make her do it."

At that, Harold roughly pulled Allen away from the den, out of Babby's hearing, and sneered, "Just shut up and think of the money we'll get. She won't get hurt. She'll be fine unless you go all soft on me," he warned.

He turned back to Babby and said, "Ah, come on, Babby, the pups are so cute. They'll lick your face and fall asleep in your arms," Harold cajoled. "They'll like you. But first we gotta get 'em out of the den, and you're the only one who can do that."

Remembering what she overheard back at the house, Babby asked, "You're not gonna hurt 'em, are you?"

Harold looked his little sister in the eye and lied right to her face. "Ah, Babby, we just wanna see 'em. They won't get hurt."

Allen stared at his older brother and shook his head disparagingly, but they were so far into this now they couldn't very well turn back.

Finally, after more coaxing, Babby hesitantly agreed to let her brothers push her into the den entrance. They held her up, lifted her hands above her head, and slowly pushed her inside.

"I don't like it! It's dark in here, but I can hear 'em. Oh, there, now I can feel 'em, and they're climbing on my hands," she said, her voice muffled by the rock.

"Come on and get 'em. Hurry up," Harold said.

"I'm trying." She held a coyote in each of her little fists and kicked her foot to signal the boys to pull her out.

Once out, she looked at the baby animals and cooed, "Oh, how cute. Can I play with 'em for a minute? They like me," she laughed, as she put a squirming pup up to her cheek.

"No, Bab, you gotta get the others first," Harold insisted. "Come on now, hurry up! Let's get this done."

They pushed her into the den for the second time and pulled her out again with a pup in each hand. She gave them to Harold, who put them in the burlap bag.

"Be nice to 'em, so they'll like us, Harold," Babby implored.

The trips in and out continued until the last one when Babby cried, "Ow! He scratched me! Lemme outta here! Pull me out! Get me outta here."

"No, Babby, you gotta get the last two pups before we pull you out," ordered Harold. "Get 'em! Then you can come out."

"But that one hurt me," she whined.

"Just get 'em, and do it now!" Harold ordered.

Finally, when she had the remaining pups, they pulled her out. She whimpered as she wiped her cheek, and her hand came away smeared with blood.

"What happened?" Allen asked.

"One scratched me, and it hurts," Babby cried.

"Here, use this and clean it off," said Harold brusquely, handing her his dirty handkerchief. "And you better not tell Ma how it happened or she'll be really mad at you. If she asks, you just say you ran into a branch, okay?"

"Aw, Harold?" Allen said, concerned with his harshness.

"Okay, we've got 'em in the bag. Now let's get outta here," Harold said.

"But I wanna hold 'em. You said I could hold one," Babby cried. "Why are you mad at me?" the little girl sobbed.

"Ah, honey, Harold's not mad—he's just in a hurry," said Allen, trying to smooth things over. Allen looked at his older brother and said, "We need to give her one, just for a minute."

"We're wasting time. We gotta get back, so hurry. Just take one out, and make it quick," Harold sneered.

"Okay, Babby," Allen said as he opened the sack and lifted out a kit, "here's one for you to pet."

Looking at the little pup, Babby said, "Oh, it's so soft and cute. Look, now it's sucking my finger. It's so sweet. I'm gonna name this one Firefly." She stroked the coyote softly. "It'll be my own pet."

After a few minutes, Allen gently took the pup from her and put it back in the sack, then set the squirming bag on the ground. Babby hovered over and began to sing to the little coyotes.

"Here, I'll pick them some flowers," she said, gathering a few drooping oxeye daisies and slipping them into the bag.

"Hey! We gotta go, right now! Now!" Harold said as he lifted Babby roughly into the wagon then tied the top of the burlap sack loosely and put it between the little girl's legs.

Babby stood up and said, "I wanna hold one, Harold. You said I could. I want Firefly."

"Babby, shut up!" Harold said. "Later. You can see him later if you do what I say. Now be quiet and let's go!"

Babby's lower lip began to quiver, and Allen thought she was going to cry again.

"It's okay, Babby," Allen said. "Just sit down and hold the bag and sing to 'em. They like that."

Still on the verge of tears, Babby sat back down in the wagon and pulled the bag of baby coyotes closer to her. As they started off, she sang to comfort the pups, who were mewing and crying piteously.

As they continued down the hill, Harold and Allen quietly discussed where they would kill the pups, cut off their tails, and then claim the bounty.

"I wonder what it'd be like if we first cut off their tails and then killed 'em," Harold speculated.

"You gotta be kidding! There's no need to be cruel," Allen retorted.

"Ah, Allen, don't be a sissy. They're just dumb animals—they ain't got no feelings."

"That's not true. And we're not gonna torture 'em like you did that poor cat!"

"That cat was last summer. You promised not to tell, and you better not if you know what's good for you."

"Sh, don't let Babby hear you say that," Allen warned, turning around to make sure she hadn't heard.

In a quieter voice, Harold said, "When we get home, we'll just stash 'em somewhere outta sight and far enough away so no one can hear 'em. We'll come back after Babby's asleep, bonk 'em over the head a couple of times, and cut off their tails."

"I hope she's not too upset when they're gone," said Allen.

"Who cares? Eight dollars is a lotta dough. Eight whole dollars and it was so easy. Babby can be our little coyote catcher—as long as she doesn't figure it all out," laughed Harold. "And all we gotta do is turn in their tails!"

Allen looked at his older brother, shuddered, and wondered how he ever agreed to do this. He wasn't too keen on killing anything, and Harold's cruel streak worried him. Plus poor little Babby would be heartbroken.

In the back of the wagon, Babby strained to hear what her brothers were saying, but with the squeak of the wheels she picked up only a few words. Wanting to hear more, she scooted closer to the front of the wagon bed and heard the phrase "cut off their tails."

Cut off their tails? That's not nice, she thought. *It'll hurt 'em, and they won't look pretty without tails.* She remembered seeing a ranch hand dock a dog's tail and recalled how the poor animal yelped in pain and whimpered for a long time afterward. *I don't like this at all. I think Harold's gonna hurt 'em. I shouldn't have helped. I shouldn't have gotten 'em out of there and given 'em to them. Now they're gonna get hurt.*

Babby thought and thought and made up her mind. She would save the pups. She wouldn't let them have their tails cut off. Once she made the decision, she moved to the back of the wagon, turned to make sure the boys weren't looking, and quietly worked the knot of the bag open. She peered over the wagon back and judged the distance to the ground.

The pups would fall, but they would be okay, and this was the only way to save them. Carefully she felt inside the bag and took hold of one pup. She brought it to her lips and kissed it. When the wagon squeaked over a particularly noisy bump, she held the creature over the back edge and gently lowered it as close to the road as she could then carefully dropped it. The first one rolled several times then got up and ran into the brush unhurt. Babby did this seven more times then put the rocks in the sack and tried to tie it.

Babby knew her brothers would be furious, especially Harold. She heard them talk about getting $8, and that sounded like a fortune to her. Because of this, she planned to jump down from the wagon as soon as they got back to the house, run inside, and stay close to her mother.

Even before the wagon stopped completely, Babby was down.

"Babby, where you going?" Allen called. "Don't you wanna see the baby coyotes, before Pa gets back?"

Knowing the bag would be empty, she called over her shoulder, "I'm gonna help Ma," and ran inside.

She was nestled next to her mother when Harold hollered her name as he threw open the door.

"Babby, you come out here, right now!" Harold ordered as the little girl put her hands over her eyes and burrowed into the safety of her mother's arms.

"Harold, don't talk to your sister like that! What did you two boys do with her? She's all dirty, her cheek's scratched, and she's real upset. She'll stay right here with me," their mother said. "Now git and leave us alone!" she added.

All that evening and into the next day, Babby was her mother's little shadow. When asked what happened, Babby wouldn't say, but she continued to stay close to her mother's side, avoiding her brothers. She never told anyone about that afternoon because she worried she might get in trouble for saving the lives of the coyotes that would grow up to be ranch predators.

The following day, their father Asa took both boys on an overnight deer hunt. With them gone, the event blew over. Babby learned her lesson about trusting her oldest brother, Harold, and the two were never close after that.

Several weeks later, Martha Kempton, Babby, and her mother Effie again visited Evelyn Cameron. Babby politely asked Mrs. Cameron if she could see her coyote pups. They all went outside to the coyotes' pen and watched them wrestle and play.

"They're so sweet at this age," Martha Kempton said. "It's too bad they grow up to be such a problem."

"Yes, they're so cute now, but I'll have to keep them caged like this all their lives," Mrs. Cameron replied.

Looking at the little girl, she said, "Here, you can hold one, Babby." She took the smallest kit from the pen and handed it to the little girl.

Evelyn Cameron with a coyote pup.
PHOTOGRAPH BY EVELYN CAMERON,
COURTESY OF MONTANA HISTORICAL SOCIETY RESEARCH CENTER, HELENA, MT.

Babby was overjoyed and sat quietly, stroking the coyote pup in her lap and singing to it while the women continued their visit under the shade of a nearby tree.

When it came time to go home, Babby kissed the pup and reluctantly put it back with the others. There were tears in her eyes as she said, "I had eight little coyotes once, and I loved 'em. But I had to give 'em up so they could live."

Effie, Martha Kempton, and Mrs. Cameron raised their eyebrows and looked at the girl quizzically.

"She did? When did this happen?" asked Mrs. Cameron.

"What's she talking about?" asked Martha.

Putting her arm tenderly around her daughter, Effie said, "Oh, my little Babby has such a wonderful imagination. She dreams up all kinds of things." She guided Babby away from the pen to the buggy for the ride back to the Kempton Ranch.

Author's note: My father told me that Harold and Allen later contrived another method to get coyotes out of their dens. They took several eight-foot lengths of barbed wire, shoved them in the den when the mother was out hunting, twisted the wire, and pulled it back out. I didn't want to hear any more of that gruesome story.

SAVING
CYGNUS BUCCINATOR

he Kempton land was blessed with ample water from over forty artesian springs, and in arid eastern Montana that was a blessing indeed. Soon after the ranch house was built in the 1880s, the family patriarch, JB Kempton, used huge scrapers pulled behind six horses to dig several large spring-fed reservoirs. The one near the ranch house also fed an irrigation system. Many a child enjoyed swimming in those man-made ponds on hot summer days, and the vegetable and flower gardens always flourished, even in the warmest weather.

A reservoir on the Kempton Ranch.

In winter, the springs became spectacular, huge fountains of ice, and the reservoir was a wonderful skating rink. When the water froze to a sufficient depth, ranch hands cut large blocks of ice and hauled them to the cooling room dug into the hillside near the ranch house kitchen. That ice, covered with sawdust for insulation, lasted through the summer to cool food before the advent of electrical refrigeration.

Harvesting ice on the Kempton Ranch.

These large reservoirs also attracted many different migratory birds that stopped there to rest during their long flights, drawn by plentiful water and the stubble left in the fields, which provided food. People in Prairie County were used to seeing snow geese, various ducks, eagles, and occasional swans. The largest of all, the trumpeter swans, usually left their wintering grounds and flew over Montana in March or April.

Most households hunted ducks and geese to add to their daily larder, and pheasant hunting was particularly popular. The Kempton boys, with the exception of Jerry, who was more interested in reading than killing, frequently hunted on the prairie, although hunting was prohibited near the ranch house. The boys brought home game birds, rabbits, and an occasional prairie dog. I'm not sure how many of these animals ended up in Martha's stew pot, but I remember when she visited us in Anchorage one summer, she cooked wild ducks given to us by a neighbor. Although I am not usually a fan of game, they were delicious, with rich dark gravy.

Two Kempton boys show off their prairie dog harvest.

In the spring of this story, Martha had been sending food to help a nearby rancher, Mike Patterson, whose wife, Bonnie, was very ill with terminal cancer. It was evening, and Pansy and Jerry were riding home after delivering loaves of fresh bread, roast chicken, and apple pie. Young as they were, both children recognized Bonnie Patterson was becoming weaker each day. They knew the family would soon be without her.

"What'll they do without their mom?" asked Jerry, who was good friends with the oldest Patterson daughter, Rose. "How sad to have her die when the kids are so young."

"I'm glad I have my mom. I hardly remember my dad. It seems so long ago. We moved here right after that, and we're kinda like part of your family now," Pansy said.

"Yeah, you are," Jerry answered.

Thoughtfully they rode farther, considering the age-old sorrow of the death of loved ones.

"I hope both my folks live to be a hundred," said Jerry, breaking the silence.

"Gee, Jerry, you'll be really old then too."

"Maybe so," he admitted, "but they're swell parents, and I'll always want 'em around."

They were almost back to the ranch when suddenly a strange, deep, trumpet-like sound interrupted their conversation. It was coming from the reservoir.

"What in blazes is that? Some kind of bird?" exclaimed Jerry.

"It must be," said Pansy. "But I've never heard one like that. Let's go look."

Both children quickly unsaddled their horses, put them in the open corral, and ran back to the reservoir.

Paddling around in the middle of the pond was a huge, white swan. Its beauty was horribly marred by an arrow that had pierced the side of the creature's neck and was still embedded. Around the arrow shaft, a stain of bright blood dripped down the bird's arched neck.

"Oh, no! It's a swan. Who would hurt a swan?" cried Pansy.

"I dunno. Maybe someone who wanted the bird's feathers," suggested Jerry. "Some ladies wear feathers like that on their hats. It's real dumb."

"But who uses bows and arrows?" asked Pansy. "Everyone around here uses guns, even the Indians."

The children ducked down into the underbrush then slowly and quietly moved closer to the edge of the pond where they could get a better view of the large bird. When they stood and showed themselves, the swan didn't seem afraid. They discussed what they could do to help the bird.

Since Jerry's father was away on a cattle-buying trip, they decided to ask the ranch foreman, Jeff Dixon, for help. Pansy stayed by the water and Jerry ran to the barn, where he found Jeff out back stacking rolls of barbed wire.

"Jeff, come quick! There's a hurt swan with an arrow in its neck," Jerry blurted out.

"An arrow?"

Jerry told him the details, and Jeff pointed to a pile of burlap sacks on the barn floor.

"Jer, bring those, and I'll find a wire cutter."

Jerry also grabbed a small sack of grain, shoving it in his pocket. Then he and Jeff headed back to the reservoir to find the large bird still swimming around. Jeff noted that the arrow had pierced only the outside of the bird's neck.

"Had that arrow been any closer to the middle, it would have killed the swan," Jeff said. "It's a trumpeter, and its scientific name is *Cygnus buccinator.* It's the largest water bird in North America," he added. "Its wing span can be more than seven feet, and it can weigh as much as forty pounds. It's the heaviest bird that can fly. This pond is just barely large enough since they need a lot of surface to take off."

"How do you know so much about swans?" Pansy asked.

"Well, before I came here, I worked on land that's now part of Yellowstone National Park. Swans are common there," Jeff explained.

"I didn't know you worked anywhere but here," Jerry said.

"Oh, there's a lot you don't know about me, Jer," Jeff answered, with a good-natured laugh.

"Is it a boy or a girl swan?" asked Pansy.

"I'm not sure. It's hard to tell males from females, but males are usually larger."

"What else do you know about them?" she asked.

"Well, they mate for life," Jeff said. "This one must have gotten separated from its mate when it was hurt. Without humans interfering, they can live around twenty-five years. Swans can usually fight off predators with blows from their wings, and sometimes they chomp down with their bills, but they certainly can't fight off arrows."

"If they mate for life, where's this one's mate?" asked Jerry, scanning the area.

"And how can we get 'em back together?" said Pansy, looking up in the sky.

"Hey! Is that another one way up there?" Jerry asked, squinting to see a single swan circling far above the ranch.

"I'll bet that's his mate, looking for him," said Pansy. "Poor things. Can we get 'em back together?"

"Well, let's see what we can do," said Jeff as he explained his plan to wrap the burlap sacks around the bird's body to immobilize the wings and then use the wire cutters to snip the arrow and remove it.

Jerry held out some of the grain he brought from the barn in hopes of enticing the swan. They were all amazed when the bird swam closer and ate the grain right from Jerry's hand.

"The poor thing is really hungry," Pansy said as she filled her palm with grain and fed the bird too.

While the bird ate from Pansy's hand, Jeff waded in, quickly covered the swan's wings with the burlap sacks, then snipped the arrow. It fell from the bird's neck without much further bleeding, and the bird seemed calm.

"I think we should keep it at least overnight because it's lost a lot of blood. Maybe we can help him get stronger then let him go," Jeff said.

"How're we gonna keep it?" asked Jerry.

"If we can get it to the barn, we'll put it in that big walled-in stall with food and water," Jeff suggested. "That should work."

Together Jeff and Jerry struggled to carry the huge bird into the barn, where they put it in the stall. The weakened swan didn't resist and seemed content to be in the enclosure. The children fetched water and grain for the creature. It hungrily finished both, and they replenished the buckets.

"Will its wife or maybe its husband stay around here overnight, do you think?" asked Pansy.

"I hope so," Jeff answered, "but there's not much we can do about that."

"Well, I can pray," said Pansy quietly.

"Yes, little one, that might help," said Jeff, as he gently put his arm around Pansy's shoulder.

The three of them made sure all was secure, closed the barn door, and left. The bird gave a call and then all was quiet.

"What else can you tell us about swans?" asked Jerry as they walked toward the house.

"Well, the male's called a cob, the female is a pen, and the young ones are cygnets. They used to nest over most of North America but became scarcer as civilization moved westward."

"I love the story of the ugly duckling that was really a swan," said Pansy. "I made Ma read it to me a thousand times until I had it memorized, and she probably did too," she added with a laugh.

"I thought of that story too when Buttons first came and everyone thought he was ugly, but he turned out to be a great horse," said Jerry.

"Yeah, swan babies, or cygnets, are an unattractive, dull-gray color with pinkish legs. They don't turn white and swan-like until they're a year old," Jeff told them. "Now it's getting late and you two should be in bed. I'll let the ranch hands know about our visitor in the barn, and I'll check on it at least once before dawn," he promised.

Both Jerry and Pansy told their mothers about the bird then finally went to bed, although they also got up during the night and went to the barn with coats over their pajamas to make sure the swan was okay.

Early the next morning when the children opened the barn, the bird greeted them with a loud trumpet call. It had finished the grain and water and wanted more. Martha fixed a special batch of mush and grain, mixed with diced apples, and Jeff brought it out for the swan.

"We have to build his strength back up for the rest of his flight," he said as the bird quickly gobbled the food.

"Can't it just stay here all winter? Pansy and me would take care of it," Jerry said.

"Yeah, we promise to feed it every day and keep its stall clean," echoed Pansy.

"I'm afraid that's not a good idea," said Jeff. "Hunters would eventually kill it."

"But we could tell everyone that it's a pet swan and keep it right here so it wouldn't get hurt," suggested Jerry.

A pond on the Kempton Ranch.

"What about its mate up there? They need to be together, and they need to be free. No, its best chance is to continue its migration. Wild creatures are meant to be wild. We have to release it," said Jeff.

A few hours later, when the children went out to check on the bird, they heard the distinctive honking from two directions—both the barn and the reservoir.

"It's his mate looking for her, or maybe it's her mate looking for him. Either way, it stayed!" said Pansy excitedly.

They finished up in the barn, closed the door, and took some grain down to the pond, where the other swan gracefully paddled around in large circles.

When Pansy saw it, she clasped her hands together and whispered, "Oh, *Cygnus buccinator,* you stayed! You stayed."

They scattered the grain and ran to tell Jeff about the swan's mate as the birds continued to call to one another.

The injured swan stayed in the barn one additional night. Its neck wound was healing, and it was well-fed and rested. Its mate remained near the reservoir and ate the grain the children left, and the two birds continued to call back and forth. Twice, the swan in the reservoir flew over the barn and around the ranch house trying to locate its mate and then settled back in the water.

Everyone in the household, and even the ranch hands in the bunkhouse, showed an interest in the swans. They began to hand-feed the pair in the barn and at the reservoir. They suggested names for them, and soon several neighbors stopped in to see the birds. The swans were becoming increasingly popular. That evening at dinner, Jeff suggested the birds might be growing too accustomed to the easy life of ranch pets.

"I think it's time to free the one swan so they can both continue their migration," Jeff said. "We'll do it tomorrow morning."

"I hate to see them go," Pansy said quietly.

"Me too," Jerry added.

That final morning, the two children and Jeff opened the barn door, pulled back the gates of the swan's enclosure, and herded the bird outside. Pansy fed it grain from her hand as it hesitated near the doorway. It looked around, took a few steps, and fluttered its wings as if trying them out.

"He'll need some room to get going before he can fly because his body's so heavy," Jeff said. "But here he goes!" The swan ran across the grass in front of the barn, flapping his wings.

"He's kind of awkward on land," Jerry said.

"Oh, but look at him now!" Pansy exclaimed as the bird rose on strong wings and circled the reservoir where it met up with its mate. The large birds trumpeted to each other, brushed one another in flight, and headed south on powerful wings. It was a beautiful sight that brought tight throats and stinging eyes, even to Jeff.

"Goodbye, *Cygnus buccinators,*" Pansy whispered.

"Good luck!" said Jerry, giving them a parting salute.

"Godspeed to you both," Jeff said.

Jeff looked at the youngsters and smiled. The three watched until the beautiful swans were just small specks in the sky, and then they walked back to the ranch house for breakfast. Pansy took Jeff's hand, and he saw she was crying.

"Aw, sweet Pansy, don't cry. Why, I'm just so proud of you, and you too, Jerry, for the way you children cared for God's creatures."

Jeff put his arms around both youngsters and hugged them.

Author's note: My family and I live in a coastal town north of Seattle, not too far from the Skagit Flats, which is one of the prime West Coast wintering grounds for many migrating birds—among them, both whistling and trumpeter swans.

In the late winter when we drive by those farm fields left in stubble, we see hundreds of these graceful, elegant birds. Each time, I always remember the story of my dad, Pansy, and Jeff's efforts to save the injured swan that took refuge in the Kempton Ranch reservoir in the 1920s, almost a hundred years ago.

INDEX

grass, 62, 115, 118, 120, 140
Gray, Zane, 98
Gray Hawk (Sioux Indian), xiii–xiv;
in conversation, 76–79, 88, 249;
friendships and, 255–256; hunting for
arrowheads, 246–248, 250; in Kempton
Hotel, 70–75, 79–85, 87; rattlesnakes
and, 242, 250–252, 254–255; swimming,
252–253
Greeley, Colorado, xiv, 55
gumbo, 92–93
gunfights, 216–217
guns, 166, 178, 208, 213–214

H

Höga Berg (High Hill, Swedish farm),
26–27
Homestead Act (1862), xviii, 57–58, 60
homesteaders, 60, 103, 131
honyockers, 131–134, 139–140
horses, xiv, **237;** Appaloosa, 204–**205,**
228; benefits of riding, 187; brands used
on, 199; broom tail, 234; in cattle drives,
207–208, 211, 213; cavalry, 64, 220, 241;
Cossack, 19, 229; in Doctor Carver's
Wild West Show, 105–108, **107;** half-
wild team, 198; Kentucky-bred,
204, 228; Morgan, 204, 228; mustangs,
228–229, 230; names for, 235–236,
240–241; palomino, 230, 241; as payment
for wife, 55, 197; Percheron, 64, 220,
228, 241; polo ponies, 90, 220–221, 226,
241; race and steeplechase, 220, 241;
rustled, 199; school children riding,
165, 167, 168–169; Thoroughbred, 220,
226; trick ponies, **221;** wild, 15–16,
228–229. *See also* Buttons (horse);
Miami (horse)
horseshoe, 79–**80**
Huffman, L. A., 234–235
hunting, 117–118, 249, 270–271

I

ice harvesting, **270**
Indians: in Doctor Carver's Wild West
Show, 15–18; Homestead Act (1862)
and, 58; hunting buffalo, 249; land,
relationship to, 49–51; married to
white men, 193–197; Nez Perce, 204;
Pilgrims and, 49–51, **50;** in polygamous

marriages, 53, 55, 196–197; raids by, 25,
44, 56–57, 61, 195. *See also* Gray Hawk
(Sioux Indian) Sioux, 16–18, **17–18,** 44,
145, 193, 247

J

J Mule Shoe Ranch, 62, 117
The Jungle (Sinclair), 97
justice system, 105, 142–143, 155, 157–158

K

kangaroos, 5, 7–8, **19–20,** 108–109
Kempton, Allen, 243, 257, 258–267, 268
Kempton, Asa, xiii, **42, 186, 192;** on
Berney Kempton, Sr., 17–18; on cattle
shipments, 150–152; coyotes and, 258;
as family historian, 190, 193–197,
199–200; family role of, 143, 147,
148–149, 186–187; as father, 243, 246,
257, 267; in friendly banter, 188–189,
191, 198; on Jerry Kempton, 156; on loss
of cattle, 153; on Northern Pacific
lawsuit, 154–155, 157–159; wolves and,
192, 258
Kempton, Barbara "Babby": coyotes and,
263–268; siblings and, 247, 259–262
Kempton, Berney Edmond, Jr., xii–xiii,
177, 204
Kempton, Berney Edmond, Sr., xii, xiv,
xviii, **11, 20, 42, 66, 90, 106, 141, 186,
222;** on ancestors, 49; Australian
friend of, 109–112; as boss, 208, 232;
in calving season, 177–178; cattle
drives, descriing, 206–208, 209–210,
211–212; character of, 21–22, 90–91, 112,
131, 230, 232–233; in conversation,
with Asa, 149–150, 152–156, 157, 159;
in conversation, with brothers, 187–192,
194–200; in conversation, with guests,
94–101; in conversation, with Jerry,
147–150, 152–155, 157, 159; in conversation, with sons, 76–77, 88, 203–206,
210–211, 216–218; on coyotes, 258;
on Doctor Carver's Wild West Show,
104–109; Doctor Carver's Wild West
Show, joining, 15–16, 229–230; Doctor
Carver's Wild West Show, keepsakes
from, 5–8; Doctor Carver's Wild West
Show, performing in, 19–20, 109;
Doctor Carver's Wild West Show,

ABOUT THE AUTHOR

*T*rudy Kempton Dana grew up hearing stories of her father's life on a large horse and cattle ranch in eastern Montana. Although her father, Jerry Kempton, became a civil engineer instead of a rancher and never again lived in Montana, the mystique of the Wild West was a major part of his childhood. After he met and married Phyllis Engdahl, they moved from Montana to Anchorage, Alaska, where Trudy was born and raised.

While attending college at the University of Montana in Missoula, Trudy grew to love Montana. She also wanted to know more about her family history, which includes pilgrims, patriots, pioneers, and Native Americans.

Trudy is a well-known expert in the field of child safety and the author of two books on the subject. Following a series of highly publicized, horrific crimes against children in the Northwest, she was involved in efforts in Washington State to pass the first sexual predator legislation in the nation. Now all states have similar laws. Trudy spoke to hundreds of groups of law enforcement professionals, school administrators, parents, and businesspeople on the topic of protecting children.

Trudy joined a large, suburban Seattle law enforcement agency as their civilian crime prevention officer, where she created several innovative and award-winning programs.

Trudy lives with her husband in a small coastal town on Puget Sound north of Seattle. Her grown daughters, their husbands, and two granddaughters live nearby. She welcomes contact by email: Trudydana@hotmail.com.